THE
METHOD
TO THE
MADNESS

THE
METHOD
TO THE
MADNESS

Donald Trump's Ascent as Told by Those Who Were

Hired, Fired, Inspired—and Inaugurated

ALLEN SALKIN
and
AARON SHORT

ALL
POINTS
BOOKS

NEW YORK

First published in the United States by All Points Books, an imprint of St. Martin's Publishing Group

www.allpointsbooks.com

Design by Meryl Sussman Levavi

Library of Congress Cataloging-in-Publication Data is available upon request.

ISBN 978-1-250-20280-2 (hardcover)
ISBN 978-1-250-20281-9 (ebook)

Our books may be purchased in bulk for promotional, educational, or business use. Please contact your local bookseller or the Macmillan Corporate and Premium Sales Department at 1-800-221-7945, extension 5442, or by email at MacmillanSpecialMarkets@macmillan.com.

First Edition: July 2019

10 9 8 7 6 5 4 3 2 1

Allen: For Sara

Aaron: For my mother, Marjorie

I have had much trouble getting along with my ideas. There was a daimon in me, and in the end its presence proved decisive. It overpowered me, and if I was at times ruthless it was because I was in the grip of the daimon. I could never stop at anything once attained. I had to hasten on, to catch up with my vision. Since my contemporaries, understandably, could not perceive my vision, they saw only a fool rushing ahead.

—Carl Jung, *Memories, Dreams, Reflections*

CONTENTS

PART THREE: SETTLING ON A POLITICAL VOICE: 2010–2013

Trump builds a political team and slowly learns
the power of social media.

PART FOUR: THE RACE BEFORE THE RACE: 2013–2014

A productive detour onto the gubernatorial trail in New York.

PART FIVE: TO THE ESCALATOR: 2014–2015

A popularist politician emerges.

CONTRIBUTORS

Gloria Allred is a women's rights attorney who tangled with Trump over the right of a transgender Miss Canada contestant to participate in the pageant.

Tyana Alvarado, a onetime Miss Cougar California, was a contestant on *The Apprentice* season 10.

Melinda Arons was a producer for *Good Morning America* and *Nightline* for 12 years before arranging TV interviews for Hillary Clinton during the 2016 campaign as Clinton's director of broadcast media.

Derek Arteta, an entertainment lawyer, was a contestant on *The Apprentice* season 6.

Bob Arum, a former federal prosecutor who once deposed Roy Cohn, is a boxing promoter who worked with Muhammad Ali, Sugar Ray Leonard, and George Foreman.

Michael Ault is a nightclub owner who opened the 1990s Manhattan lounges Spy Bar and Chaos.

Michael Avenatti, a Los Angeles attorney, represented the porn star Stormy Daniels, real name Stephanie Clifford, in a confidentiality agreement lawsuit against Trump, and was involved in an intellectual property suit over the origins of *The Apprentice*. In March 2019 he was arrested on extortion and embezzlement charges related to other cases.

Stephen Bannon was executive chairman of Breitbart News, chief executive of Trump's 2016 campaign, and White House chief strategist in 2017.

Kurt Bardella, a former congressional spokesman for prominent Republicans, switched parties in 2017 and works as a political media consultant.

Dean Barkley is an attorney, a former U.S. senator representing Minnesota (1992–1993), and a founder of the state's Reform Party who chaired Jesse Ventura's gubernatorial win in 1998.

Rona Barrett, who interviewed celebrities for network television across five decades, including Trump in 1980, runs the Rona Barrett Foundation, building affordable housing for seniors in central California.

Glenn Beck is a political commentator, author, and founder of TheBlaze.

A. J. Benza is a gossip columnist and television host who wrote for *Newsday* and the New York *Daily News*.

Caron Bernstein is a model and 1990s nightlife fixture. Trump—whom she met through her former boyfriend, the lawyer Richard Golub— once wrote her a letter of recommendation to help secure a lease on an East Village apartment.

Mark Bethea, an Air Force veteran, was working as a private jet company executive in 2000 when he came up with an idea for a business competition reality show starring Trump.

Conrad Black, a former newspaper publisher, is an investor and author who attended Trump's wedding to Melania.

Gwenda Blair is the author of *The Trumps: Three Generations That Built an Empire* and *Donald Trump: The Candidate*.

Poppy Carlig Blaseio, a dentist and champion synchronized swimmer, was a contestant on *The Apprentice* season 10.

Pat Boone is a singer, actor, and conservative political activist.

Joe Borelli, a Republican New York City councilman representing Staten Island, was an early supporter of Trump for governor.

David Bossie is the president of the conservative nonprofit Citizens United and served as deputy campaign manager for Trump's 2016 presidential campaign.

Pat Buchanan, a conservative commentator, was a Republican presidential candidate in 1992 and 1996 and the Reform Party candidate in 2000.

Michael Caputo is a political media consultant and former Trump campaign adviser.

Tucker Carlson is host of *Tucker Carlson Tonight* on Fox News.

Pat Choate, an economist, was Ross Perot's vice presidential running mate in 1996 and co-chairman of Pat Buchanan's 2000 Reform Party presidential campaign.

Corynne (Steindler) Cirilli, a writer and strategist, is a former Page Six gossip columnist at the *New York Post.*

Eleanor Clift began covering presidential campaigns for *Newsweek* in 1976, and she is currently a political columnist for the Daily Beast and a panelist on *The McLaughlin Group.*

Tony Coelho, a former U.S. congressman from California (1979–1989), was chairman of Al Gore's 2000 presidential campaign.

Sara Conca, an artist and model, frequented the 1990s Manhattan clubs Wax, Chaos, and Life.

Andrew Corsello is a senior writer at *GQ.*

Peter Costanzo set up Trump's Twitter account in 2009 as director of online marketing for Perseus Books when its imprint Vanguard Press published *Think Like a Champion.*

Katie Couric has hosted news programs for NBC, CBS, ABC, and Yahoo!

Ed Cox has chaired the New York Republican State Committee since 2009.

Doug Davenport is a political consultant who advised the Trump campaign, writing a strategic memo in 2014.

Donny Deutsch is an advertising company executive, television host, and regular guest on MSNBC's *Morning Joe.*

Fred Dicker is a political journalist and radio show host who reported for the *New York Post* for 34 years.

Bo Dietl is a former NYPD detective and 2017 New York City mayoral candidate.

David DiPietro is an Erie County Republican assemblyman who, in 2010, ran unsuccessfully for the New York State Senate as a member of the Tea Party. In 2013, he was a key force in convincing Trump to consider a run for governor.

Jim Dowd was an NBC publicist in charge of *The Apprentice* who started his own agency and represented Trump from 2004 to 2010. He died September 18, 2016, from what the Fairfield County, Connecticut, medical examiner lists as "acute intoxication due to the combined effects of ethanol and oxycodone."

Erin Elmore was a contestant on *The Apprentice* season 3. She appears on Fox News, and during the 2016 campaign, she was a frequent Trump advocate on TV.

Jon Elsen has been media and marketing editor at the *New York Times* and business editor at the *New York Post*. He is president of Elsen Strategies, a communications firm.

Erick Erickson is a conservative political writer and radio host who served as editor in chief of RedState and founded The Resurgent.

Michael J. Fox is an actor, author, and producer and the founder of the Michael J. Fox Foundation, dedicated to finding a cure for Parkinson's disease.

Paula Froelich is an author and a former Page Six gossip columnist at the *New York Post*.

Lenora Fulani is a progressive political activist and frequent independent candidate in New York and national races. She worked closely with Fred Newman, a controversial psychotherapist.

Lloyd Grove, an editor-at-large for the Daily Beast and a contributor to *New York* magazine, formerly wrote gossip columns for the New York *Daily News* and politics and media columns for the *Washington Post*.

John Haggerty is a Republican political consultant.

Jenn Hoffman, a writer and actress, was a contestant on *The Apprentice* season 6.

Dan Isaacs, an attorney, was chairman of the New York County Republican Party from 2011 to 2014.

Kwame Jackson, an entrepreneur and public speaker, was a contestant on *The Apprentice* season 1.

David Cay Johnston is a Pulitzer Prize–winning investigative journalist and author of *The Making of Donald Trump*.

Jeff Jorgensen is a political activist and founder of the Iowa-based PAC Republicans for Conservative Values. He was chairman of the Pottawattamie County Republican Central Committee from 2010 to 2017.

Carolyn Kepcher was an executive vice president at the Trump Organization from 1995 to 2006 and a judge on *The Apprentice* seasons 1–5. She is the general manager of a Connecticut country club.

Richard Kilfoyle was a University of Pennsylvania student who questioned Trump on *Hardball with Chris Matthews* in 1999. He graduated in 2001.

Tesia Kuh is an executive administrator at Wolfgang Puck Worldwide.

Gersh Kuntzman, a reporter and editor for three decades, wrote the Metro Gnome column for the *New York Post* from 1994 to 2004.

Nick Langworthy is the chairman of the Erie County, New York, Republican Committee. He served as an executive member of Trump's 2016 transition team.

Laraby was a downtown Manhattan bartender in the 1990s who used only one name professionally. She has participated in shows with performance artist Penny Lane and was the inspiration for the Spin Doctors' song "Laraby's Gang," about drinking beer on the New York club scene.

David Laska worked for the New York Republican State Committee from 2010 to 2015, most recently as director of communications.

Michael Lawler is a political strategist and adviser to the New York State Republican Party. He served as campaign manager for Rob Astorino's unsuccessful 2014 New York gubernatorial campaign.

Theodore LeCompte was a student who helped *Hardball with Chris Matthews* film at the University of Pennsylvania in 1999. He served as chief operating officer of the Democratic National Convention Committee in 2012 and was a Commerce Department deputy chief of staff.

Joe Lieberman was a Connecticut senator and Al Gore's vice presidential pick in 2000.

Michael Long was chairman of the Conservative Party of New York State from 1988 until February 2019.

Frank Luntz is a Republican pollster and television commentator known for his expertise in shaping political terminology and conducting focus groups for candidates.

Phil Madsen, a Minnesota Reform Party official in the 1990s, served as Trump's 2000 campaign webmaster; he now runs a gym in Port Orange, Florida.

Ronald Makarem is a Los Angeles attorney who represented Mark Bethea in an idea theft lawsuit over who created *The Apprentice*.

Nicole Malliotakis has been a Republican member of the New York State Assembly representing Staten Island since 2010.

Stuart Marques was managing editor of both the New York *Daily News* and the *New York Post*.

Justin McConney directed social media for Trump from 2011 to 2017. He taught Trump Twitter.

John McLaughlin, a political consultant and pollster who has worked with Arnold Schwarzenegger and Benjamin Netanyahu, met with Trump and Dick Morris in 2011 when Trump was considering running for president.

Frank Morano is a political activist and a radio host at AM 970 The Answer in the New York metropolitan area.

Dick Morris is a Republican political consultant and author.

Ralph Nader is a consumer rights advocate who ran for president as a Green Party candidate in 2000 and an independent in 2004 and 2008.

Jerrold Nadler has represented New York as a member of the House of Representatives since 1992 and is House Judiciary Committee chairman.

Jim Nicholson was Republican National Committee chairman from 1997 to 2001 and secretary of veterans affairs from 2005 to 2007.

Sam Nunberg is an attorney and political strategist who began consulting for Donald Trump in 2011 and served as an aide in Trump's 2016 presidential campaign.

Rosie O'Donnell is a comedian, talk show host, and memoirist.

Carl Paladino is a real estate developer. He was the New York Republican gubernatorial candidate in 2010 and a member of the Buffalo Board of Education from 2013 to 2017.

Katrina Pierson, an early member of the Tea Party, was a Trump campaign spokeswoman in 2016 and is a senior adviser for the Trump 2020 campaign.

Randal Pinkett, a businessman, author, and speaker, won *The Apprentice* season 4 and worked for a year for the Trump Organization.

David Plouffe was Barack Obama's 2008 campaign manager and senior adviser to the president from 2011 to 2013.

Jefrey Pollock is a pollster who has consulted for Democratic presidential candidates, governors, senators, and members of Congress.

Jessica Proud is a spokeswoman for the New York Republican Party and was a campaign aide to Rob Astorino in 2014.

Bill Pruitt, a producer for *The Apprentice* seasons 1 and 2, worked on *The Amazing Race* and *Deadliest Catch* and produced shows for CBS, NBC, the Discovery Channel, the History Channel, and National Geographic.

Katherine Pushkar is a lifestyle and entertainment journalist and editor in New York.

Dick Ravitch, a Democrat, was New York lieutenant governor from 2009 to 2010.

Ed Rendell was the mayor of Philadelphia from 1992 to 2000, the chairman of the Democratic National Committee in 2000, and the governor of Pennsylvania from 2003 to 2011.

Barbara Res was a Trump Organization vice president, senior vice president, and executive vice president.

Conrad Riggs worked closely with Mark Burnett in developing *Survivor* and *The Apprentice.*

Tom Robbins, an investigative journalist in residence at the CUNY Graduate School of Journalism, wrote for the *Village Voice*, the New York *Daily News*, and the *New York Observer.*

Marji Ross is the president and publisher of Regnery Publishing, a leading producer of conservative titles.

Anthony Scaramucci served as White House director of communications from July 21 to July 31, 2017.

Reverend Al Sharpton is a civil rights activist and the host of *PoliticsNation* on MSNBC.

Hank Sheinkopf consults for major politicians including Bill Clinton and Michael Bloomberg on communications strategy.

Dave Shiflett is a journalist and the co-author with Trump of *The America We Deserve.*

Darryl Silver was a producer involved in sponsorship and integration for *The Apprentice* seasons 1 and 2. He created and executive produced *Mama Medium* (TLC), *Half Pint Brawlers* (Spike), and *Big Medicine* (TLC).

Sean Spicer, the communications director for the Republican National Convention from 2011 to 2015 and chief strategist for the Republican Party in 2015, was White House press secretary in 2016.

Elizabeth Spiers was the founding editor of Gawker and editor in chief of Jared Kushner's *New York Observer* from 2011 to 2012. She is the founder of *The Insurrection*, a digital media consulting firm.

Tom Squitieri, a former war correspondent and political reporter for *USA Today*, is a professor at the American University School of Communication.

Andrew Stein was Manhattan Borough president from 1978 to 1985 and New York City Council president from 1986 to 1994.

Jared Paul Stern was a reporter for the *New York Post*'s Page Six gossip column. His writing on automobiles and luxury appears widely.

Roger Stone is a campaign strategist and lobbyist who advised Donald Trump's presidential explorations for decades. The subject of the documentary *Get Me Roger Stone*, he also worked on the presidential campaigns of Richard Nixon and Ronald Reagan. He was indicted in January 2019 by a grand jury on charges brought by special counsel Robert Mueller over potential involvement in the WikiLeaks release of Democratic emails in coordination with Trump campaign officials.

Neera Tanden is the president and CEO of the Center for American Progress, a liberal advocacy group. She was policy director for the 2008 presidential campaigns of Hillary Clinton and, later, Barack Obama.

Robert Torricelli was a U.S. congressman from New Jersey for 20 years, first in the House of Representatives from 1983 to 1997 and then in the Senate from 1997 to 2003.

Jesse Ventura, a champion professional wrestler in the 1970s and 1980s known as "The Body," served as governor of Minnesota from 1999 to 2003 after winning as a Reform Party candidate.

Russell Verney was chairman of the Reform Party from 1995 to 1999, director of Ross Perot's 1996 presidential campaign, and campaign manager of Libertarian presidential candidate Bob Barr's 2008 run. He is executive director of Project Veritas, a group that seeks to expose journalists' political biases, usually targeting liberals.

Jonathan Wald is the senior vice president for programming and development at MSNBC. He executive produced *Today*, *Piers Morgan Live*, and *Nightly News with Tom Brokaw*; he also created *CNN Tonight*.

Abe Wallach was executive vice president of acquisitions and finance for the Trump Organization.

Chris Wilson has written for the *New York Post*'s Page Six gossip column and is the digital director of *Maxim* magazine.

Rick Wilson is a Republican political strategist who advised Mayor Rudolph Giuliani from 1997 to 2001; he has also produced commercials for political action committees. His firm Intrepid Media worked for a super PAC that supported Florida senator Marco Rubio.

Matt Wing directed communications for New York governor Andrew Cuomo's 2014 reelection campaign.

Surya Yalamanchili, an investor and 2010 Democratic candidate for the U.S. House from Ohio's District 2, was a contestant on *The Apprentice* season 6.

Paolo Zampolli founded ID Models and introduced Donald Trump to Melania, one of his clients, in 1998. He later worked for the Trump Organization as director of international development. He is currently UN ambassador to Dominica.

Mike Zumbluskas helped found the New York Independence Party, the state affiliate of the Reform Party, and served as a delegate for the Reform Party's founding convention.

THE
METHOD
TO THE
MADNESS

PART ONE

REFORMED
1999—2000

At a crossroads, Trump test-markets
Trump the political brand.

INTRODUCTION

YES, THERE IS A METHOD

Donald Trump spent more than 15 years figuring out how to sell himself effectively in the political world. He studied long and hard and had a carefully thought-out plan before officially declaring his presidential candidacy in June 2015.

Many people do not believe Trump was so methodical. For a long time Trump created so much noise in other arenas that it drowned out his political machinations. As New Yorkers, we were well aware of his overblown image. From the hard-to-impress citizens of the money-obsessed metropolis, he had won the rare tribute of an instantly recognizable nickname: The Donald. He was the gossip-page fixture who blasted enemies, used every publicity opportunity to extol the gauche luxuries of his condo developments, and somehow drove his mistress to proclaim on a tabloid front page that with him she'd experienced the "Best Sex I've Ever Had." He lived in the Fifth Avenue sky, firing and hiring on his reality show, surrounding himself with fashion models in his box at the U.S. Open tennis championships in Queens and with socialites at his Palm Beach club. He was always good for an attention-getting quote about anything—and both of us took him up on that in our newspaper work in the 1990s and 2000s.

We weren't immune to believing the easy myth at first. It goes that Trump's political dalliances over the decades were all stunts designed to satisfy his ego or create free publicity to promote a new product. Trump, savvy New Yorkers thought, was a political ignoramus, an Elmer J. Fudd fixated on his mansions and yachts who could not possibly have serious policy ideas or a realistic vision of himself occupying 1600 Pennsylvania Avenue. This groupthink was confirmed by his brutishness when he did share an opinion on charged events in full-page newspaper ads—most infamously his 1989 "Bring Back the Death Penalty! Bring Back Our Police" ad arguing that five African American teenagers suspected of raping a Central Park jogger be executed—followed by outlandish cable news interviews to reinforce his point.[1] "Maybe hate is what we need if we're gonna get something done," Trump told CNN's Larry King after publishing the jogger ad. His un-commenced runs for office—in 1988, with a New Hampshire primary season speech; in 2000, with talk of a third-party bid; and in 2011, when, during talk show appearances ostensibly to promote *The Apprentice*, he veered into speculation about challenging President Barack Obama—seemed to confirm a tiresome pattern: he would never fully declare his candidacy.

But now? Still? After he ran for the White House, spent $66 million of his own money, and won?[2] Despite many books and documentaries painstakingly tracing the history of Trump and his family backward to Germany and the Klondike, and forward to the cheeseburgers and blaring televisions of the presidential living quarters, the myth that Trump was never serious about politics before 2015 holds on more stubbornly than the idea that you can get a good deal on a Rolex on Canal Street.

For us, the existing stories about Trump's political rise didn't add up. At best, other authors credited political advisers and campaign strategists like Steve Bannon, Kellyanne Conway, and David Bossie for formulating a viable Trump recipe in the years immediately leading up to 2016. We'd written enough about Trump over the years that we had strong sources to tap for a deeper understanding. When did he get serious about politics? Did he have a real plan when he declared his candidacy in 2015, or was it all seat-of-the-pants? Were there behind-the-scenes players we hadn't heard of? Why all the apparent chaos around him?

What we found is that Trump prepared diligently over many years, learning and evolving. There are plenty of things he does not know. He may even be, as some psychologists argue, a classic narcissistic personality, insisting on a stilted version of reality, or a victim of the Dunning-Kruger effect, a cognitive bias that leads the afflicted to transform his lack of knowledge on certain subjects into a stubborn assertion of superior comprehension. But when it comes to honing and trusting his instincts, manipulating the media, branding, timing the political tides, collecting useful advisers, engaging in public takedowns, creating and thriving in chaos, adapting winning strategies from others, and dozens of other sometimes subtle methods of getting his way, he is a master.

Trump's early presidential explorations presage what he is doing now and what he is likely to do next as president. Here we see how his years-long repetition of an anti-immigrant message culminated in the idea of a border wall with Mexico, and why he has unique reasons to believe that a lot of news reporting is inaccurate.

We narrowed our focus to 1999–2015, pivotal years that start with what we now see was Trump's first serious exploration of a presidential run and end at the moment when he unfurled a fully baked strategy and declared his intention to run and win.

Other books spend only a few paragraphs on Trump's exploration of a presidential run on the Reform Party ticket in 2000 and his near run for New York governor in 2014. Our sources show convincingly that these were pursuits on which Trump spent copious time and mental energy. They were major moments in the political education of a future president—dramatic episodes that well deserve a full unwinding.

Likewise, most Trump narratives tell a version of the birth of *The Apprentice* that makes him look lucky rather than strategic to have landed on TV. They only follow the first triumphant season of the NBC show closely. Here, we reveal new facts about the origin story, and then zoom in on a later, troubled season. With this additional light, some of Trump's strengths and flaws can finally be fully displayed and considered, along with what the entertainment industry hid.

These firsthand accounts are evidence to annihilate myths. Trump had long said he wouldn't run for president unless he thought he could win. No, he didn't know in 2015 that he *would* win. But he thought he could. And with that he stood atop the brass-and-glass escalator in the public atrium of Trump Tower and rode down to his destiny, announcing on June 16, 2015: "So ladies and gentlemen, I am officially running for president of the United States, and we are going to make our country great again."

We are not doing this to argue that one should support or not support President Trump's policies. We are journalists who saw a part of the record that was incomplete, believed we were in a position to fill it, and passionately felt our duty was to do just that. We understand that if you take away FBI director James Comey announcing a new investigation of Hillary Clinton, foreign meddling in the election, hush money to former lovers, the fog around Trump's net worth, strategic missteps by

Democrats, the Electoral College system, and other unknown factors, Trump may not have won.

What we do ask is that you consider, as we started to, that Trump was diligently preparing for decades to take advantage of opportunities such as those this particular election presented.

Here is a quick but useful trip through Trump's political prehistory. Donald J. Trump, the son of outer-borough real estate mogul Fred Trump, went into the family business full time after graduating from the Wharton School at the University of Pennsylvania in 1968. His father heavily subsidized his ambitions to become a force in Manhattan commercial development, a fact Trump successfully hid for years, building the myth that he was largely self-made.[3]

He'd become president of the Trump Organization in the 1970s, although his father still worked in the company. Trump's first notable success was converting the derelict Commodore Hotel on 42nd Street in Manhattan into the flourishing 30-story Grand Hyatt. Then, starting in 1979, he bought and razed the Bonwit Teller building on Fifth Avenue to make way for his eponymous condo Xanadu, Trump Tower.

A month before the 1980 presidential election, with Trump Tower still under construction, the 34-year-old developer sat for his first in-depth television interview with Rona Barrett, a well-known celebrity reporter. Barrett became interested in him because of New York gossip-page mentions of his youth and wealth, and of his wife of three years, the Czech model Ivana Zelníčková. Barrett sensed something lurking behind his answers to questions about current events and asked if he'd ever want to run for president.[4] He answered that he didn't think he would.

> **Donald Trump:** Because I think it's a very mean life. I would love, and I would dedicate my life to this country, but I see it as being a mean life, and I also see it in somebody with strong views, and somebody with the kind of views that are maybe a little bit unpopular, which may be right, but may be unpopular, wouldn't necessarily have a chance of getting elected against somebody with no great brain but a big smile.

He'd clearly thought about it. "One man," he said, "could turn this country around." On another topic, Trump told Barrett that the bad publicity he received for destroying Bonwit Teller's signature 1929 limestone facade reliefs rather than preserving them as he'd promised was actually good for him. Those who cared little for historic preservation and wanted prime city views had seen the critiques and bought condos.

In his answers about politics, Trump grappled with a difficult problem: How does one become president if one is not a wholesome-seeming candidate type with a smile as disarming as Jimmy Carter's or hair as thick as Ronald Reagan's? It would take him more than three decades to perfect a formula.

Donating to the campaigns of political officials in regions where he had real estate interests over the years was business to Trump, not politics. When he dove into the political fray more directly for the first time in 1987, the timing foreshadowed some of the Russia troubles he'd have as president. Two months after a six-day[5] trip to Moscow in July 1987, paid for by the Soviets, to discuss building two luxury hotels in the communist nation,[6] Trump spent about $95,000 to print a full-page open letter in the *New York Times*, *Washington Post*, and *Boston Globe*. It read: "There's nothing wrong with America's Foreign Defense Policy that a little backbone can't cure," adding that America "should stop paying to defend countries that can afford to defend themselves."[7] Trump is not known for spending money without hope of receiving something tangible in return, and the idea that American allies, including Japan, should be left to fend for their own self-defense was certainly a position Moscow would favor. Whatever his motivations for the ad buy, Trump went on CNN's *Larry King Live* to criticize U.S. trade policies with Japan, Kuwait, and Saudi Arabia and tout that he would address a Republican luncheon in New Hampshire the following month.

> **Larry King:** . . . You realize now, in just setting foot in that state, people are going to presume things.
> **Donald Trump:** Well, they can presume whatever they want. I have no intention of running for president, but I'd like a point to get across that we have a great country, but it's not going to be great for long, if we're going to continue to lose $200 billion a year. You're going to get into the early '90s—1990, 1991—and the whole thing's going to blow.

On October 22, 1987, a week before the publication of his canonical advice book *The Art of the Deal*, Trump flew to New Hampshire. He had been brought there by a mercurial political consultant named Roger Stone. Already advising former football player and Reagan housing secretary Jack Kemp on his presidential campaign, Stone saw a potential political star in Trump. The developer delivered a stem-winder about trade deficits, taxes, and his business skills, shouting to an audience of 500 people, "I'm tired of nice people already in Washington. I want someone who is tough and knows how to negotiate."[8]

Thanks to the success of *The Art of the Deal*, which rose to number one on the *New York Times* bestseller list and held the spot for 13 weeks, Trump was invited to appear on *The Oprah Winfrey Show* in April 1988, shortly after he acquired the Plaza Hotel in Manhattan. Oprah asked Trump whether he wanted to run for president. He "probably wouldn't do it," he said. But he wouldn't rule it out if Americans' lives worsened.

> **Oprah Winfrey:** You've said, though, that if you did run for president you believe you would win.
> **Donald Trump:** Well, I don't know, I think I'd win . . . I wouldn't go in to lose. I've never gone in to lose in my life. And if I did decide to do it . . . I would say that I would have a hell of a chance of winning, because I think people . . . are tired of seeing the United States ripped off. And I can't promise you everything, but I can tell you one thing, this country would make one hell of a lot of money from those people that for 25 years have taken advantage. It wouldn't be the way it's been, believe me.

He was both feeding America's anxiety about itself and suggesting he had a solution. Also worth noting is that he said he had no interest in running in 1988, and he did not run. He said that if he ever did run, he would try to win.

His August 27, 1998, interview with CNBC's Chris Matthews turned from a discussion of President Bill Clinton's legal strategy amid investigations to Trump's political ambitions.

> **Chris Matthews:** Why don't you run for president? . . .
> **Donald Trump:** People want me to all the time.
> **Chris Matthews:** What about you?
> **Donald Trump:** I don't like it. Can you imagine how controversial

I'd be? You're thinking about [Clinton] with the women? How about me with the women?[9]

Trump didn't have a winning answer—yet. Here is where we pick up the story in the mid-1990s. At the end of this book, we will leave you at the Trump Tower escalator in June 2015. We trust you can find your way from there.

This story is told with every source named and on the record, with one slight exception: we paraphrase an MGM entertainment executive who works under Mark Burnett. That executive refused to allow their name to be used in responding to charges leveled against producers of *The Apprentice* by named sources.

This is not a criticism of other works that rely on anonymous sources: anonymous sources are an essential part of many of the best pieces of journalism. It's just that in this case, we found we could tell the story we wanted to tell without them, which is always the goal.

Some of our interview subjects are household names, some not. Among them are behind-the-scenes assistants, off-camera TV producers, *Apprentice* contestants, obscure Albany political players, and spotlight-shunning New York nightclub fixtures. From those who served in the Trump White House or regularly appear on talk radio and TV we received new, revealing stories.

We repeatedly requested an interview with Donald Trump through various White House channels, including then White House deputy chief of staff for communications Bill Shine, Press Secretary Sarah Huckabee Sanders, and innovations director and Trump son-in-law Jared Kushner, but did not land a fresh interview.[10] Because Trump has given so many interviews over the years, we were often able to include his comments already on the record from the eras we examine.

We recorded nearly every one of our more than 100 interviews and worked from transcripts. To make reading easier, we fixed some grammar and condensed some quotes. Our comments are meant to provide context and fill in relevant history. The quotes are arranged in a way to move the narrative forward clearly. None of our interview subjects were in a room or on the phone together speaking directly to one another.

For decades, Donald Trump was preparing to run for president. It wasn't the only thing he was doing. There were casinos, relationships, *deals*, golf, a "university," out-of-court settlements, and big-time wrestling matches throughout his energetic life. But the evidence here shows he was puzzling out politics all along.

Some who criticize his political persona will allow that Trump possesses a preternaturally sharp intuition for what some audiences want to hear. Few consider—Steve Bannon told us during an interview at the Loews Regency hotel in New York—that Trump's approach to gut instinct is studied. According to Trump's co-authored 2004 book *How to Get Rich*, he briefly studied the groundbreaking psychoanalyst Carl Jung's book *Memories, Dreams, Reflections*. Trump noted that even with a quick reading, Jung's philosophy can help in "fine-tuning your intuition and instincts."

Some of what Trump brought to politics is already becoming the new normal, evident in the fierce social media rhetoric deployed by his rivals. More of his techniques, once understood, are sure to be adopted. Others are unique to the forty-fifth president.

Here's the news: there is a method to the madness.

1.

TIPSTER

When Trump Tower *opened in Manhattan in 1983, the* New York Times *architecture critic was impressed by the atrium that visitors entered from Fifth Avenue. Of the floors and soaring walls clad in Breccia Pernice marble in tones of peach, orange, and rose, and the polished brass escalators, Paul Goldberger wrote, "The marble is carefully cut and matched, with rounded corners that are absolutely sensuous; the balustrades of glass and brass are crafted in a manner that suggests not only a willingness to spend money, but also a knowledge of how to spend it correctly."*[1]

This charmed space, where Donald Trump would descend on an escalator to announce his candidacy for president 32 years later, would not be the only totem of his pre-political life used on his quest for the White House. Trump, who partied in the 1970s at Studio 54, was a gossip-page fixture by 1983 when he claimed for himself a palatial three-story penthouse. He spent the next few years riding high. The public largely saw a rambunctious sybarite who marketed glossy apartment buildings under the label of accessible luxury; flaunted his yacht, airline company, and professional football team; and partied with entertainers and models even though he was married. Appearances at WrestleMania, on the Howard Stern Show *and* Late Night with David Letterman, *and in various films implanted him in the public consciousness in the 1990s.*

Even around nightclub tables late at night, surrounded by a mélange of models and ice buckets of booze, Trump could stay relentlessly on message. The real person behind Trump's glitzy persona rarely showed himself, and as a result, few of those who know him personally count themselves as close friends. Throughout this book, we present insights into who the real person is—not completely different from the public face but certainly, at times, kinder, more patient, and more freckled than you'd think.

The true extent of his personal wealth has long been murky, but he appeared on a Forbes list of the world's billionaires in 1989.[2] Whether or not that list was accurate, it peddled an image of his success that clung to him despite well-publicized business setbacks over the next few years.

By the second half of the 1990s, Trump was twice divorced. The airline, Plaza Hotel, and football team were gone. For his fiftieth birthday in 1996, Trump celebrated at his Atlantic City Taj Mahal hotel. The Beach Boys were onstage, but that year vibrations at the casino company were not good, as it had lost $66 million. The stock price plunged from more than $30 in 1996 to under $4 in spring 1999, as the company lost another $82 million in 1997 and 1998.

Amid these business pressures he staked his ambitions on convincing the public that Trump the man who was also the brand was still successful. His third book, The Art of the Comeback, which came out in October 1997, purported to trace his path out of crushing debt, termed his financial problems "a blip," and offered comeback tips such as play golf, be paranoid, get even, and always have a prenuptial agreement. The book did not note that some of his comeback was due to his father's backstopping him financially when bank loans came due.

Even with the family support, Trump's strategy was to rely more than ever on what he had that no banker could seize: the persona. Thanks to his relentless marketing of himself, including through books, Trump the name still connoted over-the-top luxury. While the Trump Organization never left the construction business, Trump made deals to license his name to new buildings others owned. Erected billboard-tall in gilt letters, TRUMP was affixed to new structures in the belief that it, and Trump's input into design touches, added value—and studies proved it worked.[3]

Many reporters at New York City's newspapers in the 1990s had Trump's office number handy. Dial it and his personal secretary Norma Foerderer would pick up. Foerderer was one of Trump's most loyal aides: she worked for his company for 26 years before retiring in 2005. Within minutes, no matter what the story subject, Trump would be on the line giving quotable opinions when he didn't have facts. Trump rubbed shoulders with television personalities like Katie Couric and Tucker Carlson at New York nightclubs, society parties, and galas when the cameras weren't running. His long involvement in professional wrestling and boxing circles put him in contact with another subset of friends in Las Vegas and Atlantic City, including boxing promoter Don King. Through King he met civil rights leader Reverend Al Sharpton, an equally media-savvy figure with New York roots.

In these years when Trump—a professed teetotaler who witnesses said drank beer and champagne—partied at downtown clubs and chased European *models, he dropped morsels about himself and the celebrities he knew into the eager ears of the city's gossip columnists, including Liz Smith, Lloyd Grove, and A. J. Benza at the New York* Daily News *and, at the* New York Post, *Cindy Adams, Bill Hoffman, and reporters for the paper's widely read Page Six gossip column, Richard Johnson, Paula Froelich, Jared Paul Stern, and others.*

This is Trump as we find him right before he starts exploring politics more seriously. He was not yet directly using his self-marketing skills for political gain, but they would eventually serve him in that sphere too.

Paula Froelich, *reporter for the* New York Post's *gossip column, Page Six, 1990s:* I went to his house for something once, a drinks event, and I thought, *Yeah, I love real estate porn, I'll go check it out.* Ugh. It was all white carpet, all gilt, all mirrors, and they only served white wine because he didn't want anyone to stain the carpets. It was so tacky. It was styling that my grandma used to call Mosholu Parkway* Renaissance. It was very Persian glamour.

A. J. Benza, Newsday *and New York* Daily News *gossip reporter:* The first call I had with him, I picked the phone up and it was Trump. As he's talking to me—I forget what he was giving me or talking about, because he didn't know me from Adam—at that point, the phone rings and I have to pick it up, and it's David Dinkins [mayor of New York City 1990–1993, when he lost to Rudolph Giuliani]. I said, "Mr. Trump, I've got to put you on hold. It's David Dinkins." The first thing Trump said was, "Tell him he lost because he didn't carry the Jews." I didn't know what to say. He said, "You can quote me. He lost because he didn't carry the Jews." And then he hung up.

Stuart Marques, *New York* Daily News *and New York Post writer and editor:* My start with him was in the late '80s when he was divorcing Ivana and cheating with Marla Maples. Liz Smith was at the *News.* Cindy Adams was at the *Post.* Liz was on Ivana's side, and Cindy was on Trump's. It was hilarious because one day the *Post* would have this bombshell, obviously from Trump with nasty shit about Ivana, and "Best sex I've ever had," supposedly from Marla. And then the next day Liz would have the bombshell from the other side about Donald being a womanizer. He courted the gossips. A lot of them just fawned over him. He was a master of it. It's all about getting out there, keeping your name in the

---

* A boulevard in a Bronx neighborhood once known for its middle-class, striving nature.

paper, and changing direction and changing the subject, keeping people hanging on. He was always orchestrating it.

A. J. Benza: We worked with Trump a lot. In the morning you have a phone call with people over coffee. You bullshit about where was the party last night, who's getting laid. And then eventually [Trump] needs a favor, he needs copy, he drops a name. At that point he was doing all sorts of things in New York to try to get back on his feet.

Lloyd Grove, *gossip reporter,* New York *Daily News and the Daily Beast:* You knew that if worse comes to worse and you're down on your story quota, you could always get something from Donald. He definitely knew how to write a tabloid story. He just had a natural ability to communicate in bold headlines.

Stuart Marques: A lot of times I would ask a reporter, "Who's your source on this?" And it was always Trump. Norma or Trump. He knows how to play the game.

Jared Paul Stern, *Page Six reporter:* At the U.S. Open, he'd have a model agency night, and I would go to that every year and hang out with models in his suite next to where John McEnroe is commentating.

A. J. Benza: "Come to Mar-a-Lago. Give a helicopter ride. Let me know what you want to do." He just was very open to helping anybody. And you got the impression that if you accepted that gift, you owed him a favor.

Katie Couric, *TV newsperson:* When my daughter had a birthday party at the Wollman Rink, it was shortly after my husband died, and I needed to stay in there for a half-hour longer because of the timing of the birthday party. He had refurbished Wollman Rink, and I called him, and he was great about it. He said, "Yeah, absolutely."

Tucker Carlson, *Fox News:* Probably 20 years ago I was hosting a show on CNN, and I had this throwaway line, "That's the state of Donald Trump's hair." The next day I was with my kids at the swimming pool, and I got a message on my cell phone. I was sitting next to my wife, and the message, this is verbatim: "Tucker, it's Donald Trump. I saw what you said about my hair. It was true you have better hair than I do, but I get more pussy than you do." Click. And I called [political consultant] Roger Stone. "That really isn't Trump? Like, did he really send that in a message?" He's like, "Oh yeah, that was absolutely Trump."

Reverend Al Sharpton, *activist and MSNBC host:* Around '87, maybe '88, I get a call from Don King. King had been a supporter of my youth movement. And Don told me he wanted me to go with him to Atlantic City. And I said, "For what?" "I want you to go down, because we're thinking of doing fights down there, and I want you to meet Donald Trump, and I know you all got differences. He's not a bad guy." I said, "I don't want to meet Donald." Finally, he convinces me to go. We meet at the heliport on the West Side [of Manhattan], and we get on Trump's big black helicopter, and I'm sitting facing Don King and Donald Trump. And it was the most surreal 45 minutes of my life, because it was two guys talking nonstop about themselves. It didn't feel like either one of them even stopped for air and totally were not listening to each other. We get to where we're over Atlantic City, and Trump says to the pilot, "Circle the boardwalk. I want to show Al what I own. I got Trump whatever Plaza here, and I've got something here. And right there I'm going to build the Trump Taj Mahal." And I say, "Yeah, but you see all them huts over there? You're lucky I don't live down here, because we'd all be marching on the boardwalk. Because none of that's being invested in the community." Trump says, "Well, I want to work on the community."

Katie Couric: If the city is a play, then he's a character in that city, a Damon Runyon–type guy. He was never really embraced by New York society or the big swinging you-know-whats of Wall Street. He never had the street cred that he was searching for or got the imprimatur of some of those more sophisticated social people, and it drove him crazy.

Tucker Carlson: Trump touches a lot of people in a day by phone, which is an old-school habit. Trump's just checking in, asking, "What's going on, what do you know?" Six-minute conversations with 10 people a day, and that's one of the ways that he stays current.

A. J. Benza: One day, on my desk landed naked pictures of Marla. They had just gotten married, and they were the talk of the fucking town. I said, "Holy shit, these look real. These aren't doctored." So I called him. "Listen man, I've got naked pictures of Marla. They came in the mail."

He said, "Send them to me. Let me see." So, I sent them. I didn't make a copy of them. I didn't go to the supermarket tabloids, which a lot of people nowadays would have done in a second. And he goes, "These are real. That's her. What do you think of her?" I said, "She's a beautiful girl." And he goes, "You did me a solid. I owe you."

Reverend Al Sharpton: He feels that me and him navigated New York, and there's some feeling of camaraderie there, though we navigated much different parts of New York, and our politics are as different as could be. We're survivors, because he and I have been out here since the '80s, and there's not too many of us like that. Don King and him, though, are fellow travelers. They are both self-promoters. Trump defines friends as people he thinks have skills in what they do that he can reach out to. I don't think he has intimate friends. I've never met anybody who says, "This is my homie."

Tucker Carlson: Trump is much more transparent than anyone will acknowledge, like there's no real agenda with Trump that you can't see. It's all on the surface. Trump is exactly the way that he is in public, in private. His lines might be slightly saltier, just slightly, not much more. But he's exactly the same. He curses, he's a little bit disconnected, he's going back to things he's interested in, he's funny, he's a little weird. I've known the past four presidents. In their role as Mr. President and outside of that, they're totally different. Most politicians have a public face and a private face that have a bare resemblance to one another but are not the same thing. Trump? Exactly the same. I doubt you're gonna meet anybody who says, "Who is this guy? I don't even know this guy, that's not the Trump I know." Bullshit. That's exactly the Trump you know.

Trump often claims that he does not now nor has he ever imbibed alcohol, explaining that he wanted to avoid the fate of his alcoholic older brother Freddy, an airline pilot who died at 43 in 1981.[4] It has always seemed unlikely that Trump, who has regaled other writers with raunchy tales from partying in the 1970s at Studio 54, never tried an intoxicant. But sobriety has been part of the persona he peddles. Let everyone else get sloppy, the subtext goes. He wants consumers of the Trump brand and would-be lenders to believe he always keeps it together.

Trump separated from his second wife, Marla Maples, in May 1997, but he was out on the town for years before that. Nights among the famous and infamous during his 1990s bachelorhood gave Trump meat to feed gossip writers. Downtown, especially SoHo, had become home to a new type of nightclub. Small lounges like Spy Bar, Wax, and Chaos drew fashion models, artists, and a few Wall Streeters, along with Trump and his friend John Casablancas, founder of Elite Model Management. On any given night, the A-list at Wax reported in gossip columns might include Yankees shortstop Derek Jeter "cozying up to a stunning blonde" or indie film actress Parker Posey hosting a party with MTV News personality Serena Altschul, designer Alexandra von Furstenberg, and actor Chris Noth. Meanwhile, film actors Nicolas Cage and Stephen Dorff were "escorting three ladies to Chaos for Candyland night."

There beside Casablancas and in pursuit of European models, Trump drank, according to Laraby (a bartender who has long used only one name professionally, sometimes spelling it Larabee) and Michael Ault, a titan in clubland who is credited with inventing bottle service. One of the models Trump met in this era was Melania Knauss, a Slovenian invited to New York by the founder of the ID Models agency, Paolo Zampolli.

Donald Trump at a 2018 press conference: I'm not a drinker. I can honestly say I never had a beer in my life. . . . Whenever they are looking for something good, I say I never had a glass of alcohol.

Caron Bernstein, *model:* I was at clubs like eight nights a week in those days and ran with an entourage. We'd have all these club kids and models, and the night would start at a place called Pure Platinum on 21st Street, which is basically a strip club. There'd be all these girls that were known for their bodies, like Maureen Gallagher. They would get onto the poles with the strippers. It was more lax about doing drugs out in the open in public than the regular nightclubs, so we would start the night out at these strip clubs and it became a frenzy. I would see Epstein,* Trump, like all the old geezers, at that place too. It would be the prequel to whatever club we were going to, like the earlier part of the night, 11:00, 11:30.

Laraby, *bartender at various 1990s clubs:* I served him. And he drank at the bar. He'd come in with John Casablancas. He'd go to the side of the bar [at Spy] by the waitress station, because he liked the waitresses. He would order light beer. It was usually Miller Lite or Bud Light. John ordered vodka-based drinks. If they could get some large-breasted beautiful young European girl's attention, they would get a nice bottle of wine, sometimes champagne, and move to a table. He drank his beer

---

* Referring to the infamous registered sex offender Jeffrey Epstein.

out of the bottle. He would nurse his beer. Even if they were there for hours, he would have three beers at the most.

Michael Ault, *owner of 1990s Manhattan lounges Spy Bar and Chaos:* I would hear from the doorman that he was on the way to our table. I'd think, oh, it's going to be one of those nights. People talk about how he's such a genius PR guy and marketing guy, and I guess that's true. But it felt like you were in the presence of someone who was constantly selling you something. He would talk about his successes, he would talk about how he started from nothing. At the time, he was opening his Atlantic City casinos, and he was talking about how big they were going to be, like they were going to be the best casinos in the country and no one had spent this much money on a casino. He didn't want to know how my day was, but he was certainly prepared to talk about how his day was. Maybe that's what you do when you're a real estate mogul, you're selling something all the time. I just wish occasionally he would turn that off and say how are you, what are you doing? It was boring.

Laraby: John was really nice, he would say, "Hey Lara, what's going on? Where you been?" Whereas Trump was very fucking awkward, and it was like John was Trump's wingman to get him laid. That was his dynamic. Like, this is how you be a human in a club.

Michael Ault: We had champagne on the table, always, and we had vodka usually, some scotch. He was drinking champagne or vodka, a liquor and not really a beer so much, but I could be wrong on the beer, I just never saw him with one.

Laraby: Trump was not a good tipper at all. He would stand at the bar, and if he was paying, which he sometimes did, John would have like three drinks, and he would have his beer and then they would get their bottle of wine, and the wine was expensive, and then he would leave me, like, two dollars. He never paid with a credit card. He'd have a wad of cash, and he'd leave me two dollars. I wanted to kill him.

Sara Conca, *model, artist, and patron at Wax, Chaos, and Life:* Everybody would couch surf and end up at a table and have a drink. Donald Trump was there, and he was always a gentleman with me. He would hang out with John Casablancas and there was a bunch of Brazilian girls, but it was John who really loved the Brazilian girls.

Michael Ault: We paid girls to come every night. Modeling agency bookers were on our payroll. Owners of agencies were on our payroll. Plus, when all these girls were there, they attracted all the other girls.

Paolo Zampolli, *ID Models founder:* We were at the Kit Kat Club, and I introduced them. "Melania, please meet Donald." You could see champagne and vodka on the table, but for sure Mr. Trump had only Diet Coke. That's what he drinks since I've known him. This was a Fashion Week party. Melania was a successful model. I met her in Milano. I invited her to come to my agency in New York. She was hanging out a lot with my girlfriend, eating healthy, going to the gym, what girls do. Two weeks later I did a dinner at my house with Roberto Cavalli and [Donald and Melania] show up together.

In his calls to reporters, Trump tattled about who showed up where and with whom, and asked for something in return. Sometimes it was a mention of a new project or a book. More typically, he wanted the adjective "billionaire" preceding his name when the New York Post's *Page Six, the New York* Daily News's *Hot Copy, or* Newsday's *Inside New York mentioned him. Whether or not he was a billionaire—and many Trump experts doubt it—was not a concern of gossip reporters who had a hunger for usable items to fill column space seven days a week and little interest in fact-checking. A New York* Daily News *gossip-page item about Sean Combs's twenty-sixth-birthday party at SoHo's NV bar reported that Trump was there "with two voluptuous blondes and presented Puffy with the perfect gift: a copy of* Trump: The Art of the Comeback."

In September 1998, the National Enquirer *began an article with "Donald Trump is the sexiest billionaire alive," revealing results of a poll of three hundred women. Trump garnered 70.3 percent of the vote. Fashion designer Ralph Lauren was second at 9.7 percent. Texas billionaire Ross Perot got 3 percent. The article accompanying the poll quoted an "inside source" at a Hamptons party dishing that two models, Kara Young and Celina Midelfart, tussled over Trump. One of the "world-class beauties" was left behind "screaming and crying."*

Everything was fine if you played along, and most reporters did.

A. J. Benza: One of the main things you had to do to put him in a column as a payback was that he always liked that we got the word "billionaire" in there. You couldn't just write "Donald Trump." You had to say "billionaire Donald Trump." That's fine, because we like to use adjectives. He didn't care what other adjectives preceded the word "billionaire." We could have said "pompous billionaire." He didn't care. The word "billionaire" was what was important. We got a kick out of it. I care as much about [whether he was really a billionaire or not] as I do about Kylie Jenner. I don't give a fuck. All I know is they have more money than I'll ever see in 20 fucking lifetimes.

Donald Trump, *from March 25, 1999, interview with Allen Salkin:* I'm much bigger now than I was in the '80s. I'm actually a little bit more conservative now. I've learned that ultimately it's good to be conservative because bad things come. I joke that I'd like to see a real estate market collapse because I'm in a position to buy a lot of things.

Wayne Barrett, spurred by investigative reporter Jack Newfield, a colleague at the weekly Village Voice, *had started reporting on Trump's dealings in the 1970s.*

Tom Robbins, *journalist,* Village Voice *and New York* Daily News: Newfield spotted Trump as an up-and-coming power broker type, someone who was trying to elbow his way into the big time and had all of the signs of a faker. He suggested Wayne go after him. Trump tried to bribe him. "Wayne, you don't have to live in Brownsville [Brooklyn]. I have apartments." It was in the middle of interviewing him. Wayne realized that he was being bribed. He said, "That's okay. I like living where I live. I don't have to move."

Jon Elsen, New York Post *business editor:* One time, Chris Byron writes a column about Trump, very critical, and one of the main points he makes is that Trump is not worth nearly as much as he says, which since then has surfaced many times in many different ways from different writers. I get a call from Trump, and he says, "Listen, Jon, I don't want to sue you, and I don't want to sue the *Post*, but I'm going to sue Byron." I laughed, because I'd never heard anything quite like that, and to me it reflected that he basically showed no understanding of how newspapers work or how the world works in general, yet it was outside-the-box thinking, because he was flattering yet threatening. I said, "I appreciate the thought, but if you sue Byron, then you're suing the *Post* and suing me." He said, "Well, I don't want to do that." And I said, "Well, do what you have to do, but if it involves a lawsuit, you're going to have to talk to our lawyers." He never sued. After he called me to complain about Byron, he had Howard [Rubenstein, a publicist] call me to see if he could come in for a lunch, and I said sure. A bunch of editors joined us. He never brought up Byron's column.

Stuart Marques: There was a period in the '90s when the *Post* kept writing that he's not a billionaire, that he was only worth about $700 million, $800 million. He would call up and complain to the business editors and to Ken [Chandler, the editor in chief], "I'm a billionaire. I'm a billionaire." Finally, one day he comes into an editorial board meeting for a lunch. He was talking about different things, and how wonderful and great it all is.

Jon Elsen: Trump told a funny story about Mike Tyson at the lunch. He said there were some reports that he had slept with Tyson's wife, Robin Givens. This is when he was promoting Tyson's fights. He said Tyson asked to see him, and when he got there, Tyson sat down across his desk and said—and here Trump tries to mimic Tyson's high voice—"Donald, there's a rumor that you're sleeping with Robin, is it true?" Trump says, "I see my life flash before my eyes, and I look at him and I'm thinking. And finally I say"—and here he begins to slowly shake his head side to side—"No. Mike it's not true." So Tyson says, "I didn't think so," and leaves. The beauty of the story is that Trump never tells us if the rumors were actually true. The clear implication is that they were, and he got away with it. So basically he's bragging about his sexual prowess and his ability to get away with anything.

Stuart Marques: And, of course, me, I threw out a couple of snarky questions, which he danced around. When he got up to leave, he shook everybody's hand. He grabbed my hand, he held it extra tight and put a second hand on it, and he turned and looked—I don't know if Rupert [Murdoch, CEO of *Post* owner NewsCorp] was there, but I know Ken was there and some others. He grabbed it really hard. He looked at the others and said, "You better keep an eye on this one."

Tom Robbins: When Wayne Barrett finally decided to do a book about him, Trump had him locked up. Barrett goes to his party up in the Taj

Mahal. These off-duty cops were doing security, arrest him, and hold him in the Atlantic City jail. Wayne thought that he could get Donald to cooperate with the book. He has a great line in his book where he says, "This is where I realized that Trump wasn't going to cooperate." He was handcuffed to a wall in the cell.[5] When Wayne's book came out [in 1992], he was devastated, because at that point Trump's star had fallen, he was going under in Atlantic City. Trump did everything he could to try to sabotage the book in addition to getting [Wayne] arrested. Warning people not to talk to him, trying to cut off all his access. But he laughed about what a failure the book was.[6] The people who did tough stories about him were few and far between. He was able to really just duke it out with editors, beat them back.

A. J. Benza: Fortunately for us, he gave up dirt on people and information that fleshed out other stories. So we didn't mind dropping in the story about him with so-and-so at the Knicks game, the billionaire blah blah blah.

Lloyd Grove, *gossip reporter:* I didn't really challenge him on the facts, so I guess in that sense I was being an enabler and lazy. But he was a colorful personality. He wasn't the president of the United States.

Jared Paul Stern: Page Six deserves credit for building his profile. I don't know if credit is the right word.

Donny Deutsch, *advertising executive and CNBC host:* Trump is not well read. He's not a sophisticated thinker, but he's an evil genius. Call him an idiot savant, whatever you want, but I've never seen a guy who understands messaging and consistency of messaging and staying on brand and being able to be true to the brand but also evolve the brand at the same time. The guy's a genius.

2.

THE TOUGH AND TIRELESS ROGER STONE

Donald Trump's political upbringing had three fathers. He learned about government from his biological father, Fred, about power from attorney Roy Cohn, and about campaigns from Republican strategist Roger Stone.

Fred Trump grew up in Woodhaven, Queens, and lost his father to the 1918 Spanish flu pandemic. In 1927, he founded a real estate company with his mother to build single-family homes and expanded the business after World War II to develop apartment complexes in Brooklyn and Queens with the help of generous federal loans. Donald Trump often accompanied his father to survey construction sites, greet tenants, and butter up politicians.

Roy Cohn was chief counsel to Senator Joseph McCarthy during the infamous anticommunist congressional hearings in the 1950s. Cohn met Donald Trump through Eugene Morris, one of the city's top real estate lawyers, who Fred Trump had hired for real estate transactions. Cohn went on to become Trump's favorite lawyer, an irreplaceable henchman and the immoral center of Tony Kushner's Pulitzer Prize–winning drama Angels in America. *Trump kept a framed photo of Cohn on his desk, and the pair often held court at 21 Club and Studio 54. Cohn talked up Trump to his reporter friends, including Cindy Adams. "This kid is going to own New York someday," Cohn told her in the early '70s.[1]*

Barely two months before Cohn died from an AIDS-related illness in 1986, the Washington Post *anointed Roger Stone as "the next generation's Roy Cohn."[2] Stone started his career as a 19-year-old aide to President Nixon's re-election campaign in 1972 and became known as a master of the black arts in politics. He covertly donated to a Nixon rival under the moniker of the Young Socialist Alliance and sent the receipt to a New Hampshire newspaper. He also successfully placed a mole inside the Hubert Humphrey campaign who became Humphrey's driver. Stone met Cohn while working on Ronald Reagan's 1980 presidential campaign.*[3] *Stone embraced his dirty trickster reputation and formed a lobbying firm with Paul Manafort and Charlie Black in 1980, taking on clients, such as foreign dictators, few others in Washington, DC, would accept.*

Stone viewed Trump as a charismatic outsider with the potential to upend a presidential race. In the opening pages of his 2000 book The America We Deserve, *Trump acknowledges "my friend and associate, the tough and tireless Roger Stone."*

Roger Stone, *Republican political consultant and lobbyist:* I met Donald Trump in 1979 when I was sent to New York to run the Reagan campaign for president for 1980 for the three-state region—New York, New Jersey, Connecticut. Mike Deaver, who was President Reagan's man, gave me a card file—President Reagan's friends in New York. Most were dead, but there was a card for Roy M. Cohn, Esquire. I contacted him cold. I went to ask him for help because I needed a headquarters, I needed people, I needed telephones, I needed a finance committee. He introduced me to Trump. Trump liked Reagan. He had been visited by [John] Connally, [James] Baker, [George H. W.] Bush. Everybody had taken a trek to get him on their finance committee. He was sour on Jimmy Carter. We became friends.

Dean Barkley, *Independence Party U.S. senator from Minnesota 2002–2003:* Roger's a good old political operative. He always seems to appear where there's power and money.

Robert Torricelli, *Democratic U.S. senator from New Jersey 1997–2003:* They had a genuine friendship, and they see the world in a similar way. Roger's also very smart, and understood politics and how to build campaigns and communicate in ways that Donald Trump did not at the time. In a lot of ways, he probably saw Roger as a successor of Roy Cohn—smart, focused.

Roger Stone: Roy was the first one to spot the potential for Donald Trump, an outer-borough son of a homebuilder, who was tall and handsome and audacious. Roy was Donald's guy to the fast-track, cutthroat world of Manhattan real estate, quite different than what they do in Queens.

Dick Morris, *Republican political strategist:* My father was Donald Trump's lawyer on most of his important real estate deals. He handled the legal work for Trump Tower, which Trump told me "is the most important and complicated job I ever did, and the only one I really needed a lawyer on." My father, whose name was Eugene Morris, was the dean of the real estate attorneys in New York City, particularly among Jews. His first cousin was Roy Cohn, Trump's mentor. My father and Roy weren't brothers, but they might as well have been, because my father's mother lived with the Cohns when my dad was young. I grew up knowing Donald Trump as a household name. He came over to dinner a few times when he was young. That really began my relationship with Donald.

Roger Stone: Roy was extraordinarily pugnacious. He was very combative and very aggressive and got things done, and Trump liked those qualities. He wanted a bulldog in his lawyer, he was a bulldog in the boardroom in terms of deal-making. He admired Roy's ability to bring in a whole new element of the media coverage. That's what made Donald Trump. It has been reported that after Roy's illness became known that Donald became cruel to him. I don't know that firsthand. After the election, he has always said fond things like, "Boy would Roy be proud of us or what?" or, "Don't you wish Roy was here to see this?" So those do not indicate a lack of respect.

Rick Wilson, *Republican political strategist:* It's an absolutely symbiotic relationship. For all of Roger's years in politics, he's never been rich, he's never been one of these guys to walk out of a campaign with $20 million of consulting [fees]. Roger's great at being Roger. Roger's not so good at putting together legislative programs or doing the mechanicals of actual campaigns. He's a one-trick pony, the dirty trickster emails or direct-mail pieces or pranking some candidate into saying something stupid. That's great and a useful task, and he's very good at those things, but he's not a modern campaign guy. Roger could never spin data if it bit him on the ass.

Tucker Carlson: When I knew them in the '90s, Roger was [Trump's] self-described "bag man." Roger wore a pinky ring to signify his involvement in what he described as the gaming industry with Mr. Trump, and he would always be with Mr. Trump and Mrs. Trump in a John Gotti Jr. way.

Roger Stone: What Trump does is he has somebody print out for him every story that mentions his name—and he reads the clips. Then sometimes he would write in the margin, "Send to Roger Stone, what about this?" He would have it sent to you by a secretary, "Please see the attached note from Mr. Trump." Nixon also did it, interestingly enough.

Eleanor Clift, *political reporter for* Newsweek *and the Daily Beast:* Roger has been committed to a Trump presidency for a long time.

Robert Torricelli: Roger doesn't get enough credit. All this was Roger's idea, and he was the only architect.

Many people were confused about Trump's political leanings. His Democratic friends, including former City Council president Andrew Stein and then–New Jersey senator Bob Torricelli, thought he was a moderate Democrat or an independent because he gave money to their campaigns and professed socially liberal views. Yet Trump Tower was a perennial stop for Republican leaders, such as Republican National Committee chairman Jim Nicholson, looking to replenish the party's treasury.

Roger Stone: In 1988, when I first put this idea forward, he liked the idea of it, the publicity of it, the speculation. He's a genius showman when it comes to getting press and getting focus on your idea. Even then he was talking about the trade imbalances and the fact that our trading partners are screwing us, and even the imbalances at NATO and why our allies aren't paying their fair share. He's been amazingly consistent. And his speech in New Hampshire where he spoke in the Chamber of Commerce got enormous free coverage. I had engineered the invitation from a friend of mine in the chamber named Mike Dunbar[4]—he's a city councilman—just so Trump could go up there and show some leg. He had a good time, but he didn't seriously think about running in 1988.[5]

Andrew Stein, *Democratic Manhattan borough president:* He was an independent. I never thought of him in any box. First of all, he just supported people as a practical matter through his real estate stuff. But I never thought of him as particularly liberal or particularly conservative.

Roger Stone: He had a low regard for politicians, a low regard for the political system, a low regard for all the suppliants who came sniveling for money. He disdained the system even though he was participating in it by giving.

Robert Torricelli: Donald had friends in both political parties in the New York region for years. If he wasn't intellectually interested in issues, he at least had a business interest in issues like casino gaming. He was as involved in New Jersey politics as he was in New York City because he had a massive investment in Atlantic City.

Roger Stone: Donald was always a generous contributor to both Republicans and Democrats, because he knew how the system worked. He was a Republican. In '88 he had a reception at the Plaza Hotel for George H. W. Bush, and he raised more than $100,000. All of his lawyers and vendors and friends are there. He knew you would have [Congress] members' attention if you made contributions. He had always maxed out to the Republican Senate Committee and to the presidential. He understood it was part of being in business in New York.

Andrew Stein: He contributed a lot of money to my campaigns and others'. He just has a natural affinity for politics.

Tom Robbins: Donald gave Andrew Stein a lot of money. In turn, Andrew Stein backed him on every single thing he ever wanted. He was the borough president of Manhattan. I was looking at the list of all the Trump entities that Donald would give through—$10,000 from each one of them.

Barbara Res, *former Trump Organization construction manager:* Donald didn't like any of them. He just wanted influence, that's all. Donald doesn't have convictions. He doesn't feel any way about an issue. What can it do for him? How can he make it work for him?

Jim Nicholson, *Republican National Committee chairman 1997–2001:* I had a couple meetings with Donald Trump in Trump Tower to see about getting money for the RNC, but I do not ever remember talking to him about his presidential aspirations. I was quite aware of his real estate prowess, and I have a real estate background, so I was very respectful of what he accomplished in real estate in a very tough city. He was a person of high visibility and wealth and involvement, and those are the people

I called on to raise money for the RNC. I had an organization called the Team of Hundred, which was that people would give $100,000 a year to the RNC, so that's what I asked him for. I got rebuffed.

Robert Torricelli: I always thought of Donald Trump more in those years as being a moderate Democrat. When I was chairman of the Democratic Campaign Committee, he contributed to that. He helped me raise money and came to fundraisers. He certainly was socially progressive. I certainly never thought he was a conservative Republican.

Roger Stone: Well, he was a conservative. Donald was a Republican for virtually all of his life. Both of his parents were staunch Republicans in their private leanings. I discussed it with both of them. Locally, his father contributed to Democrats, because the Queens machine controlled zoning and building. If you went to his office, he would have pictures of the mayor and the borough president, but in his personal politics, in his national politics, he was a subscriber to the *National Review,* he was a major donor to Barry Goldwater, he had given to Billy Graham's revival. He had given to those who worked on anticommunist crusades.

Joe Lieberman, *Democratic U.S. senator from Connecticut 1989–2013:* He was very cordial and interesting. I asked him for a contribution, and he wrote out a check, about $1,000, which was the max then.

Ed Rendell, *Philadelphia mayor 1992–2000 and Democratic governor of Pennsylvania 2003–2011:* He gave me a little money to run for mayor. When I got elected, I had him down to a Rangers–Flyers hockey game, and then I also had him come down for the Welcome America celebration.[6] We had local fighters fighting the Irish Olympic team, and we gave the award to Muhammad Ali. Joe Frazier was there to help me present the award to Ali, and Donald came down for that. So it's fair to say he was somewhat of a friend of mine, and when I ran for governor in 2002, he gave me significant money, somewhere between $20,000 and $50,000.

Tony Coelho, *Al Gore campaign chairman and Democratic congressman from California 1979–1989:* When I was the Democratic Whip in the House of Representatives and Jim Wright was Speaker of the House, he contributed to the Democratic Congressional Campaign Committee. Jim used to be a boxer, and he wound up taking us to a boxing match in Brooklyn and flew us in his shared helicopter. I felt that it was him trying to gain credibility by being engaged and involved and to be able to say that he took the Speaker to the boxing match.

Dick Ravitch, *Democratic lieutenant governor of New York 2009–2010:* Don't you think it's interesting that somebody like myself who has been immersed in New York [politics]—I was chairman of several civic organizations, I was in the government—you would have thought I would have run into Donald Trump? Practically every businessman from David Rockefeller to all kinds of people in the real estate business played active roles in all of these organizations. Donald Trump never did. He had no presence, wasn't a member, didn't involve himself.

Reverend Al Sharpton: Mike Tyson bought a mansion up in Connecticut [in 1996], and Don King invited me to the housewarming. I went up to the master bedroom, and on the balcony stood Don King and Donald Trump and all of these guys from the hood, which Tyson's crowd was. This was not your upper-echelon black entrepreneur crowd. And Trump and Don King standing there and talking about fight deals and all that. That's when he and I start talking again. And he told me, "I'm helping a lot of Democrats. You call me."

When Trump declared his candidacy for the presidency years later, part of his speech can be traced directly to these very experiences, buying politicians for what amounted to a pile of pennies. "So I've watched the politicians," Trump said at the bottom of the Trump Tower escalator in June 2015. "I've dealt with them all my life. If you can't make a good deal with a politician, then there's something wrong with you. You're certainly not very good. And that's what we have representing us. They will never make America great again. They don't even have a chance. They're controlled fully—they're controlled fully by the lobbyists, by the donors, and by the special interests, fully."

3.

ROSS FOR BOSS

Populism in American history can be traced through the Boston Tea Party in 1773, the presidency of Andrew Jackson from 1829 to 1837, and the formation of the Populist Party in 1892, when heartland farmers demanded the federal government regulate railroads and boost grain prices. With the populists' help, former Nebraska congressman William Jennings Bryan won the Democratic Party's nomination for president in 1896 following his "Cross of Gold" speech praising farmers and miners while chastising businessmen and urban elites.

Populism upended the Republican Party when Arizona senator Barry Goldwater ran for president in 1964 calling for limited government, lowered taxes, and repeal of the Civil Rights Act. He lost in a landslide but appealed to Southern conservative Democrats, whom Republican Richard Nixon courted in 1968 and 1972 in a geographic realignment that led to Ronald Reagan's victory in 1980.

By 1992, more voters described themselves as independent (36 percent) than Democratic (33 percent) or Republican (28 percent).[1] A charismatic Texas billionaire named H. Ross Perot appealed to white non-college-educated voters by chastising the country's stultifying political class, promising to eliminate the national debt, and saying he would curtail the outsourcing of manufacturing jobs to Mexico, which he called a "giant sucking sound."

In many ways, Perot was Trump before Trump, not only in having a populist agenda, but also in adeptly using alternative forms of media. Trump would have Twitter; Perot made 30-minute television infomercials and launched a dial-in number for an electronic town hall. One of Perot's many folksy and memorable quotes was, "War has rules, mud wrestling has rules—politics has no rules." With the slogan "Ross for Boss," he led the polls over President George H. W. Bush and Arkansas governor Bill Clinton in June 1992 and ultimately received 19 percent of the vote.

Whether it was Perot or someone else, the electorate was displaying a hunger for an alternative, someone outside the two-party system. Leftist activists, frustrated with Clinton's "New Democrat" centrism, established a Green Party in more than two dozen states and encouraged consumer rights activist Ralph Nader to run for president in 1996 and 2000.

Perot's success in 1992 led him to found the Reform Party. In 1996, he captured only 8 percent of the vote but created a national party infrastructure. Whoever would be the Reform Party presidential candidate in 2000 was entitled to $12.6 million in federal matching funds for the general election campaign.

Starting in 1999, a range of political candidates began circling, including paleoconservative populist Pat Buchanan, leftist Lenora Fulani, fiscally conservative former Connecticut governor Lowell Weicker, socially liberal former wrestler Jesse Ventura, retired four-star general Colin Powell, actor Warren Beatty—and Trump. Perot, according to his former campaign manager Russell Verney and former running mate Pat Choate, had not ruled out running again himself.

Roger Stone: Trump liked Perot. Like everybody else, his confidence in Perot was undermined when Perot dropped out of the race [in 1992], claiming the Bushes had tried to disrupt his daughter's wedding, and then dropped back into the race. Recognize there was a time when Perot was leading both of his opponents in the polls. There was a window in which we may have elected somebody who was not a Republican or a Democrat. Russell Verney was a very capable guy who had run Perot's campaign.

Russell Verney, *former Reform Party chairman:* Perot in '92 focused on economic and government reform issues. Reducing deficit spending and cutting the national debt were major. Fair trade was major. Campaign finance reform and a lot of other government reform issues including the IRS were issues. I also managed his campaign in 1996.

Ralph Nader, *Green Party presidential candidate in 1996 and 2000:* Perot wasn't a complete candidate. He wasn't well versed in some stuff, but he certainly was about not messing around in other people's backyards, even though he was big on helping POWs. He didn't think they should have been sent there in the first place.

Russell Verney: Perot needed his family to get his business started, but he wound up creating EDS [Electronic Data Systems], which had over 200,000 worldwide employees, and then a second, similar company, Perot Systems, which eventually had another 100,000 employees worldwide.

Pat Choate, *Reform Party politician:* The two parties control the debates. Ross only got in in '92 because H. W. [Bush] agreed to let him in. In '96, Clinton and Dole refused to let Perot and me into the debate. The moment it was impossible to get into the debate, he was just dead meat. If Perot had run in '96 as a Republican, he could have won the presidency. This is something that Mike Poss, then Perot's chief of staff, in '95, and I argued with Perot about at some depth. We argued that it was possible to take over the Republican Party and that if we took over, the Republicans would fall in line. Perot didn't want to do that. He wanted a clean party, start from scratch.

Russell Verney: As a result of the 1996 election results, Perot was eligible for public funding in 2000, and he assigned that right to the Reform Party once he created it. Therefore, whoever we chose to be our nominee would be eligible for that money. Nobody besides the Republicans and Democrats had ever qualified for general election funding.

The Reform Party blossomed before 2000. Former professional wrestler Jesse "The Body" Ventura had won the election for mayor of the Minneapolis suburb Brooklyn Park in 1991, but the state's political establishment largely ignored him. The love many Minnesotans had for him, however, was noticed by political activist Dean Barkley, who had formed the state's Independence Party, which would become affiliated with the Reform Party.

Dean Barkley: I first ran for office in 1992 as an Independent. When Ross Perot decided to run for president, I paid a lot of attention to what he did. I helped form the Independence Party, and in '96, I was running for U.S. Senate to get major party status in Minnesota. That's when I met Jesse Ventura. He was a talk show host on KSTP, and he had just won the mayor's race in Brooklyn Park. The Democrats and the Republicans both ganged up on him, and he called them the Republahcans and the

Awfulcrats, and the Crips and Bloods. I called into his show quite a bit to get some free press. I asked him if he would join me at a Fourth of July parade in Annandale, Minnesota, my hometown. A third of the way through that parade, I first noticed the Ventura phenomena, where everybody was cheering for him and ignoring me. The lightbulb went on, and I said, "Gosh, I wonder if this could be turned into political power?" I said, "Jesse, the wrong guy's running. Next time, you're going to run." He laughed and said, "No, I'm not going to move to Washington," and I said, "Well, in two years, we've got a governor's race." I worked on Jesse after my '96 campaign. I finally convinced him to run for governor when his wife reluctantly said, "Alright."

Jesse Ventura, *Minnesota governor 1999–2003:* I always vote third party. The Democrats and Republicans, they cause the problems. They don't solve them.

Dean Barkley: We put him anywhere and everywhere there was a crowd, the Minneapolis Aquatennial or the St. Paddy's Day parade, put him in my little '69 Camaro convertible. Usually in a parade like that you almost have to go up to people and have them take your literature. He was being mobbed. We have a national CBS crew following us. I said to the crew, "What's this about?" They answered, "We want to see what this wrestler is gonna do." That's when we first got the inkling that it was more than just a Minnesota story. When we made Jesse available, the media would show up. I always told Jesse, "Tell the truth, and if you don't know the truth, just admit you don't know and you'll figure it out. And that'll make you completely different than your opponents." We had two career politicians, [St. Paul] Mayor Norm Coleman and Attorney General Hubert H. "Skip" Humphrey in their little gray suits saying the typical crap you hear from Democrats and Republicans. Little canned speeches they say no matter what the question is without answering the question, and it was the perfect foil. You've got Jesse the big bad wrestling guy in there who tells it like it is. Traditionally they'd say he didn't have a chance. But it was status quo versus somebody different.

Ventura, running as a Reform Party candidate, the successor to Barkley's Independence Party, won 37 percent of the vote, edging out Republican Norm Coleman (34 percent) and Democrat Hubert Humphrey III (28 percent), earning headlines around the country[2] and demonstrating the Reform Party had the power to elevate outsiders to high office. Roger Stone was among those who recognized that the Reform ticket held promise for the right presidential candidate in 2000. Trump happened to be friendly with both Perot and Ventura, one through business connections and the other through wrestling promotions.

Jesse Ventura: Six of us, after the election in Minnesota, we were sitting in my kitchen the next day with the afterglow, and we all looked around the table and started laughing. "What the hell do we do now?" Because we had no experience. We were now going to run the state of Minnesota.

Roger Stone: The local Reform Party people, they had pulled off a miracle. It was a three-way race with three heavyweight candidates, including Skip Humphrey, Hubert Humphrey's son, who was the state attorney general.

Dean Barkley: After he won, my God, the attention Ventura got. The whole world paid attention to what the hell happened in Minnesota.

Roger Stone: Donald did not have a high regard for the other potential candidates in 2000, Al Gore and George W. Bush. He had known Jesse Ventura for many years, because Jesse did WrestleMania at Trump Plaza.

Jesse Ventura: Trump's link to wrestling was we had the fastest sellout he's ever had at his big Trump place in Atlantic City. He held WrestleMania IV and V [1988 and 1989]. Big money. Donald likes that. He likes the high profile. He likes to be seen at things like that. He treated all of us wonderful, all the talent.* He'd come in and shake our hands and talk to us all. He's a very personable guy.

Dean Barkley: It was show. It was entertainment. And it was manipulating crowds. Trump liked the limelight, and that's what pro wrestling was, a big dog-and-pony show that marketed itself well, and people liked it.

---

* Ventura, retired from competition, was a commentator.

Roger Stone: They had a good relationship and very similar views, anti-interventionist and so on.

Pat Choate: Trump was a person who had money, and he was a New York personality in the tabloids at that point. Anyone who has a lot of money and is a personality and is media savvy is someone you would take seriously.

Perot tapped into the dissatisfaction with trade policies that led to a decline of manufacturing jobs, and a Washington-based political class that didn't seem to care. Ventura's success in Minnesota signified that the Reform Party could attract populist leaders who could win elections by speaking to the public's anxieties. Seizing the Reform Party helm was a rare and tempting opportunity.

4.

THE AMERICA
WE DESERVE

By the start of 1999, it was clear the 2000 election would be wide open, with Texas governor George W. Bush, New Jersey senator Bill Bradley, Arizona senator John McCain, and publishing executive Steve Forbes expressing interest. Other candidates who sought the Republican ticket included Tennessee governor Lamar Alexander, New Hampshire senator Bob Smith, Elizabeth Dole, Ohio congressman John Kasich, and conservative pundit Pat Buchanan, who had twice run for the presidency in the 1990s. Ralph Nader prepared another run, and "radical centrist" Lowell Weicker,[1] who had left the Republican Party and won Connecticut's gubernatorial race in 1990 as an independent, sought a party from which to launch a presidential bid.

As presidential hopefuls began soliciting campaign cash, Roger Stone convinced Trump to consider a run. He argued that an exploration might demonstrate that the mogul had a real chance of winning—and there was a $12.6 million pot in federal matching funds and, possibly, a podium on the debate stage awaiting the Reform Party's nominee.[2]

Stone knew Trump needed a policy book if he was to be taken seriously. His rivals were well ahead of him. Bill Bradley had published a memoir in 1996 and a meditation on lessons from his professional basketball experience in 1998. Pat Buchanan authored The Great Betrayal *in 1998 and* A Republic, Not an Empire, *on foreign policy, in 1999, the same year that George W. Bush published an autobiographical collection of stories called* A Charge to Keep *and John McCain released his family memoir about war,* Faith of My Fathers.

Trump did have policy ideas about trade with China and Mexico, nuclear proliferation in North Korea, terrorism, taxes, and healthcare, but the Trump brand was about over-the-top luxury and a mythos of gutsiness in business. The occasional op-ed and full-page advocacy advertisement in the New York Times *were not enough to make Trump a convincing political product.*

Trump had long said he didn't think someone like him could win. But if Jesse Ventura could be elected governor, why not Trump for president?

Roger Stone: I saw very early on that he had the capacity to be elected president. I didn't really care what party. I was just looking for that opportunity. I recognized that the voters would have to reach their saturation point with conventional politics and parties, but I thought that moment was coming. It ultimately came.

Jim Nicholson, *Republican National Committee chairman 1997–2001:* I had three meetings with Trump—in '98, in '99, and then again in 2000. The first two meetings were not very pleasant. He kept me waiting a very long time, and then all I got from him was a lecture about how screwed up we Republicans were, and I did not get any money. He thought we weren't doing enough about reducing the debt and reducing taxes. We were too caught up on social issues and not enough on economic issues.

Roger Stone: Ross Perot had performed so well, the party was entitled to a $38 million check from the federal government once they nominated a candidate.* You could run for president on other people's money.

Tucker Carlson, *Fox News:* That's always the problem, and Stone will tell you that again and again—"Trump is incredibly cheap, and that's why he's rich and I'm not." Trump hates to spend money. It's a point of principle for him that the less you spend, the better you are. So the fact that Perot was funding the Reform Party and had the national stage, there was that promise you could run for president on the cheap.

Rick Wilson, *Republican political strategist:* Roger told him, "Hey, you don't have to do anything, really. Just get your name out there, it'll be fun. You'll be more famous."

---

* It was $12.6 million.

Phil Madsen, *Reform Party operative:* They were doing exactly what you would be doing if you were thinking about running for president. You're making contact with people. You're listening. You're testing the waters. You're asking questions. You're wanting to see what's going on.

Roger Stone: Yeah, it would be fair to say, and he has said this publicly, Roger was always more enthusiastic about it than I was, and that's true.

Phil Madsen: The Reform Party was of interest because Ventura had just won. He made history by becoming a third-party candidate. And he was not an independent. This was a true third party.

In early 1999, Stone enlisted a service founded by ghostwriters for Republican presidents, the White House Writers Group, which assigned the job of a Trump policy book to Virginia-based writer Dave Shiflett, who would complete the manuscript in April 1999. The book displays some Trump foreign policy and economic objectives that have carried through the years and some that don't.

Dave Shiflett, *co-author,* The America We Deserve: The phone rang and someone asked me if I'd be interested in writing a book for Donald Trump. I said, "What does he want a book written about?" And they said, "He's writing a book about what he would do if he were president." At the time he was nothing but a real estate guy, a Manhattan jet-setter. I said, "This would be my first published work of fiction, but I'll be glad to talk to him about it."

Roger Stone: We were going after a different constituency. We were running more as a centrist for the Reform Party nomination, hoping to have a candidate to our right and a candidate to our left. That's why the book Trump published, *The America We Deserve,* is more centrist on health insurance, on abortion.

Dave Shiflett: That was the first I'd heard of the Reform Party. I guess someone had convinced him he needed a book that contained all his political beliefs. I went up to his office, and it was a lot of fun. It was a little gaudy. It's got all that pink marble. He had a modeling agency, so you were surrounded by beautiful women. They looked like they'd been cooked up in a laboratory, flawless beauties. Roger was there. He's the only person whose name I knew. And then he had these three guys who were lawyers or assistants in blue suits. He would tell a joke, and they would all laugh. It was like a B-movie. "That's a good one boss!"

We sat down at his desk, and he would talk. He's cracking jokes, and he took a call from Bob Torricelli, the Torch, the senator from New Jersey. At the time Torricelli was dating Bianca Jagger. So they were talking about Bianca for a minute, and then he hung up. We'd bring up a subject, and he talked in general terms. I was in there for an hour and 45 minutes.

It was a deal where they said, here are the chapters, here's roughly what they're going to say, here's the points we want to make, and I filled in the blanks. He was most animated about terrorism. This was a couple years after the first attack on the World Trade Center, when a bomb went off in the parking garage, so that was most on his mind. He had an uncle at MIT [John G. Trump] who explained to him that somebody could bring a suitcase bomb into Manhattan and that would be the end of Manhattan. And he talked about North Korea and how they must never be allowed to get nuclear weapons or the ability to deliver a nuclear weapon to the United States, because they would do it. He also talked about Iran. He said if North Korea gets away with creating those big nuclear problems, you're going to have the same problem with Iran. Trump's view was that to get North Korea to the table, you might have to use military force, and you would blow up one facility and say you want to come back to the table? No? Then you blow up another one. He was also very much for single-payer health insurance. That was something that he said he had looked into. Trump didn't have a whole lot of details about any policy, but he felt that the Canadian system was a good system to emulate.

He was very pro–gay rights, and he liked his entertainment friends, and he talked about Muhammad Ali, how much he liked him, P. Diddy, and all these people. He denounced the murder of Matthew Shepard.

I enjoyed him. It's like being with a frat house guy. He's easy enough to get along with. At the time, he had been rumored to be a germophobe, so he seemed like he took special care to shake hands with the people who were there.

Abe Wallach, *Trump Organization vice president of acquisitions:* In '99, when he was thinking of running, he was writing position papers and doing a far more traditional campaign. He gave me a stack of material to read over the weekend. I was lying on a mat in my pool reading and fell asleep, and the papers went all over the pool. I gathered them up and put them under some drying machine. When I gave them back to him Monday, he said, "Why are these all in such bad condition?" I just said, "Oh, the dog got to them." They were just so dull and uninteresting that it put me to sleep. But he was building.

Dave Shiflett: I had turned in the draft for it and I got a call from his assistant, Norma Foerderer. She was a very sharp woman, very piercing, and had a very keen intellect.

Barbara Res, *former Trump Organization construction manager:* Norma was revered by everybody because she knew how to handle Donald. She knew what he wanted, and she filled his office with women who looked like models.

Dave Shiflett: Norma said, "You need to come up here and talk to me." I had to get on a plane, fly up there, and go to the office. She said she thought that the tone was too strident and that it needed to be toned ' down. She didn't want Donald looking strident. I said, "I thought I'd captured his voice, but it's no big deal," and that was it. It was like a three-minute meeting, and I was thinking, did you really need me to come up here to tell me that in person? That was a pain in the ass, but it was that important to her.

Trump's father, Fred, died from Alzheimer's disease on June 25, 1999, at age 93. Melania Knauss and Ivanka Trump both attended the funeral at Marble Collegiate Church in Manhattan four days later.

Andrew Stein: There's a big difference between Donald and Fred. The other big real estate families were much more low-key. Donald was a showman from the get-go. He always loved the publicity and attention. [Fred] came to see me and said I should stop The Donald from getting so much publicity when he first started to get publicity. I said, "Fred, I'm not taking this contract. There is no way you're gonna stop Donald from getting a lot of publicity. Forget it. You can just enjoy it, because he's not gonna stop."

Barbara Res: I didn't see his father much on the Hyatt. But when Trump Tower started, he became a thorn in my side. He hated the fact that

Donald hired me. Hated it. I was a woman, and I was a kid also. I was only 30 years old. He gave me a hard time: "No, no, no. You don't know what you're saying." That was very much his demeanor. "No, no, no." He was borderline abusive verbally. He never called me stupid, but he implied it. I think it rubbed off on Donald a lot. Donald was intolerant. Donald thought he knew everything. That was the biggest problem that he sort of got better at was that he thought that he knew everything. Donald had more personal skills than Fred. Fred was not charming. Donald was charming.

Dave Shiflett: One of these rare moments, at least for me, was when he was speaking about his parents, and he talked about their long-standing marriage, and he felt that he had not lived up to that ideal they had set. He talked about his brother who drank himself to death, and then he's talking about how he himself didn't drink or smoke, and his parents came up then. His mother lived in the building. He felt that he came up short in that area. That's the only humility I recall, the only vulnerable thing he was saying.

5.

THE TRUMP RV

The Shiflett book would not be published until January 2000. Reform Party de-liberations were moving more quickly than the wheels of book publishing, and Stone needed to make sure Trump wasn't out of the race before it began. Leading up to a crucial national Reform Party gathering on July 23–25, 1999, in Dear-born, Michigan, Stone and Trump began to make their case for a Trump candi-dacy. In May 1999, Trump attacked former senator Bill Bradley in a Wall Street Journal *op-ed for chilling real estate sales by eliminating a tax shelter, which Trump claimed "precipitated" an early 1990s recession. Trump also nee-dled Al Gore for losing ground to Bradley in a* Time/CNN *poll.*

On June 30, 1999, Washington, DC–based research firm Schroth & Associ-ates surveyed 421 national and state Reform Party officials about their favorite presidential candidates not affiliated with a major party. Retired general Colin Powell topped the list with 39 percent, followed by Ross Perot (18 percent), Jesse Ventura (11 percent), and Donald Trump (10 percent). A handful of others, in-cluding former Connecticut governor Lowell Weicker, received one or two points. In the July 19, 1999, edition of Newsweek, *writer Matt Bai cited the poll in a story about Ventura's power struggle with Ross Perot over the direction of the Reform Party. "And here's a strange thought," Bai wrote. "A close friend of Donald Trump's tells* Newsweek *that he was also toying with a bid."[1] Both the* Daily News *("Trump Mulling White House") and* New York Post *("Trump 'Toys' with Prez Run") ran with it. Trump played it down and then up, telling the* Daily News, *"I'm honored by the poll results, but I'm having an awfully good time doing what I'm doing." He then issued a statement for wide release: "If the Reform Party nominated me, I would probably run and probably win."*

A Ventura spokesman told USA Today that he was not aware Trump had done anything with the party but encouraged anyone to get involved. Reform Party chairman Russell Verney scoffed to the Associated Press that the poll was bogus. "Is this a joke? I have never once heard his name mentioned in the Reform Party."
He would soon hear more.

Mike Zumbluskas, *New York Reform Party strategist:* In the '99 convention I ran for vice chairman of the party, and this is where some of the Trump stuff comes in. I didn't have a shot at winning. But I went and ran to prevent Lenora Fulani from winning the vice chairmanship. Do you happen to know who Lenora Fulani is?

Lenora Fulani, a New Yorker and onetime neo-Marxist political activist, joined psychotherapist Fred Newman's minor New Alliance Party, running as its presidential nominee in all 50 states in 1988. Newman's leadership—and his therapeutic practice of encouraging sleeping with patients—has been described as cultish.[2] In 1994, Fulani and Newman joined the Independence Party of New York, aligning with fringe politicians at both ends of the political spectrum. Fulani nevertheless developed strategic alliances with the Reverend Jesse Jackson, the Reverend Al Sharpton, and Nation of Islam leader Louis Farrakhan and ran for office multiple times at the state and national levels.

Lenora Fulani, *New York Reform Party leader:* It was the first time that African Americans were present and included in the founding and shaping of a national political party. We wanted to bring people together from the left, center, and right and see if we could set aside social issues and focus on the need for political reform. Social issues were being used by the major parties as a way to divide Americans.

Mike Zumbluskas: The Fulani organization, Fred Newman organization, is a cult that came into the party.

Lenora Fulani: We used to have these political conventions where white men would come in triangle George Washington hats, and some of the younger people of color would come into the conventions wearing Malcolm X t-shirts. We were breaking through some of the unnecessary divisions between Americans who needed to be on the same side together, and it was cool to sit back and watch some of these relationships develop.

Mike Zumbluskas: A few people from New York decided to try to prevent Fulani from becoming vice chair. She knew how to control conventions, and most of the people in the Reform Party were neophytes. We decided we can get more people if we rented an RV and drove to Michigan. I had to go down to Cape May, New Jersey, to pick up the RV. All of a sudden [New York party members traveling with me] started putting on the RV "Trump for President" signs. I'm going, "What is this?" I bought t-shirts and hats saying "Vote for Mike Zumbluskas for Vice Chairman," with a Big Z. That's when I first knew Trump was thinking about running for president on the Reform Party line. So our RV starts being called the Trump RV, even though he's not paying a cent for anything. I paid for probably about 70 percent of this trip, and I'm not a rich man.

Lenora Fulani: We focused on political reform, government accountability, fiscal responsibility, creating opportunity for people to be able to participate, and opening up the process of voter registration.

Mike Zumbluskas: I had a suite, and, basically, I had a party up there. The alcohol was flowing, the reporters, the convention people are up there, and I was taking down Fulani's people. We were able to get one of Fulani's playbooks. They had it set up who would stand up, speak, push this motion, and who would second it. I don't know how we got hold of it, but it was very helpful in convincing people to stay away from her. Roger Stone did have a suite there. They were running around the entire convention with Trump stuff on, pushing him when they were supposed to be stopping Fulani and pushing me.

While the Reform Party could sometimes descend into a wild party, Trump learned more in his dealings with it than just the nasty machinations of party politics. From Ventura's push to slash income taxes, Perot's rejection of the North American Free Trade Agreement (NAFTA), and Buchanan's immigration alarmism, populist ideas stirred audiences.

The fight for the vice chairmanship was emblematic of the tension at every level of the Reform Party. Those who wanted Perot to maintain control fought against those who wanted the party to expand beyond its founder. Gerry Moan, a New Yorker, and not Fulani, was elected vice chairman. With the internal drama, the Reform Party had not come to any consensus over its 2000 presidential nominee. A host of political independents, has-beens, and ne'er-do-wells fantasized about a bid, but none committed. Arianna Huffington floated a Warren Beatty candidacy in an August 10 column in the Huffington Post. At a Hollywood gathering attended by 150 reporters and hundreds of film industry vets on September 29, the Bulworth star gave a speech advocating campaign finance reform and chastising President Clinton. Ventura favored Weicker, who backed out by October 5, comparing the Reform Party's bickering to a "food fight."[3]

Meanwhile, Republican Pat Buchanan considered a third-party switch, strategizing with Perot's ex–running mate Pat Choate and seeking a blessing from Reform Party chairman Russell Verney. When Buchanan went on NBC's Meet the Press *on September 12, 1999, he said he was "taking a hard look" at changing parties so he could head the Reform ticket. This shocked Republican elites who worried that a Buchanan–Perot alliance could tip the 2000 election to a Democrat. RNC chairman Jim Nicholson rushed to Buchanan's Northern Virginia home on September 28 to convince him to stay in the fold.*

Jesse Ventura: I got criticized for not taking the reins and running the party. That was not my job. That is a job of the party leaders. My job was to govern Minnesota and to be successful so that people would not be fearful to elect another Reform Party candidate.

Dean Barkley: I worked on Lowell Weicker for a month to get him to run for president. I stayed at a little apartment in the basement of his house in Arlington, Virginia. I thought Lowell would have been great. I got him for two or three hours, and he said okay, but obviously somebody or something changed his mind. Warren called, too. That had to be about one or two in the morning. My wife hands me the phone and says, "It's Warren Beatty." Warren Beatty. He told me he was thinking about running for president. We talked for a little bit and that didn't go very far.

Pat Buchanan: Perot's people got in touch with my sister [Bay Buchanan, a prominent Republican organizer and commentator] and said if I wanted the Reform Party nomination, I could pretty much have it. Perot and I had national organizations, and together we could get the nomination and use that to get into the debates and establish a new party, which would represent the economic patriotism, economic nationalism, port of control, no more foreign wars, end this interventionism—all the other issues I had run on in '92 and '96.

Russell Verney: I spoke to Mr. Buchanan about the possibility of him running in the Reform Party. I was supportive of him. I told him the Reform Party doesn't take a position on social issues. Whether he opposes or supports abortion is irrelevant to us. We were about economic issues and government reform issues.

Jim Nicholson: I went to Pat's house in Virginia, I sat down with him and had a long amiable conversation about the damage that he could do to our party and to our country, because it could jeopardize our chances of winning the presidency. He had no chance of winning the presidency.

Pat Buchanan: The main point he made was that I could cost Bush the election. That would mean the opportunity to change the Supreme Court, which I had been working on since the mid-'60s with Richard Nixon. It was a very compelling argument. But I went ahead and did it.

Jim Nicholson: He looked me right in the eyes, seeming to me to be totally convinced in his own mind that he could win. He said the time is now, he could do this, and people want somebody more conservative, more straightforward and blunt and very experienced. I think Pat thought he could win. I really think he thought that.

Pat Buchanan: I thought I could win the election? How could I win the election when I couldn't win the Republican nomination? No, I never thought I could win. And that's not why we did it. I believed I might be able to get in the debates and create a new party to represent these ideas.

6.

STANDING PAT

Roger Stone recognized that Buchanan would be Trump's main opposition in the Reform Party. This triggered Trump's first real political slugfest, and he showed he had a taste for it. An hour before Buchanan was to appear on CBS's Face the Nation *on September 19, 1999, producers received a statement from Donald Trump via fax:*[1] *"Pat Buchanan's stated view that we should not have stopped Adolph [sic] Hitler is repugnant. Hitler was a monster, and it was essential for the Allies to crush Nazism."*

Trump was referencing ideas in Buchanan's 1999 book A Republic, Not an Empire, *and the fax led the host to ask about it. The point of Buchanan's appearance was to announce his switch from the GOP to the Reform Party in the coming weeks. But now Buchanan had to defend himself on air, meaning Trump had masterfully inserted himself into the conversation. "That's a silly and false caricature of my position," Buchanan said.*

A Republic, Not an Empire, *a defense of isolationism, includes the contention that World War II could have taken a different course had some countries not declared war so quickly on Germany. Buchanan argues that Hitler offered "no physical threat to the United States" as of late 1940. It was not a work of Holocaust denial or a treatise praising Hitler in general. In another section, Buchanan criticized U.S. foreign policy, writing, "After World War II, Jewish influence over foreign policy became almost an obsession with American leaders."*

Trump and Stone took this book and combined it with editorials Buchanan had written over the years about Nazi Germany and synthesized it into a two-word sobriquet: "Hitler lover."

Jim Nicholson: Pat had published this book, and it was very offensive to Jews. My Jewish Republican friends, after I was going to make an effort to keep Buchanan, were imploring me to tell him to go to hell.

Roger Stone: Pat's a friend of mine. You can go back and look at the clips. Trump taunted him for praising Adolf Hitler, taunted him for finding no fault with the Third Reich.

Pat Buchanan: I'm not gonna get into that. I can give you the history I've given you, but I'm not gonna get into that.

Stone conscripted Dave Shiflett to write an anti-Buchanan op-ed under Trump's byline. Published in the Los Angeles Times *on Halloween 1999, it accused Buchanan of having a "psychic friendship with Hitler," excoriated him for arguing that concentration camps did not kill Jews during the Holocaust, and vowed to stop him from "hijacking" the Reform Party's nomination.*

Dave Shiflett: It was a pretty good op-ed. I thought that was a good reflection of Trump's basic viewpoint.

Pat Buchanan: Trump called me a lot of names but, as we've come to understand, these are terms of endearment.

Tony Coelho, *Al Gore campaign chairman and Democratic congressman from California 1979–1989:* Pat had a core, he really believed his stuff. In my view, he's honest and real to his views. I may disagree with him, but I don't have trouble with people like that.

Trump and Stone kept up a media campaign about Trump's political intentions. They enticed New York Times *reporter Adam Nagourney to the twenty-sixth floor of Trump Tower, where Trump touted a* National Enquirer *survey of readers who were "clamoring" for a Trump candidacy. "Those are real people. That is the Trump constituency," Trump said, insisting he would run on the Reform line only if he determined he could win the entire thing.*[2] *Skeptics argued this was Trump's out, indicating he never intended to follow through.*

    To Dateline NBC's *Stone Phillips, Trump, who'd started dating model Melania Knauss, hinted that if he were president he'd have a first lady, although it was "not a priority." When* USA Today *reporter Tom Squitieri was interview-*

ing Trump, he "turned to Roger Stone, his political consigliere, and said, 'Let's make him White House press secretary when we win.'"[3]

Tom Squitieri, *journalist and professor:* I took him moderately seriously, guessing he would stay in as long as it was easy and he got his way. I also knew it was partially designed to boost his book. The serious factor was an obstacle with editors who thought it was all a stunt.

Trump sat in CNN's New York studio on October 8, 1999, and told Larry King he would open an exploratory committee for a presidential run. He extolled lower taxes, railed against NAFTA, and said Germany, France, and Japan were "ripping off" America.

> **Larry King:** Can you say it is a major step?
> **Donald Trump:** I don't think I can say it's a major step, I'm looking at it very seriously. I have a lot to lose, Larry. I mean, I'm the biggest developer in New York by far. . . . But I really want to see, if you get that nomination, what happens from there? If I couldn't win, if I felt I couldn't win, I wouldn't run. . . . I'm not looking to get more votes than any other independent candidate in history. . . . There's a great lack of spirit in this country . . . and I think the spirit has to be brought back.

Trump floated a running mate—Oprah! "I mean, she's popular, she's brilliant, she's a wonderful woman. I mean, if she would ever do it." He continued, "I haven't even started campaigning yet. Now, maybe when I start campaigning, I'll do worse. Perhaps I shouldn't campaign at all, I'll just, you know, I'll ride it right into the White House."[4]

Trump was trying out the idea of a presidential run on himself, the media, the public—and the Reform Party. What challenges would surface, what would be easy? He had invited Ventura to dinner that night at Jean-Georges in the Trump International Hotel.[5]

Roger Stone: We talked about Oprah for vice president, that was catnip for tabloid media. He's on the cover of both the *Daily News* and the *New York Post.* There were cartoons at the time.

Jesse Ventura: We were simply looking for viable candidates. All third parties, when they're growing, do that.

Dave Shiflett: Trump was big on Jesse. He liked Jesse's attitude. He just said what he wanted to say. That was always important with Trump, to say what you believe, say what you think.

Roger Stone: Jesse couldn't stop talking about the improbability of his own election in Minnesota and how it could be done nationally, and how Donald was the guy to do it.

Jesse Ventura: Don't build me and Trump into more than it was. There was no plan ever laid. We didn't do any type of meeting to determine this could happen, that could happen. We were casual acquaintances before that. I happened to win governor. And if he wanted to use that politically, my win as governor, fine. I didn't give him any recommendations to do anything. So anything he did, he did on his own. Did he watch us? Maybe.

The next morning Trump went on NBC's Today Show, *and Matt Lauer asked whether women were his Achilles' heel. Trump said there's "nothing in the closets" and blamed media "scum" for making things up.*

> **Matt Lauer:** What's it going to take to make you decide to do this?
> **Donald Trump:** Well, I'll be deciding sometime early next year, and there's only one really important thing, and that's if I can win. Not if I can get the Reform Party [nomination], because I believe I can get the Reform Party. It's really if I can win. . . . The Reform Party has a huge obstacle. You have Democrats, and you have Republicans. And you have 25 or 30 percent of the people are going to vote for one or the other or both, no matter what. . . .
>   If the economy is bad at the time of the election—and you know, we have a long way to go, and lots of things can happen—the Reform Party candidate would, if it's the right candidate, have a good chance. If it's Pat Buchanan, there's no chance. He'll get a hard-core group of wackos. But the Reform Party candidate, if it's the right candidate, would have a good chance of winning the election, depending a little bit on the economy at the time of the election.

Phil Madsen, *Reform Party operative:* Trump was not messing around. This was an authentic exploratory effort. At this point, it was Roger

Stone I was talking to, but I'm sure he wasn't operating alone. They had this committee established. They wanted to know more about us. It's exactly what any logical, reasonable person would do who was thinking about running for president and had not done so before. Trump was not campaigning, but Stone was setting up events that would give Trump a real good opportunity to get a sense of what it was like. They had a book written already, his policies. That book was done before they ever met us. So, Stone put together the structure of a campaign and some of the content. And then Trump was experimenting with this new entity. It was truly an exploratory committee.

Russell Verney: I didn't then, and I'm not even sure I do now, view Donald Trump as a very partisan person. He has a lot of policy positions that would cut across both parties. He wasn't fixed in a specific dogma, so an independent third party made a lot of sense.

Both in his forthcoming book, The America We Deserve, *and in appearances, Trump argued for raising taxes on the wealthy, banning assault weapons, helping charter schools, applying the death penalty more, halting interventions in overseas humanitarian crises, terminating NAFTA, and slowing immigration. "We must take care of our own people first," he and Shiflett wrote.*

Reform Party members were interested in him, and Trump clearly stated his intention to run if he thought he had a real chance of winning. Yet few members of the establishment political class could envision it. We spoke with political and media leaders, including Ed Rendell, Andrew Stein, Tony Coelho, Robert Torricelli, Dean Barkley, Jim Nicholson, Joe Lieberman, and Ralph Nader, who said they never took a potential Trump run seriously.

Mike Zumbluskas: There were a number of Reform Party people, not just in New York but all over the country, who wanted Trump. A lot of these people came up through the Perot organization. They wanted a businessman to run the country. A lot of them saw the national debt running up, and they wanted somebody to go in and change Washington.

Lenora Fulani: People liked Trump because he could finance [a run]. His heart was not necessarily connected to building something outside of the two-party system that would advance the role and participation of ordinary people.

Dean Barkley, *Independence Party U.S. senator from Minnesota 2002–2003:* Donald Trump seemed like a very flamboyant, self-centered businessman who liked getting his name out there. I found him an opportunist. He flies around in his own Trump plane. He liked being in the news. He liked being the center of attention.

Lenora Fulani: I liked Governor Ventura. I was glad he was part of the movement, whether we agreed on everything or not. Trump was interested in running, and he was a real estate developer, he had money, and the person who brought him around was Jesse Ventura. Ventura did that because Pat Buchanan had reached out.

Jesse Ventura: Buchanan is a hard-core, right-wing Republican. Plain and simple. I'm fiscally conservative and socially liberal.

Ralph Nader: At the time I thought Trump was just bluffing to get publicity and that he would never run, because he would never disclose his financials. See how right I was?

Tucker Carlson, *Fox News:* Trump has a very constant need, a huge appetite for entertainment. And I recognize that because I'm exactly the same way. That's one of the reasons I went into the media. Trump just likes getting out there, flying around in the plane, sitting and bullshitting with people. But I also think it was a commercial calculation, designed to self-explode.

Polls showed the public was skeptical, too. Three out of four Americans did not take Trump's candidacy seriously in a July 1999 Gallup poll.[6] Forty-seven percent viewed Trump negatively, and only 41 percent had a favorable opinion of him in a Gallup poll two months later.[7] Voters preferred Pat Buchanan (28 percent) and Jesse Ventura (24 percent) to Trump (11 percent) in a September Time/CNN *poll. Only 6 percent of registered voters said Trump would be the best Reform candidate behind Buchanan (24), Perot (16), Ventura (13), and Warren Beatty (10) in an October* Newsweek *poll.[8]*

Stone arranged a new flurry of interviews and public appearances. On NBC's Meet the Press, *host Tim Russert pressed Trump on past negative comments about women. Trump answered that women would respect what he said and added that women are "cunning" and "so tough they make us wince."*

Trump said Buchanan should not be taken seriously because he was a "Hitler lover."[9]

Tim Russert: Why are you joining the Reform Party?

Donald Trump: Well, for one thing, I really believe the Republicans are just too crazy right. I mean, just what's going on is just nuts. And I'm seeing the Democrats as far too—I mean, Bradley and Gore are so liberal, it's just too liberal for me. And I really think they've hit a chord, they've hit a very good chord, and I guess I'm very popular in that party.[10]

Pat Choate, *Reform Party politician:* I was very unsupportive of Trump coming in and being part of the Reform Party. I just didn't think Trump fit. During that period he had done an interview from his bed after having sex with the lady who eventually became his wife, on *The Howard Stern Show.* He had had business difficulties. He had bankruptcies. He was not of the people that made up the bulk of the Reform Party, which were basically Reagan-type Democrats, independents, and conservative Democrats.

The November 9, 1999, call from bed to Howard Stern's radio show reveals the one-of-a-kind political confection of Trump all coming together—the business-man, tabloid tantalizer, and crafty campaigner selling, selling, and selling. Trump touts his presidential aspirations, insults Bill Clinton for his taste in mistresses, and hands the phone to his love interest, Melania Knauss, who admits she is wearing nearly nothing.

Howard Stern: I know that you have a book coming up pretty soon, right?

Donald Trump: Correct.

Stern: Right. I believe that this is advance publicity for the book.

Trump: Well, that's true, but I really am considering this. But it would be very, very important to have your endorsement.

[Trump eventually hands phone to Knauss]

Stern: You're perfect. And what do you do, you go out with him every night and you guys have sex?

Melania Knauss: That's true. We have a great, great time.

Stern: Every night, you are saying?

Knauss: Even more.

Trump could play in places low and high. The same day as the call to Howard Stern, a Trump-bylined article ran in the National Enquirer: *"Why I Should Be President." Meanwhile, University of Pennsylvania student Theodore LeCompte, who ran a speaker series and would later manage two Democratic presidential conventions, had been working to lure MSNBC to shoot an episode of* Hardball with Chris Matthews *on the campus. Trump brought Melania Knauss, Donald Trump Jr., and his bodyguard Keith Schiller to the November 18, 1999, event.*[11]

Theodore LeCompte: I had seen *Hardball* do a campus town hall at the Institute of Politics at Harvard on TV and I was like, "That's really cool. I wish they would do one here." And so I reached out to a producer. A month or so after I sent that, [*Hardball* producer] Phil Griffin called and said, "Hey, we want to do *Hardball* on campus with Donald Trump," because he had gone to Wharton.

Roger Stone: We would prepare talking points for him. He would really look at them. He would go out and perform magnificently and say most of what we wanted him to say but in his own words. He's his own man. No one puts words in his mouth. It didn't work then, doesn't work now. He can't be managed or handled like a traditional candidate. He's not George W. Bush to Karl Rove. Puppet mastery. Sometimes he would take a few notes, that was a major concession.

> **Chris Matthews:** Are you running for president?
> **Donald Trump:** I am indeed [audience cheers]—maybe.
> **Matthews:** When you run for president, will you release your income tax returns?
> **Trump:** You know, it's something I haven't even thought of, but I certainly, I guess, as I get closer to the decision, which I'll probably make in February, it's something I will be thinking of. They're very big. They're very complex. But I would probably have—I probably wouldn't have a problem with doing it.

Theodore LeCompte: Chris Matthews goes, "Are you running?" And Trump said, "I'm running." And when everybody was cheering he said, "Maybe." There was an AP reporter who didn't catch he said "maybe," so a wire report went out that he announced. It wound up getting more attention than we anticipated, because there was this AP report that said he was running.

Hardball *had information on specific Trump policy ideas included in his forth-coming book. He proposed a onetime 14.25 percent tax on individuals worth over $10 million that he claimed would raise $5.7 trillion to reduce the national debt.*[12] *Matthews asked Trump about the idea, and a student asked a follow-up question.*

Richard Kilfoyle, *former Penn student:* Theo was looking for volunteers to ask questions at the event. I was the token Republican in my group of friends.

> **Richard Kilfoyle:** I still see problems where people would be shift-ing their money to other nations . . .
> **Trump:** I don't see it, because this nation will boom, the economy will boom, and ultimately they're going to shift their money anyway if our economy isn't booming. Look what they did with Asia. When Asia went down, money shifted into Asia because they thought they were buying things cheap. So money's going to shift where the economy is good.
> **Kilfoyle:** But they only have to ship it out for a year. So I don't see where the . . .
> **Trump:** Well, I just think that the booming economy that we cre-ate by my plan would keep the money here because it's incentive. They're going to want to be where the action is, they're going to want to be where the good economy is. And they move their money around—hey, including me—you move your money around where the action is, and now it's a real world economy. But this country would be booming. We'd have no debt. It would be unbelievable.

Richard Kilfoyle: I don't know if he understood his own policy or not. My friends liked it. They thought it was funny. Afterward they called me Trump Killer, because they thought that my response had put Trump in his place.

Russell Verney: The first time I met him was in his office at Trump Tower in November at the request of Jack Essenberg, chairman of the Independence Party, our Reform Party affiliate in New York. It was a very long, narrow office with a spectacular view of Central Park and all the buildings around it. All of my discussions with him were about the process. They wanted to know what they have to do to achieve the nomination of the Reform Party and what were the logistics of it. Conversations about the campaign if it was to ever materialize.

Pat Buchanan: I went about my business, which was this: Our party was on the ballot in only about 19 or 20 states, so I had to get the Reform Party on the ballot. We drove in vans from one state to another getting the required signatures to get the Reform Party and my name on the ballot. And this took all the way from October 1999 to the summer of 2000.

Pat Choate: At that point I was co-chair of Pat Buchanan's campaign. I was confident if Trump did run we could take him down.

Throughout December 1999, Trump gave speeches as part of motivational guru Tony Robbins's Results 2000 seminars around the country. At stops in Miami, Hartford, Connecticut, and Southern California, he met with Reform Party bigwigs before heading to arenas. Trump was to give 10 speeches with Robbins at a reported $100,000 each. This fed skeptics. How could he be simultaneously running for president, giving paid speeches, and pushing a forthcoming book?

Roger Stone: We met with Reform Party people privately. He gave a speech and toured the Holocaust Museum in Los Angeles. We visited the Bay of Pigs Veterans Museum in Miami, and he gave a speech.

Phil Madsen: On the trip to Miami I was in a room with Trump, Melania, Stone, and four others. These were people Stone had selected to talk to Trump about what it would mean for him to run as a Reform Party candidate. Regarding Trump and Melania, she did not speak. He said almost nothing. He just listened to people as they talked. But I noticed that the two of them seemed very happy together. And it was little things, like, he would wash his hands, and she'd hand him the towel. She'd go to read something, and he'd read it ahead of time and get it for her. It was obvious that they were accustomed to being together. They were showing each other kindnesses, and I was touched by that.

Trump met with 40 members of the Reform Party at a hotel in Hartford on December 1 before giving another Results 2000 talk at the Hartford Civic Center with Tony Robbins. Trump fed off the energy of the thousands of fans who paid to see him and Tony Robbins speak. He told stories, recited business mantras, and asked, "Who thinks I should run for president?" in a freewheeling style he would elevate on the campaign trail in 2015. When Trump advised patrons at the Hartford Civic Center to "always sign a prenup," one aide marveled to the New York Daily News, "Trump is making money running for president."[13] At Anaheim's Arrowhead Pond, Trump offered his business maxim: "When somebody screws you, screw 'em back a lot harder."[14]

On December 7, 1999, at a gathering of 100 Reform members at L'Ermitage Hotel in Beverly Hills, with Melania Knauss in attendance, Trump argued that donors should be able to make unlimited contributions to candidates and said, "Nobody knows what the Reform Party platform is."[15] Roger Stone told reporters that focusing on traditional media and gatekeepers was a mistake in understanding how Trump might appeal to voters: "You can laugh at the . . . Entertainment Tonights and the Hard Copys if you want . . . but millions of people are watching those things and forming opinions based on what they see."[16]

That night, Trump was on The Tonight Show with Jay Leno, where he was brought out to the band playing "Hail to the Chief."

Leno had Trump admit he'd never been elected to anything and pointed out that being in charge of the Trump Organization was more like a dictatorship. ("That's true," Trump replied with a smile.) Leno also asked about alcohol ("I had a brother who had a big problem with alcoholism. . . . I've stayed away, not for any other reason, that and I just don't like it") and about Bill Clinton's legal strategy ("His lawyers did an absolutely atrocious, terrible job. They could have fought harder for him not to answer that question . . . 'Did you have an affair with this woman?'").

Trump said that despite his divorces he believed in marriage.

"If you got married in the White House and got divorced would she get, like, everything west of the Mississippi?" Leno asked.

"You'd need a good prenup," Trump replied jocularly.[17]

7.

I PLEDGE
I WILL NOT RENAME
THE WHITE HOUSE

Trump was keeping tabs on the response to the political trial balloon he'd been floating. On January 5, 2000, two-and-a-half months after telling Larry King he would explore a run, Trump descended—via elevator, not escalator—to a lectern in the Trump Tower atrium to announce the release of his policy book The America We Deserve.[1]

> **Trump:** We've done three books, they've gone to number one, but they've been much different than this book. This is a little bit about what I think on the country, what could be done, what should be done, and we hope this also becomes a number-one bestseller.

A reporter asked if this presidential talk was promotional, not serious.

> **Trump:** It's something that has turned out to be very serious. If you look at the crowds, if you look at our internal poll numbers have been amazing, the ratings on television have been the highest of anyone by far.

Trump moved to a desk flanked by American flags to sign books for the public and answer a few more questions, including from New York Post *reporter Gersh Kuntzman, who first wanted to know how Trump had gotten over his aversion to shaking hands.*[2]

Trump: It's not necessarily something I'm in love with, but it's fine. I do it.

Kuntzman (minutes later): How do you think you're going to appeal to Middle America?

Trump: I really think just as well. I supply lots of jobs, lots of work, lots of money for lots of families. I think it's the same as here. I think the people that don't like me are the rich people.

A reporter introduced herself from Pseudo, an "internet broadcast company" (which was famously ahead of its time, sending interactive video onto the Web when almost no one had broadband fast enough to use it).[3] *She asked if Trump had any thoughts on the internet and politics. He gave a generic answer that the future of the internet was unlimited.*

Pseudo reporter: Do you think you'd like the opportunity maybe to talk to some of the people in America, maybe interact with them online?

Trump: Maybe someday.

He paused to sign a book and then continued the thought.

Trump: I still understand NBC, ABC, and CBS better. Isn't that terrible?

The America We Deserve *mapped out Trump's most complete policy stances on trade and diplomatic policy, and even included a warning that America was at risk of a terrorist attack thanks to its unchecked "military adventures"—a year before 9/11 occurred. Trump wrote that he wouldn't rule out a "surgical strike" if negotiations failed to prevent North Korea from developing nuclear weapons. He called China a "growing military threat abroad and an oppressive regime at home." And he advocated restricting the flow of immigrants to the United States, writing, "Let's be extremely careful not to admit more people than we can absorb. It comes down to this: We must take care of our own people first."*

The book made the point that "a Trump candidacy would do best in an economic downturn when American voters would likely turn to a can-do businessman prepared to make the tough decisions. No one can tell what the economy will be like in 2000, but it will impact my decision."

Trump's most biting observations were reserved for political opponents: Lowell Weicker ("one of Washington's premier windbags"), Bill Bradley ("as phony as a twenty-dollar Rolex"), Jerry Nadler ("one of the most egregious hacks in contemporary politics"), and Buchanan ("he called Hitler 'an individual of great courage'"). Ironically, in light of the 2016 election cycle, Trump in 2000 called Jeb Bush "exactly the kind of political leader this country needs now and will very much need in the future," and praised Hillary Clinton as "definitely smart and resilient" and "very nice to my sons Donny and Eric."

Gersh Kuntzman, New York Post *reporter:* The editors thought he might announce for president, so they were sending us to everything he was doing. And it always turned out to be a book signing. He loved moving books, that guy.

Dave Shiflett: The book helped the Trump brand. Here's a different way to think of Donald, not only as a real estate guy and a celebrity but as a politician. It was a campaign book for a campaign that was very short-lived and a candidate who was not at all serious about doing this. This was just something they needed to have. For all I knew, Roger Stone had sketched stuff out. I don't know if Trump would've thought about it that much. We'd want to write something about taxes. I'd say, "Well, what are the basic ideas?" and then I would get a bunch of documents and boil the stuff down. There were people who were doing research. They would put packages together and send it to me.

Roger Stone: I worked very closely with him and I edited large parts of it myself because I have always had some ability to write in Trump's voice because I've known him for 40 years. He's prescient on a lot of things in the book: terrorism, 9/11, North Korea. But, I mean, the book was really formulated by Shiflett sitting with Trump and just letting Trump talk.

Jerrold Nadler: He had a chapter on the three worst politicians in the United States—Senator Bill Bradley, Lowell Weicker, and Jerry Nadler. That was some pretty good company.

Russell Verney: My impression is that he was deadly serious. He could have picked any subject in the world—real estate development, any type of business advice—and he could have sold a book. Public policy? That was a little harder sell for somebody like Donald Trump.

In the chapter "Should I Run?," Trump pledges, joking, "I would not rename the White House. I would only want my name on the desk in the Oval Office."

The reviews were mixed. New York *magazine's Walter Kirn scoffed that Trump was "America's greatest living comedian," writing, "As befits this master of unconscious camp, the only jokes in Trump's campaign book . . . are unintended." Kirn was tickled by Trump's comparisons of himself to the Founding Fathers and his obsession with terrorism, writing, "One almost pities Trump here. The fellow is petrified."*[4]

Dave Shiflett: Later I got a card from Roger Stone saying, "Dave, thanks for the good work, and you'll see that your name is on the front of the book. It's in the smallest font I could find."

On January 7, 2000, Trump, Donald Trump Jr., and Roger Stone[5] *flew to Minnesota. Melania Knauss was not along for the ride. The couple had split in the previous days, a drama that would play out in the gossip pages over the next few weeks even as Trump's political aspirations were examined in news columns, the two topics sometimes intersecting.*

But Trump was in the Gopher State following through on plans to hold a Reform Party fundraiser and press conference with Ventura. On the acknowledgments page of The America We Deserve *Trump thanked the governor: "And to Jesse Ventura, whose breakthrough in Minnesota caused me to start thinking about the role people outside government must play to help our country."*

Dean Barkley: At NPR in downtown St. Paul, I happened to walk by and saw a sign that Trump was coming to Minnesota to talk to Team Ventura. I thought, Oh, that's interesting. No one told me that. I went to Ventura to see what he knew about this, and he told me, "Trump's coming, and they're going to do a rally and raise a little money. He wants to meet you and learn about what we did with our campaign and know how we pulled it off."

Phil Madsen: At the Northland Inn in Minnesota, two women who were part of his advance team were there a day or two ahead of time. I happened to be standing next to them when a call came in that Trump and Melania had split. They were shocked. It didn't matter to me. I had other things to think about and worry about, and I barely knew who Melania was. But to them it was a big, big deal. This was a fundraiser for the Independence Party [which the Reform Party was also called in Minnesota]. The thing I cared about most was party growth. And this was a big, fun thing for me. I had Jesse Ventura and Donald Trump raising money for the party.

Dean Barkley: He had a Trump plane then, and he flew it into Minneapolis. They took a motorcade with Jesse, and I met them at the Northland Inn, where the rally was going to be. It's the nicest hotel in Brooklyn Park, Jesse's hometown. We went to the top floor. It was a large suite. I had a sportcoat on, and Jesse had his black suit on. His governor's suit. I was staring at [Trump's] hair the whole time trying to figure out if it was real. It was puffy and blow-dried and stuck together with whatever it's stuck together with. It looked like a nice comb-over job.

We were together up there in the hotel room for a good two, three hours before the rally. He was talking, and Roger Stone was doing a lot of note-taking. Basically Trump asked a lot of things. What was your strategy? What did you try to do? How did you think he could win without spending a lot of money?

I told him we were outspent 20 to 1, and it's win-by-doing. We won a lot of debates. We did well on doing as many events as we could do. And just being different. Being honest to people rather than just telling them what they want to hear. Number one is how we managed to monopolize the press and get all of the free press we could. We wouldn't have won the governor's race in '98 if Jesse hadn't been a masterful manipulator of the press.

Trump asked a lot about the status of the Reform Party. What it was like dealing with Perot. What my feelings were about him. He was sizing up Perot as an impediment. That's when I explained my dealings with Ross, which weren't all that positive. Jesse had the same feelings that I had about Perot's likelihood of letting someone else take up the mantle of the party.

Jesse Ventura: He came to Minnesota on a book tour. That ain't a campaign stop. I've done plenty of book tours.

At the press conference, Trump promised he would support a lawsuit to get the Reform Party nominee onto the presidential debate stage during the general election. Trump added, "If people think that I'm running, we do great" in the polls. He didn't ask for Ventura's endorsement but promised to return soon to seek it if he decided to run.[6] Behind the lectern, a Ventura banner with a toll-free phone number hung next to a Trump pennant with the URL www .donaldjtrump2000.com, the website Stone hired Madsen to set up. He also emphasized a point from The America We Deserve, *saying that a Reform Party candidate would stand a much better chance of winning the presidency if the U.S. economy were to tank.*

This was not merely a stop on a book tour, Trump insisted. "I don't need this for that. The book, whether it goes to number one as the other three have or whether it doesn't, is not a major factor economically. It's not a lot of money in a book no matter how successful it is."[7]

Dean Barkley: I didn't get much of what his actual political philosophy is or why he wanted to run, other than he thought it was interesting to do, so we parted ways after that meeting.

Jesse Ventura: I don't cross a bridge until I get to it. I'd have to see what he stood for. I'd have to see what his policies were.

Pat Choate: I saw Trump as an opportunist. I saw the same thing with Roger Stone. I had written a book in 1990 called *Agents of Influence*. It basically was taking a look at lobbying inside Washington, DC. I had spent time on [the lobbying company] Black, Manafort, and Stone. The *New Republic*, in '85, had done a cover story calling Stone the sleaziest operator in Washington. And Trump had used Roy Cohn, and it just didn't seem the right fit. [Paul] Manafort is the guy who really pioneered the whole activity of representing sleazy dictators. I was looking at Trump, that he has a lot of money and is media savvy, and was very good at the New York tabloids. I saw that his run was a hustle, that he was selling books, he was promoting his hotels, he was promoting his business activities. I thought it was not serious, that it was just a way to get cheap publicity.

Ralph Nader: Perot's got a good family life. He didn't screw his creditors and consumers, and his businesses, his workers. You list all of Trump's infirmities and a lot of them are just the opposite with Perot.

Russell Verney: They have different styles, sure, but they're both successful businessmen. They bring an outside perspective to governance. They're not creatures created by the establishment and promoted by the establishment and dependent on the establishment. So they're free to develop their own policies, traditions, and promote them independently.

Pat Choate: Ross Perot wasn't enthusiastic about Trump. We had conversations I'd rather not repeat. There was no enthusiasm there, let's just leave it that way.

Trump had boasted that Knauss would make a great first lady and alluded that a wedding might come soon. Ronald Reagan had been divorced, but voters had not picked a bachelor president in more than a century. Only Ralph Nader was unbetrothed among major candidates in 2000. Losing Melania not only left Trump in personal upheaval—it could have had political consequences.

Hoping to pressure the Slovenian model to return to his bed, Trump tipped the New York Post's *lead gossip writer, Richard Johnson, whose January 11, 2000, story was headlined "Trump Knixes Knauss: Donald-Dumped Supermodel Is 'Heartbroken.'" A "Trump friend" said his decision to split with the 29-year-old was "the hardest thing he has ever done."[8] The next day's paper had a photo of Trump surrounded by beauty contestants to promote the Miss USA pageant that would be broadcast on CBS, the caption noting it was taken "just five days after dumping girlfriend Melania Knauss. 'She meant a lot to me,' said Trump in between showering the girls with kisses."*

Jared Paul Stern, *Page Six reporter:* On the item from January 11, where Trump dumps Melania, it's really a funny item. This ran as a news story with Richard's byline. This is obviously dictated directly by Trump that he has given Melania the ax, and she's heartbroken. [Laughs.] With all of his quotes from friends of Trump.

Conrad Black, *Canadian financier and publisher:* The *New York Post* used to show up at Trump's place in Florida. I don't know the exact arrangement, but Trump was definitely courting Richard [Johnson]. He paid for him to come down there, and he even let him have his wedding there. I assumed he was deemed to be a friendly journalist.*

Maybe Knauss learned from the master? On January 13, the New York Post's *Jared Paul Stern had a story with an alternative version of events, sourced to a Knauss "pal." This had it that Knauss booted Trump after finding a towel smeared*

---

* Johnson declined to comment.

with unfamiliar makeup, evidence he'd rekindled a former flame, model Kara Young. "A Trump friend" presented another explanation: the towel was from his daughter Ivanka. She's "up there all the time and she uses that bathroom," the friend said.[9]

Jared Paul Stern: Then he's in Palm Beach trying to convince Reform Party members that he could be a presidential candidate.

On January 14, 2000, a New York Post *follow-up gave a positive political spin as Trump prepared for a Reform Party gathering at Mar-a-Lago: "Although Trump was glum yesterday over reports that his relationship with Knauss ended because he cheated on her, the brash tycoon got a bit of good news when Reform honcho Russ Verney accepted an invitation to attend."*[10]

Russell Verney: Just before I went down, I was still working for Perot, and he called me and asked, "Are you going to this meeting at Mar-a-Lago with Trump?" I said, "Yes, I am." He said, "Why are you going there?" I said, "Because I want to see how a billionaire lives." He said, "You work with a billionaire." I said, "Yeah, but he doesn't live like a billionaire!" Mar-a-Lago was spectacular. It is certainly five stars.

My wife and I were his guests that weekend. We went down to the dining room, sat down, and had a cocktail, and Donald came in the room. He pulled up a chair and was talking with us, and during the conversation he said, "I'm going to give you a recommendation. I told the chef when I was on the flight down here my mother's recipe for meatloaf. You've got to try it, it's to die for." So here I am in a five-star restaurant, and I ordered meatloaf, and believe me, it was to die for, it was phenomenal. It was a spectacular place. Beautiful verandas, beautiful views. He took us on a tour of his apartment, which was beautiful.

Mr. Trump and Melania were no longer dating, and he expressed several times how much he missed her and hoped to get back together. I did not inquire about the cause of the breakup or how he planned to get back together with Melania.

Trump hosted more than 100 Reform leaders in Palm Beach. "I'm very proud to be in the party of Ross Perot and Jesse Ventura," Trump told the gathering, promising a decision by mid-February on whether he would seek the nomination.[11]

Roger Stone: We hosted at Mar-a-Lago a reception for the Reform Party national committee members, three from each state, chairman and national committee people and other activists. It was a very, very public campaign. This was pre-internet in many ways.

Russell Verney: It was primarily the nuts and bolts of how to accomplish the nomination and whether they anticipate the difficult parts in an independent campaign. We put together a great campaign team out there. So he had contacts and knowledge of what it would take and the ability to get it done if he decided to do it and had the liquid cash to do it.

Everything was working. The Wall Street Journal *reported on January 19 that Trump was visiting the construction site for Trump World Tower near the United Nations. Although the article questioned Trump's claim that he was worth $5 billion and quoted Abraham Wallach saying, "Donald exaggerates sometimes," it quoted Trump first: "I'm rich and I'm successful. Isn't that the kind of president you want?"*

By January 27, Richard Johnson was reporting in the New York Post *that Trump and Melania had made up. "The reconciliation was sparked late last week at a romantic candlelit dinner at Le Cirque 2000 where they kissed and cuddled between courses."*[12]

8.

THE UNREFORMED

The challenges of running a presidential campaign on a third-party ticket were becoming clearer to Trump. The media part was easy. But candidates needed to spend big money to hire knowledgeable organizers to submit petitions to get onto state ballots. Only when a candidate won the nomination would he receive the $12.6 million in federal matching funds, and his top rival wasn't going anywhere. Pat Buchanan could count on social conservatives who felt left out of the Republican Party and would volunteer for his campaign.

Trump likely would have had to spend millions to fight an experienced presidential candidate he might not beat. He had not even convinced some Reform Party officials that he had the cash or the willingness to spend it.

Mike Zumbluskas, *New York Reform Party strategist:* It was still just him and Roger Stone and a handful of people going around. Especially as late as it was, you had to start having organizations in different states, because the Reform Party wasn't that strong.

Rick Wilson, *Republican political strategist:* A lot of Roger's career is basically Roger being Roger and bullshitting. He's a master of it. He is the god-king of bullshit. Roger doesn't have the temperament to do the other things of politics.

Lenora Fulani, *New York Reform Party leader:* Trump may have been around, but he wasn't that involved. He supposedly was interested in getting our nomination, but he didn't really go after it. I knew he was floating here and there and that other people were talking to him.

Russell Verney: I'm not aware that Donald Trump ever initiated any petitioning activities to get on the ballot in any states. I know he had some posters made up, and his staff appeared at Reform Party gatherings around the country. He was serious about it and going over how we could win in a three-way race. He was simply exploring the possibility of running.

Mike Zumbluskas: We didn't promise him that he would have a free ride at the Reform Party. Pat Buchanan had an interest. You had Lowell Weicker. You had a number of people, and we were talking with all of them.

Russell Verney: Matter of fact, in '99 me and a couple people opened up an exploratory committee to try and draft Colin Powell. I was pushing for him, because he might have won in 2000 if he were on an independent line.

Mike Zumbluskas: Too many of the people in the Reform Party and early Independence Party were people who said, "We don't like this system, and we're not going to learn the system, because we want to overturn the system." I said the opposite. Yeah, I want to overturn the system, but you need to know how it works to get in there to overturn it.

Zumbluskas was one of more than a dozen people paid $1,000 to $2,000 each in early 2000 by the Donald J. Trump New York Delegate Committee—an organization officially started on December 24, 1999—for delegate petition circulation. Trump was the only listed donor to the group, having given $50,000. Most of the money went to two petition circulation consultants.

Mike Zumbluskas: We had ballot access in about 12 to 14 states where we could put Trump on. But for other states he was going to have to petition to get on. And a lot of those states we weren't strong in, so unless you were going to start putting a ground organization together, getting on the ballot is quite difficult. Roger initially went to the convention in '99, and then he had time to organize and he didn't do it. Roger knew how to do it with the Republican Party, so that's why I didn't take it seriously, because he has political operatives, and they weren't doing that.

Russell Verney: You get time constraints in every state, and you've got a lot of different requirements state to state. So it would've run about $10 million to staff it, research it, implement it, gather the signatures, verify the signatures, and get on the ballot for all states. You could cut that cost if you've got a huge cadre of volunteers, but obviously Trump didn't have that.

Phil Madsen: There would have been time. Perot started his original petition drive, I think it was early in the year in January or thereabouts. It would have been easier this time, because the Reform Party was already on the ballot. Had Trump decided to jump in in early 2000 and go for it, yeah, there would have been time to get the signatures and get on the ballot in most states, if not all of them.

Roger Stone: The ballot access question would have cost him, we estimated $6 million to get on the ballot everywhere you needed to go.

Pat Buchanan: You have people who care. People tell me stories about people coming out of the subway and saying, "Would you like to sign a petition for Pat Buchanan?" They'd have real encounters. The money wouldn't have done it. People came out for me because they believed in me.

Eleanor Clift, *political reporter for* Newsweek *and the Daily Beast:* Buchanan understood the value of grassroots organizing. Trump's whole life is prepared for him. He really didn't do any of the nuts and bolts you're supposed to do as a candidate. He didn't organize his followers. He didn't raise much money. He thought he could make a couple of speeches, and that would be it. From the outside it looked easy, and that's all he would have to do. Buchanan had just simply out-organized him.

Lenora Fulani: He's not stupid, and he had a lot of money, so I don't quite know why they did it the way they did it, but it wasn't the way that would work.

While Trump was trying to figure out if under ideal circumstances a third-party candidate could win the general election, the circumstances suddenly became far from ideal. Simmering divisions within the Reform Party widened into major rifts. New chairman Jack Gargan had taken over in January only to be confronted with one crisis after another. The party's Perot and Ventura factions went to court over where to hold their 2000 convention, several state party organizations were dissolving or in disarray, and members of the party's executive committee attempted to overthrow Gargan.[1]

Phil Madsen: The Reform Party collapsed before Trump's very eyes.

Jesse Ventura: They didn't really want to grow a third party. It was all about Ross Perot.

Pat Choate: There were power plays inside the party. You had Republicans moving to undermine it. They saw the party taking votes away from W., so you had that outside undermining going on. It became a potpourri. Here's a party that had $12 million, so you had people involved in other agendas.

Phil Madsen: The shorthand within the party was the Perotbots and the Schaumburgers. Schaumburg, Illinois, we had a meeting in that city and the name stuck with us. The Perotbots were looking for a leader to rally behind. They wanted a dictator. They wanted somebody to follow and to promote and defend. We were looking more for a process in which the people could be empowered. So that was the difference, within every state, that split, Perotbots and Schaumburgers.

The chaos pushed Perot to make clear he would "not rule out the possibility of running" if the party "needed some adult supervision," a Texas newspaper reported.[2] *The party had difficulty among voters who could choose from Gore, Bush, McCain, Bradley, and Forbes. Buchanan and Trump drew only about 5 percent of voters in general polls. Nearly 70 percent of adults liked the direction of the country, a January* USA Today/CNN/Gallup *poll showed.*[3] *The economic collapse Trump had said was a key to him winning was not developing.*

Trump skipped the Florida Reform Convention on January 22—Pat Buchanan had already locked up its delegates—sowing doubt that he would ultimately run. "I am deeply concerned about growing divisions in the Reform Party. I strongly urge party leaders to sit down and negotiate their differences,"[4] *Trump told the Associated Press.*

Trump had other problems. Lenora Fulani, who had forged an unlikely alliance with Buchanan, successfully sued to get the New York Board of Elections to throw Trump's delegates off the March 7 primary ballot.

Lenora Fulani: I guess he didn't have somebody who worked with him who knew what they were doing to get him in the running.

Pat Buchanan: I know what we did. I don't know why Trump didn't make a comparable effort if he wanted the nomination, or his people didn't.

A week after John McCain upset George W. Bush and Al Gore edged Bill Bradley in the New Hampshire primaries, Trump joined Tony Robbins for another Results 2000 motivational speech on February 8 at the Kiel Center in St. Louis. But reports surfaced that Trump was thinking of quitting. He wouldn't appear on Missouri's primary ballot the next month because his campaign whiffed a filing deadline.[5] Roger Stone told the Associated Press that Trump would huddle with campaign strategists over the weekend at Mar-a-Lago and decide what to do.[6]

In the intervening days, former Ku Klux Klan leader David Duke said he admired Pat Buchanan's pro-Christian and anti-immigration stances and might switch from the GOP to the Reform Party to help Buchanan.[7] Ventura announced on February 11 that he was cutting ties to the national organization, calling it "hopelessly dysfunctional."[8]

Trump told the New York Times *that Ventura's decision was a "devastating blow" to the party. With his strongest potential ally gone, Buchanan gaining steam, and the Reform Party in disarray, Trump was in an untenable position. Had he been the only candidate on a stable party's ticket, he might have lingered longer, seeing if the situation broke in his favor—perhaps hanging around the race to see if the economy went bad, improving an outsider's chances. Instead, Trump issued a statement that pulled the plug. "I have consistently stated that I would spend my time, energy and money on a campaign, not just to get a large number of votes, but to win. There would be no other purpose, other than winning, for me to run. I have therefore decided not to seek the presidential nomination of the Reform Party."[9]*

Trump went on the Today Show *on February 14 to explain why he would not seek the presidency. Host Matt Lauer seemed determined to get Trump to admit he'd never been serious and never would be.*

When Trump argued that "many states want me" and New York supported him, Lauer reminded him that he was dumped from the ballot. When Trump cited polls that "came out great," Lauer noted a poll where only 3 percent of voters backed him. When Trump said he was "totally serious" about running, Lauer countered that critics said he just wanted attention and pressed for a vow from Trump that he was done forever with presidential aspirations.[10]

Lauer: You're scaring me, though. You're saying, I'm looking at my options.

Trump: Yes.

Lauer: Okay, but let me just make sure we're on the same page here. Those options in your opinion do not include a run for the presidency or the vice presidency?

Trump: Right, this year. It may include something in the future. But at this point the answer is no.

Lauer: Here we go with this flirtation again. No?

Trump: No. Well, I'm just—I'm just saying that in—in a number of years I might consider it.

Katie Couric: It was part entertainment, a large part entertainment, a small part news, when he flirted with the presidency, with running. He had an open invitation to be on television because he was so unpredictable, entertaining, and outrageous. Those three things make pretty good television. But also he was available.

Russell Verney: I was of the impression that he clearly wanted to run but had the issue of liquidity, and eventually decided before March not to run because of the liquidity issue. Many rich people don't have liquidity. So my understanding from Mr. Trump at that time was that he needed to sell his casino in order to have the liquidity to run for president.

Roger Stone: He did not walk away for financial reasons. He was attracted to the idea partially for financial reasons. First of all, the inherent fighting inside the party was discouraging. But beyond that he came to the correct conclusion that when you are a Republican in this country, you start the race somewhere around 35 to 38 percent of the vote—today probably higher—regardless of who you are as a person. If you're a Democrat, you start with around 40 percent, regardless of who you are. When you're the independent you start at zero, and you have to build from there. It's very difficult to do.

Frank Luntz, *Republican pollster:* George Bush and Al Gore represented everything that most Americans were looking for. The only time that a third party ever takes hold in America is when there's something missing. Gore was positionally liberal. Bush was positionally conservative, and nobody felt the need to seek an alternative. Bush represented the anti-Washington sentiment. Al Gore was a mainstream progressive. That was enough for the American people.

Conrad Black, *Canadian financier and publisher:* Trump saw you couldn't win if you're leading a third party, but he also saw how many loose votes there were, that if you could get the nomination of one of the main parties, and if you ran a campaign right, you could pick up a lot of disgruntled people. When Trump is in the Reform Party with Jesse Ventura and just the oddest collection of people, it was hard to take the whole thing seriously, and Trump himself concluded that it shouldn't be taken seriously.

With Trump out of the way, Pat Buchanan completed a takeover of the Reform Party with help from Perot's allies. They removed Gargan from office in a chaotic meeting the day after Ventura quit, installing Buchanan strategist Pat Choate in his place. But Buchanan lost some allies, including Lenora Fulani, who resigned from the campaign on June 20, criticizing him for "transforming the [Reform] party into a party of social conservatives."[11]

Jesse Ventura: I left when he got the nomination. I said, "I'm not going to be part of a party that nominates Pat Buchanan. Are you joking?"

Roger Stone: This is the Reform Party, which is populist but not right-wing. Pat, in truth, was really too conservative for the party.

Reverend Al Sharpton: Buchanan wanted to meet with us. We never had the meeting. Me and Buchanan were always at each other's throats. Buchanan was an absolute supremacist. Buchanan was to the right of the right, and the difference between Buchanan and Trump was that Buchanan was serious about it. Buchanan was a true believer.

Jim Nicholson, *RNC chairman:* I didn't worry about Donald. I would have much preferred Trump be their candidate than Pat. Trump was disruptive, bombastic, plain-speaking, and politically incorrect.

Roger Stone: People said Trump ran in 2000, and he lost. No, he never ran. He came to the cusp of it, and he thought the better of it.

Trump won the Michigan and California Reform Party primaries—the only two states he had qualified for. In November's general election, Buchanan won

449,895 votes out of 105 million people, or 0.4 percent, not a significant showing except in one crucial way. Palm Beach County poll workers invalidated 6,607 ballots cast for both Buchanan and Gore on poorly designed "butterfly" ballots. The confusing Palm Beach ballots were likely what cost Gore the state of Florida and the 2000 election. Nader received 22,198 votes in Florida among 2,882,955 votes nationally—2.74 percent—and is sometimes blamed by Democrats for tipping the election to Bush. Bush won the state by 537 votes in the final tally.

Roger Stone: Given where he would've been ideologically positioned for the race, Trump probably would've nearly elected Al Gore.

Ralph Nader: [If Trump had been on the ballot] between Gore and Bush, I probably would have been blamed less by the Democrats. Who knows. Who could predict Trump, even in 2000? You couldn't predict anything. Al Gore knows if he won Tennessee and everything else happened that happened, he would have been president. He was a senator from Tennessee. You can't win your home state?

Pat Buchanan: Trump sent me some ties, and he called me once. I thought he was very gracious. He was saying I admire what you're doing. There might have been some rough things back there, let's let bygones be bygones.

Roger Stone: Trump correctly concluded you couldn't win as an independent. You had to be a Republican or a Democrat. Our country probably was not yet ready for an outsider businessman president.

Dave Shiflett: It was probably a smart move. He did succeed in getting the part of the public that was interested in reading anything about Donald Trump to start thinking about him as maybe becoming a politician.

Conrad Black: I had lunch with him at Jean-Georges in 2000, and he said, "I had a lot of good polls," but he'd come to the conclusion that he couldn't win in a third party. I said, "Not even Teddy Roosevelt could do that." He was obviously still thinking about it. I said, "You're one of the most famous people in the country. Is it your view in effect that celebrity can be transposed into votes? If so, the thought of some of these Hollywood people getting into high public office—I'm not talking about Ronald Reagan, obviously, but others—would be quite frightening. He said, "Celebrity alone won't do it, but it can be levered upon."

In every interview about his Reform Party ambitions, Trump had offered a version of "If I can win, I will run." He repeatedly said he would make his decision by February 2000. So he explored, decided he could not win, and, true to his word, announced in February he was dropping out. And he learned lessons that would serve him in the future: that it was unlikely a third-party candidate could win, that his celebrity could be leveraged in the political sphere, that there was a constituency and a class of activists motivated by outsiders like Ventura, that Stone's longtime insistence on his political viability was probably accurate, and that his people at the Trump Organization could be depended on to help those ambitions, as Foerderer did by helping produce the book.

Trump's public image remained that of a flamboyant, tabloid-friendly real estate developer who flirted with politics. The time and the strategy were not yet right for more.

PART TWO

PLAYING THE PART
2000—2010

Trump finds a TV persona,
sharpens his skills at attacking rivals,
and grows in national stature.

9.

C.E.O.

C.E.O. is a reality-based game show where the selected contestants compete with each other in a corporate environment for promotions, perks and benefits. The ultimate winner will be named C.E.O. of a real corporation.

—*Slide 3, PowerPoint pitch created by Mark Bethea in 2000*

Many observers credit one person above all others for Trump landing in the White House: Mark Burnett, the California-based creator of The Apprentice *and* Survivor. *Without the prime-time TV exposure of* The Apprentice, *which for 14 seasons over 11 years presented Trump as a decisive business titan, hiring and firing in a wood-paneled conference room, many Americans would not have encountered a fleshed-out conception of Trump as a leader.*

The Trump on The Apprentice *was a character inspired by the real Trump. Having abandoned his exploration of a presidential run in 2000, Trump paused most of his political talk and returned to the private sector as a real estate developer and casino operator.*

After a Hollywood writers strike in 2001 took scripted shows out of production, producers were looking for ready-made characters for reality TV. Unscripted programs were cheaper to produce and less reliant on writers. No reality TV maker was more powerful than British émigré Burnett after Survivor *debuted on CBS in 2000. With huge ratings,* Survivor *offered a way forward, with a hybrid of documentary and game show—a competition that put non-actors under stress and gave them time and space to crack. A key member of Burnett's brain trust was his manager Conrad Riggs, who helped develop the series.*

Competition reality shows of this era generally were about love quests or physical challenges, including the ratings bonanzas Joe Millionaire *(women compete to win the heart of a supposedly rich guy, 2003),* The Bachelor *(women compete to win the heart of a handsome man, 2002),* American Idol *(singing, 2002),* The Amazing Race *(geographic obstacle courses, 2001), and* The Biggest Loser *(weight loss, 2004).*

The widely believed story of how The Apprentice *was born has Burnett on the set of* Survivor *in the Amazon in late 2002 contemplating ants as they swarmed over an animal carcass and then transposing this to the rat race of the urban jungle of New York, soon settling on Trump as the perfect host.*[1]

Another California dreamer had a similar Trump reality show idea two years before Burnett. In early 2000, Mark Bethea, an Air Force veteran who was working for a private jet company and trying to break into the reality TV business, had an idea for a show called C.E.O. Bethea set about creating a killer PowerPoint presentation and finding someone with pull in the TV industry to pitch. He met with Conrad Riggs about it in 2001.

According to Riggs and Burnett, The Apprentice *was developed along a completely separate track, and the idea of Trump as host came fresh from Burnett, who had never heard of or met Bethea. The question of who invented* The Apprentice *led to lawsuits in which the controversial lawyer Michael Avenatti was involved.*

The point here is not to question Burnett's Apprentice *origin story, but to underscore that Trump's consistent publishing of books, goosing of his press coverage, and talk show stops were a strategy that forged a memorable and easy-to-comprehend persona recognized by more than one creative mind.*

Once that image was further honed by the star-making forces of weekly prime-time network television—with producers like Bill Pruitt, Darryl Silver, and Jay Bienstock, who formed plotlines, exaggerated character strengths and flaws, and extracted distillates of drama from hours of raw footage—Trump's persona emerged exponentially more powerful. Television remade Trump into an avuncular and commanding character with a catchphrase that caught on in every corner of the country. The medium also taught Trump new skills that would translate to politics and the White House, such as staging (the escalator entrance), cliff-hangers (who will be fired next), and the potential kindness of outdoor lighting (Rose Garden videos).

Mark Bethea, *aspiring TV producer, former executive at a private jet company:* My friends joke with me that I am the reason Donald Trump is president.

All of the contestants will start their corporate lives as entry-level executives.

Promotions and demotions will be based upon performance in a variety of challenges.

Performance reviews and scoring sessions will be accomplished at meetings of the Board of Directors. (Slides 8 and 9, *C.E.O.* Power-Point pitch)[2]

Mark Bethea: *C.E.O.* was the first reality show idea I had come up with. When I was thinking about somebody with a corporate background who was also a caricature of what we think about when we think about a big-time executive, Donald Trump is the name that came to mind immediately and very strongly. Love him or hate him, *The Art of the Deal* was pretty great. He had a bombastic personality, he played to the cameras, and you never knew what was going to come out of his mouth.

The President of the Corporation will serve as the Show's host and the contestant's main contact. The President will be selected for their past corporate experience as well as their on-screen presence and credibility. (Slide 24, *C.E.O.* PowerPoint pitch)

Mark Bethea: I had Trump in mind first, and then I had Lee Iacocca because as I was developing this, I went to a speech Iacocca gave.

Candidates for President: The Donald. Chairman Iacocca. (Slide 25, *C.E.O.* PowerPoint pitch)

The Office environment and living spaces will provide the perfect "showrooms" for companies to develop brand identification through product placement.

Major consumer and business retailers may also wish to negotiate "exclusive" deals for their own branded or inventoried products. (Slide 49, *C.E.O.* PowerPoint pitch)

Conrad Riggs, *reality show producer:* Mark Bethea came in and pitched. There were two ideas, an airplane racing show with fighter pilots, and the other was car racing. They were expensive and dangerous. Also too formulaic and uninsurable. I also found them boring. There is an old saying that it is exciting to learn how to fly an airplane and boring to watch someone learn how to fly an airplane. On the way out the door he says, I have this other one, it's called *C.E.O.* and if you win you will become the CEO of a company. It wasn't *The Apprentice*. It was one of dozens in this genre. I said no thanks.

Elizabeth Spiers, *media reporter, Gawker and the* New York Observer: I'm sure *The Apprentice* was probably—I don't know what the origin story is, but I know Trump was rubbing shoulders with and sucking up to network executives for the entirety of his career, so it's not entirely surprising that at some point the media would give him that kind of opportunity.

A. J. Benza, Newsday *and New York* Daily News *gossip reporter:* By putting Donald in the column on a weekly basis and talking about his women, his jobs, and how he's turning around New York, that made him a figure for television to give him a show. Television comes running when somebody is dynamic and they've got people talking about them.

Jim Dowd,* *NBC publicity representative for* The Apprentice:[3] Donald Trump's reputation in the 2003 to 2004 time frame, right before *The Apprentice* launched . . . He was a larger-than-life figure who most people would say had stalled a little bit in terms of his awareness and progression. People would talk about the past, the wives and divorces, and talk about his amazing hotels and what have you. But there was really nothing new—there was no momentum in his career at that point. So the reputation would be, this is the modern-day P. T. Barnum who is looking for the next big thing.

Conrad Riggs: Burnett called me one day from the set of *Survivor*. We were always trying to figure out an idea of how to take the success of *Survivor* and do something else in the space of competition reality. He said he'd come up with an idea that would stand alone and apart. He hadn't figured it all out. Later, I had dinner with Mark at Geoffrey's in Malibu with his girlfriend and my wife. He wanted to call it *Protégé*. For me titles are very important. You want to provoke mystique and emotion. *Survivor* had been developed as *Survive* by Charlie Parsons. When

---

* Dowd started his own agency and did public relations work for Trump from 2004 through 2010. Dowd passed away on September 18, 2016. The Fairfield County Connecticut Medical Examiner lists the cause as "acute intoxication due to the combined effects of ethanol and oxycodone." His quotes are from a 2016 PBS *Frontline* interview conducted by producer Jim Gilmore.

I'd talk to people about it, they thought it sounded like a military thing or an athletic test of skill and strength. But it's really a psychological and social experiment. "Survivor" had more entendres. He liked *Protégé*. I didn't like it. I didn't like *Mentor* or *The Sorcerer's Apprentice*. But there was something about *Apprentice*. There were a lot of things you could draw from that word. The winner becomes *The* Apprentice. It's the prize. The show isn't about *an* apprentice. It's *The* Apprentice. There were many hours of conversation about a two-word title.

At the dinner, Burnett also said he had a mogul in mind. A few months prior, in May 2002, Burnett had met Trump for the first time during a finale event for the fourth season of Survivor *hosted by Rosie O'Donnell at Wollman Rink in New York City. Burnett had an earlier impression of him. "Back when I was selling T-shirts on Venice Beach," Burnett wrote in his autobiography* Jump In! Even if You Don't Know How to Swim, *"and getting my start in America, I had read and been inspired by his book* The Art of the Deal.*"*

In a speech Mark Burnett gave in 2013 at the Entrepreneurial Leaders Conference, he told the story of meeting Trump and selling him on The Apprentice.[4]

Mark Burnett, *TV producer:* I get offstage. He says, "You're a genius for this *Survivor* show. I'd love to work with you someday."

Conrad Riggs: I had seen Trump at the *Survivor* finale. The guy was pretty imposing and kind of commands an audience. He had this reputation. But there are a lot of people with reputations. The question is, does it translate to hosting a TV show? We did look at other people because we didn't know if Trump would say yes. I met with [former CEO of General Electric] Jack Welch. He seemed to have moved on with his life and didn't want to make the time commitment. I talked with Richard Branson's team, and we could have pursued that if Trump wasn't an option. I really admire [Branson], and he would have been good, but he didn't have the electric personality of Trump. I talked to people who worked with Warren Buffett, but it never got to a meeting with him. When the team started researching it, it turned out Mark's instinct was correct. We thought, who is super charismatic, and you either love him or hate him but you're going to watch him either way?—and that's Donald Trump. He had written a lot of books. We looked at tapes of interviews he'd done, and decided he was a super-interesting guy.

Mark Burnett: I call the number I've got for Trump's office thinking I'm going to get some receptionist. He answered the phone himself.... "Who's this?" "It's Mark Burnett." He said, "Oh, *Survivor* genius. What's up?" And I said, "Well, I've got this—You said about doing a show together a couple years ago." He said, "Yeah, *Survivor*'s gotten bigger than ever. It's the number-one show. You want to do a show with me?" I said, "Yeah, I do." He said, "Well, I'm at the office now. Come over right now to Trump Tower and let's talk about it."

Conard Riggs: Mark went to Trump's office and pitched him the idea. Trump said ABC had been asking him about doing a reality show with cameras following him around. Trump said, "This is better, because it's not just about me. It's about the American Dream, it's about giving someone an opportunity." So we had the host. We said now we can pitch this. We brought it first to ABC. They said, "We have one question: Who is the host?" They were surprised, because ABC had just tried to make a deal with him. They weren't being super aggressive, and the terms weren't A-plus. We were white-hot with *Survivor*. I thought, let's hedge our bets. We brought it to CBS, because of *Survivor*, and third we went to NBC. NBC was hurting the most at the time. It was me, Mark, Jeff Zucker, and Marc Graboff [an NBC executive]. They loved it. We said this is the best way to do *Survivor* without *Survivor*. When we said we had Trump committed to host, it turned it from a good idea to a great idea. NBC said don't leave the room without a signed deal.

None of Mark Bethea's pitches went anywhere, and he kept working in private jets. A federal copyright suit brought by Bethea over who owned the show idea for The Apprentice *was dismissed. A California state "idea theft" suit was settled out of court shortly before trial, with Burnett and Riggs paying Bethea an undisclosed amount.*

Just as he watched political poll results, Trump kept an eye on TV ratings. He knew who the gold standard in reality TV was, and when opportunity came, he grabbed it. Big TV ratings gave someone power, and Trump wanted that power to further his ambitions. ABC had been pursuing Trump for what was at the time thought of as an Osbournes*-style show (the vérité program starring the slurring and aging rock-and-roller Ozzy Osbourne and his family), a format that in later years would evolve into the heights of lowness in* Keeping Up with the Kardashians. *Trump, riding his intuition about what would work for his brand, had refused. The format risked doing to Trump what it had done to others—making stars look vacuous. Trump showed he understood better than anyone how to sell his persona to get what he wanted.*

10.

BOUND FOR GLORY

Trump the reality star was in pre-launch mode. He was uniquely suited for this complex role, an image self-constructionist nonpareil, but would Trump be a compelling character for an entire television season?

Many talented people were working hard to make it so—even if some on the inside were highly doubtful about the show's prospects. One of them, Darryl Silver, originally met Conrad Riggs while pitching a sports reality show idea of his own called Bound for Glory.

As famously fancy as Trump's penthouse apartment was, his business offices were utilitarian and dated. What viewers saw instead was a set built into raw space on an unoccupied floor of Trump Tower. Here was a walnut-paneled conference room lit like a vault in a heist film with squeakless chairs and a gleaming table—an office fit for a modern king whose burgundy leather chair was higher than the others. Like Arthur pulling the sword from the stone, something almost magical happened with Trump on the television set of a boardroom. Everything came together and a myth was made: one that would last and be known throughout the land.

Darryl Silver, *co-producer of* The Apprentice: I signed my contract, and Conrad goes, "Okay, here's the show: it's *Survivor* in the city, and the winner gets to be Donald Trump's apprentice for a year. You guys need to figure out the rest before Jeff Zucker asks me what it is." Then I walked into a room with about twenty people around a conference table for a first production meeting.

Bill Pruitt, *co-producer,* The Apprentice: I got a meeting with Conrad Riggs through my agent. They were at the time living large out in Santa Monica. Beautiful offices. That triggered a meeting with Jay Bienstock, who was the showrunner. Jay sat at a desk in a much smaller office, but a decent one. The couch was a good foot, maybe even a foot and a half shorter than the table. You were literally like knees in the air looking up at him, and he was towering over you at the desk, and that sort of set the tone for what was to come, with Jay in particular leading the power dynamics. He asked, "Are you cool if I look into your references in case I want to hire you?" And I said, "Yeah, I think you would be a fool if you didn't." And he snapped his fingers and said, "I like that attitude. That's the attitude I need." I thought, what did he mean by that? He thought I said he'd be a fool not to hire me. I was talking about the references. By then I think he had had a couple meetings with The Donald. It was very Trumpian. He was getting excited. So then it came time to do the deal. All of us had these thick, rich nondisclosure agreements. My agent remarked how he had never seen anything like this before.

Conrad Riggs, *reality show producer:* Everybody sat in a room for several months and came out with what might seem like an obvious idea, but it became *The Apprentice.* Who really created the format of the show was writers on a work-for-hire contract. It wasn't really Mark Burnett. He created the concept.

Darryl Silver: I sat down, and while they were doing the intros, I started writing what I thought was a vision of the show, because I knew nothing other than the concept. A lot of what I wrote in that first 20 minutes actually made it into the show. The first thing I wrote was "Lemonade stand 101." Jay Bienstock* said, "No, no, let's make it a pretzel stand." And I'm like, "Jay, what are you talking about? Lemonade stand. It's business 101." And, obviously, it became a lemonade stand. It all seems so ridiculous now.

Conrad Riggs: The marketplace had not been flooded with reality competition shows. If this was launched today, it may not have taken off. The first *Apprentice,* the contestants were so authentic, and most were

---

* Jay Bienstock did not reply to multiple interview requests.

there for the right reasons. They truly thought a job for Donald would be life-changing, this high-profile real estate developer.

Darryl Silver: Of course I knew who Donald Trump was. A New York real estate guy. I didn't think anyone really took the guy overly seriously. In fact, if anything, we thought, would anybody want to see people doing business tasks with Donald Trump? There was no huge confidence that this was going to be a smash hit, at least when we were sitting in rooms developing it with the team. I mean, why would you? Why would you think that it would be a huge show?

Bill Pruitt: He was ready-made, no question about it. He needed the show. We needed him, but he needed that show. He understood the marketing value, the branding potential, all that stuff.

Darryl Silver: There's a saying in the reality business, and I'm out pitching every day: "Larger-than-life characters in worlds we haven't seen before." And Trump's that. There's also an aspect of wish fulfillment; I could be some business guy sitting in Chicago, and I could get on this show, and the next thing you know, I'm running a division of Trump's company.

Jonathan Wald, *NBC and CNN news executive:* The real offices are kind of dingy.

Ronald Makarem, *Bethea's lawyer, who took a Trump deposition in 2005:* The conference room was so '80s: carpeted up on the wall, really grubby furniture, and clearly indicating to me that he's not high-level. That's honestly what I thought. Just, really, second-class furniture and offices. His second-in-command, George Ross, didn't even have an office. He was sitting in a cubicle.

Bill Pruitt: We were exposed to the gilded life of Donald J. Trump, and it involved the escalator, the apartment, the lobby to some degree, the waterfall, the helicopter definitely, which you never knew if it was going to fly. That was the airplane actually. Day to day. The helicopter was on the sales docket. At the time, we didn't know if we were going to have a helicopter to film with, but we did. He hung onto it. There's that famous meme with him and the eagle. That's his office and it's very New York.

You don't hold meetings in offices. You go to boardrooms, and so there's shit piled everywhere. It's the way business gets done. I appreciated all of that. That was the New York I was very familiar with. But we wouldn't be telling that story so much. This wasn't a documentary after all, and you had to justify why some kid from Boise, Idaho, would kill to get a job with this guy.

Roger Stone, *political consultant and Trump adviser:* They created that boardroom for *The Apprentice.* That's not a real boardroom at the Trump Organization. They took an entire floor of Trump Tower in its unfinished condition. They converted that into a soundstage, which is where they built the boardroom and the other spaces they shot in.

The opening moments of The Apprentice *as it debuted on January 8, 2004, featured an advertisement for the jewels of the brand, showing Trump, tuxedoed, stepping from a limo to a chopper, which sliced through the Gotham sky while Trump delivered the opening spiel:*

> My name is Donald Trump, and I'm the largest real estate developer in New York. I own buildings all over the place, model agencies, the Miss Universe pageant, jetliners, golf courses, casinos. And private resorts like Mar-a-Lago, one of the most spectacular estates anywhere in the world.[1]

As with many reality shows, the rules evolved and changed with each season. The setup of season 1 of The Apprentice *had 16 contestants, who were called "candidates." They ranged in levels of accomplishment from those who'd started businesses straight out of high school to some with multiple degrees. They introduced themselves to viewers. "I'm Katrina Campins. I rank in the top 3 percent of real estate agents nationwide, and I'm 23 years old." "My name is Omarosa Manigault-Stallworth. I grew up in the projects, but I am now a PhD candidate and work as a political consultant. Four years ago, I worked in the White House for the president of the United States."*

They were led to the freshly constructed boardroom set to meet Trump. Gold and burgundy carpeting ran under a conference table made of wood so shellacked it looked like it could be repurposed as an Italian pleasure craft. Trump sat with beams of stagelight over his folded hands. He introduced his assistant judges, the owlish, gray-haired George Ross, a 25-year veteran of the Trump Organization, and Carolyn Kepcher, an executive vice president Trump described as "a killer. There are many men buried in her wake."

Bill Pruitt: I helped create a myth that people bought that turned into the leadership of the free world—which I carry around with me as someone indirectly responsible for the story that was told. Never once thinking that it would lead to this.

Kwame Jackson, Apprentice *season 1 runner-up, Harvard and Goldman Sachs alumnus:* I went on the show because Donald Trump had this, like, business, marketing, brand, glitz, Hollywood, showman, real estate. All these things were, to a child in the '80s seeing Donald Trump from the outside and understanding what his brand supposedly represented, I thought that would be a great cocktail along with the NBC brand to tell these stories of business and entrepreneurs.

Bill Pruitt: It's reality TV. These things really happened. That's a real guy who went to a real school called Harvard and went to Goldman Sachs and decided he got bored with that. Now he's vying to be the apprentice alongside this other guy. Holy shit. This is really happening. This is my job. Right down to the fake paneling in the boardroom. People buy that—rightfully so, because we did a good job in telling that story. These stories we tell become mythology and they stick.

Katherine Pushkar, *former editor of* Time Out New York *magazine:* You know how Michael Kinsley said of Al Gore that he's like an old person's description of what a young person should be? Trump is like a nonpowerful person's idea of what a powerful person should be.

Bill Pruitt: The truth is we told stories that involved Donald Trump. Were they a con? I don't know. A con would imply malice or forethought. I told you a story. That's all we did. Tell a story. It was a fabrication about a millionaire, a made-up story with realistic intonations. I use those terms in a very pointed way to get people closer to thinking that maybe storytellers and myself helped shape their views on this person. And if he was going to go as dramatically forward with his own self-promotion and wage psychological war with truths and lies, we could do that too.

We all need to understand at the end of the day what's happening to our minds when we're being told a story.

Darryl Silver: Yes, he lives in this ivory tower, but the ivory tower was created as a front to be able to market himself. Whether that's really who he is or not is up for discussion. But when I was hanging out with him, he talked to the construction workers and the boom guy. He was very friendly. I didn't find him some sort of aristocrat.

Candidates were divided into two teams, males versus females, the male team named Versacorp, the female Protégé. Each week there would be a challenge between teams. Members of the losing team would come to the boardroom. One person would be fired.

The first challenge was Darryl Silver's lemonade stand idea. Each team was given $250 to set up a stand, and the winning team would be the one with the highest sales. The women won, largely by promising kisses to lemonade buyers.

Trump was authoritative. He communicated gravitas and charm, although these were not world-shaking problems: "Versacorp was getting desperate, but when I told the teams to manage Planet Hollywood, Bill thought Kwame went too far when he sold autographed basketballs." Trump could exhibit kindness and regret. "You, Bowie, really have shown a lot. I'll be honest. But you failed miserably at merchandising at Planet Hollywood. . . . I have to say you're fired."

Although she did not win the competition, the breakout star of the series turned out to be Omarosa—best known by her first name. Chaotic and mean, she seemed to understand the game the way Trump did. As presented, the prize was a $250,000 one-year job with Trump. But the long game was to be a memorable character on television and see what rewards that might bring.

Bill Pruitt: In every reality show or every documentary, for that matter, whether it's *Dancing with the Stars, The Voice, Real Housewives, Amazing Race,* or *The Apprentice,* there's three versions: there's what happens, there's what gets filmed, and there's what gets cut down to 43 minutes and 30 seconds and squeezed between commercial breaks.

Darryl Silver: To call *The Apprentice* a reality show isn't accurate. It's actually a game show. There's rules that you have to follow. There were times where if we were driving one of the teams to a location and the car broke down, we had to call the other team to say, "You guys have to stop on the side of the road." We didn't have Starbucks cleared [to have the right to film there], so when we went into Starbucks, I'd have to stand with people and be like, "You guys can't talk to each other." Having said that, one of the things I thought was the most genius about *The Apprentice* was that I'd be sitting under the desk in their little compound room where they'd be figuring what to do, and I'd have my little earpiece in. They'd be talking about strategy, and it'd be like, "We need a fabric store." And I'd be talking to all the people in the production office a floor above or below, and I'd be like, "Okay guys, we need five fabric stores cleared." All of a sudden, you have a room full of people trying to clear fabric stores. Because it all has to happen in real time. And then they'd be like, forget about the fabric stores. And I'd be like, "Okay guys, cancel the fabric stores." The beauty behind this show, if they would have said, "Hey, let's just take all the seed money, hop on a plane, and go sit on a beach in Florida and see what happens," we would have followed them. They would have lost. But they really had that freedom.

Bill Pruitt: You could fly helicopters down Fifth Avenue on a moment's notice and say, "We're driving, we're about six blocks north of Macy's. Get 'em coming through." And there would be that overhead shot of them driving in formation down to the task delivery. It was a creative high. It was a very satisfying experience for what the series was supposed to be about, that seat-of-the-pants entrepreneurship. And then we'd come back and edit it all together. We were focusing on the contestants. Trump would come at key moments and dispatch wisdom. Send them off to do a task, welcome them back to the boardroom.

Kwame Jackson: We basically created business competition reality shows. That was the first, before *America's Next Top Model* and *Top Chef*, to say this is how you can come out on top and create that form of television. There was no model for *The Apprentice*, so when we did it, we were all exploring the Wild Wild West.

Trump could be tart, as he showed in an episode midway through the first season.

> **Trump:** How did Heidi do?
> **Omarosa:** Heidi was fantastic. And I will tell you that I haven't always been a fan of Heidi. I haven't always thought that she was professional, nor does she have much class or finesse. . . .

Trump: That was very nice. This is one of the worst compliments I've ever heard.[2]

Bill Pruitt: One episode, they had to come up with an ad campaign for Marquis Jet. The prize was a jet ride up to Boston to eat at this dinner. The loser went back and decided who got fired. Men versus women. The women came up with a phallic ad campaign, and the guys were really mindful and trying hard. One guy fell asleep in the war room just exhausted, and we caught the whole thing. It looked like he was going to get fired. The team leader misdirected the guy and got him to stay. And Trump launched the whole cobra hand gesture in the boardroom, so it was an electrified boardroom, which we always wanted. Omarosa doing her thing. And Donny Deutsch, who was our chaperone.

Donny Deutsch: I didn't know whether it was going to be cheesy or not. Because, pre–*The Apprentice*, he was Donald Trump doing Pizza Hut commercials who had gone bankrupt seven or eight years earlier. There was a little bit of stench to reality TV. People turn their nose up at it. And you didn't know, with Trump, what it was going to be. But I said, you know what, it was NBC, it was a network show. I think had it been on a lesser cable network, we might have passed. Walking down the halls of my agency, Trump would go, "Oh, that's a piece of —." He just always talked about women. He just went right to that. You could not get into a 30-second conversation where he wouldn't take it to something, "That girl's beautiful." We were taping *The Apprentice*. He was that guy. But it turned out to be some wonderful exposure for the agency in every way, shape, and form. We were in the second episode of the first season. I actually think—I'm going to sound like Trump—it was their highest-rated episode.*

After three months of taping, 14 candidates had been fired. No episodes had yet aired, so moments that would become famous like Trump's "cobra" hand gesture—an uncurling of the fingers and a quarter flip forward of the wrist made when firing someone—had not yet captured pop culture. The contest was down to Bill Rancic, the founder of an online cigar shop, and Kwame Jackson, an investment banker. The game was about to turn ugly and real.

---

* It wasn't. But it got 20.2 million viewers on its initial airing, one of the highest. The season finale had 27 million.

11.

THE N-WORD

It had come down to two finalists. Kwame Jackson was a graduate of Harvard Business School and a former investment manager at Goldman Sachs. He is African American. Bill Rancic owned a cigar business in Chicago. He is Caucasian. Jackson's task was producing a concert at the Trump Taj Mahal in Atlantic City. Rancic ran a celebrity golf tournament at a Trump-owned club north of New York City. The final episodes would air in April 2004, but the challenges were taped months earlier.

Bill Pruitt, *co-producer,* The Apprentice: Two rival teams had done their tasks and now we were in "task resolution." It was a "huddle," where Trump and the others who are going to weigh in discuss with producers what they're thinking, what they might say, before the cameras start rolling, just so producers have an idea. This conversation was recorded for FCC purposes. This was before what we call "final remarks," which is a chance for them all to duke it out in front of the two finalists. In the huddle, we find out, what will Carolyn say? What will George say? This was before coming back live for the resolution episode. This was before any editing had been done. The tasks had just been completed. Omarosa and Amy Henry, all the fired Apprenti, were brought back to help in the final episode. The argument went toward Kwame, mostly by Carolyn, who was legally allowed to weigh in on the decision, because she was a Trump employee. The producers, by FCC rules, are not legally allowed to push for who they want Trump to decide on. In Carolyn's mind, Kwame had won. He had overcome major problems. And this was really against her interests, because she was working, for real, on promoting the Trump golf course in Westchester, where Bill had been doing his final task.

The assertions in these statements were emailed to Carolyn, who responded in a series of emails.

Carolyn Kepcher: REALLY? How does anyone know what I am thinking—give me a break!

Bill Pruitt: What Carolyn said in the huddle was, "As a Trump Organization employee, I think Kwame would be the best representative of this company. The most authentic, justifiable choice would be Kwame." Then she went through pointing out what he'd overcome.

Carolyn Kepcher: You're asking me to verify something I said 14 years ago. Really? And in the end didn't I choose Bill to win?? Hmmmm.

Bill Pruitt: It was surprising that Carolyn would not choose Bill. So Carolyn is advocating in the huddle, cameras are not running, this is between takes. Trump says, "But will America buy a—" [*Pruitt would not repeat but did confirm Trump's use of the word "nigger"*]—"winning?" He's staring right at Carolyn, who is standing in silence. Her alabaster skin turned a deep shade of red. We were hanging on her words, and she says nothing. Carolyn was standing, leaning two hands on the table supporting her. And she says nothing. I'm not sure what happened next but most likely, Jay Bienstock tells everyone, "Okay, let's move on."

Carolyn Kepcher: I assure you if I heard the N-word being used I would remember, and I'd be disgusted. I do not remember such an incident.

Asked to comment on the possibility that Trump had chosen a winner based on their race, and if any video or audio recordings exist to prove or disprove it, a spokesperson for Mark Burnett offered a "background" interview with a long-time Burnett associate who insisted that his name not be printed. He spent just over two hours insulting journalists in general, explaining why releasing or discussing outtakes from reality shows was bad policy because it could unwittingly lead to collateral damage, offering as an example the career harm Billy Bush suffered following the 2016 release of the infamous 2005 Access Hollywood *"grab them by the pussy"* tape, and expressing a preference for Mormon politicians above all others because *"they always park between the white lines."*

Bienstock did not reply to numerous requests for comment.

When the show returned for a live finale where the runner-up would be fired and the winner hired, Kepcher, on camera, extolled Rancic. He was hired. Rancic did not respond to requests for comment. Kepcher was vague when asked to explain her final preference.

Carolyn Kepcher: I particularly think both gentlemen were outstanding, and either could have won. I have great respect and admiration for both of these gentlemen who showed respect, endurance, and persistence throughout their time on *The Apprentice.*

Pruitt gave his account to us in September 2018. Kepcher commented in a series of emails in late October. In November, Vanity Fair *reporter Emily Jane Fox wrote that former Trump lawyer Michael Cohen recounted a late 2000s conversation he'd had with Trump about past* Apprentice *winners: "Trump was explaining his back-and-forth about not picking Jackson. He said, 'There's no way I can let this black fag win.'"*[1]

We emailed Kepcher right after the Vanity Fair *article ran, asking if she wanted to add anything. She attempted to retroactively put our communication off the record, which someone with Kepcher's vast experience with the media surely knows is not how exchanges with journalists work.*

Carolyn Kepcher: All my email communication with you I wish to be off the record. Thanks.

Kwame Jackson: Yes, there were many people who thought I should have won. There was obviously a preponderance of black Americans and also folks well outside black America. Bill Rancic was a great contestant, a sharp guy. I think he's a wonderful entrepreneur, and he won because he had a better track record of winning individual challenges, and in the end Trump felt like he did a better job on our final task. Now, if I were going to unpack that and try to get inside Trump's head, Trump had no experience with understanding someone like me. Because he probably never even met with somebody like me, which is Harvard pedigree, Goldman Sachs, better schools than he had gone to, better professional experience than him, and confident with who I am. I'm a

6-foot-3-inch, dark-skinned African American man named Kwame. I think that was a bit of a shock for Trump—it was, Why did this guy leave Goldman Sachs to come on my show? What's his backstory? I'm trying to understand him—and it's easy to understand people if you've had experience with people that are similar. Trump's circle, as we know, if you just look at his White House staff, it's very vanilla, it's very older, it's very country club. His experience with African Americans to that date had been mostly in the celebrity world, the Mike Tysons, the Don Kings of that world, no disrespect to any of them, but obviously we're very different. I think with Bill there's much more of a "I understand this guy, he's one of us, he's in my tribe." I don't discount or try to belittle anything that Bill did on *The Apprentice*, but I do know that Donald Trump, at a very core level, probably just felt a lot more comfortable with Bill.

Bill Pruitt: The cut went down judiciously, giving every reason that anyone wanted to think that either guy could win. But in the raw footage, you saw everything, including just short of smelling the rotting carpet at the Taj Mahal, what Kwame was up against.

Kwame Jackson: I have heard that producers were in my camp, not all, but there were producers who were, like, you won this thing. I'm proud of what I did. In the South we have this saying, "Act like you have a little home training." I always acted like I had a little home training on *The Apprentice*. Everyone who had contributed to who I had become could watch that show and say, "Kwame, you made us proud," whether it was a Boy Scout leader or my third-grade teacher or my preacher or my coach.

Jonathan Wald, *NBC and CNN News executive:* It wouldn't have mattered to the network. It might have mattered to Trump's vision of the Trump brand.

Anyone who watched season 4 of The Apprentice *could see that Randal Pinkett, a 34-year-old black man, was by far the best candidate. In the finale, Trump hired him but simultaneously suggested breaking with protocol and also hiring the runner-up, financial journalist Rebecca Jarvis, a 23-year-old white woman.** *Pinkett protested, and Trump dropped it.*

---

* After *The Apprentice*, Jarvis found success in TV journalism, first at CNBC, then at ABC.

Randal Pinkett, *winner of* The Apprentice *season 4:* My impression of Carolyn's behavior in my finale was that she was very much in my corner. I felt energy from everyone, from Donald, from George, from Carolyn, from the producers, in varying ways. I felt positive energy from Carolyn throughout my season.

Kwame Jackson: Had he picked me, I would've had a problem when he came out against Barack Obama with the birther movement. He would always have the trump card to say, I picked the black guy as my first winner.

Randal Pinkett: The only thing that happened during the taping of the show that gave me additional evidence that Donald was racist was my finale. Seven seasons of *The Apprentice*, you've got seven winners, six white, one Randal. And the only person he asks, across all seven seasons—and I could throw in *Celebrity Apprentice* on top of that—the only person he ever asked to share the title was me, and with all humility and with all due respect, my season was not even close. [Rebecca Jarvis] wasn't even second best. So to ask me to share the title is insulting. And I can only reconcile such a move if I give him the benefit of the doubt—which I don't—[and] say he's racially insensitive. If I do not give him the benefit of the doubt, then he's a racist. He didn't want to see an African American win his show, not outright.

I was not aware until I joined the Trump Organization that there were absolutely no ethnic minorities in any executive capacity for any of his companies. And, keep in mind, when I worked for Donald, it was the heyday of his licensing deals. And there were a plethora of companies that Donald launched in that era: Trump Ice, the water; Trump Mortgage; *Trump Magazine*; GoTrump, the travel website; Trump University; Trump Institute. And that's a short list. I met most of the leaders of those organizations. I worked for Trump Entertainment Resorts, which was his casino holdings at the time. All white. So when I look at the Central Park Five, I look at housing discrimination, I look at his leadership team, I look at his treatment of me on the show—and that's all before he ran for president, right? If I layer on top of that his campaign and his administration, to me, there's no room for ambiguity. It's crystal clear, at least to me.

12.

TRUMP ASCENDANT

*It worked. The show was a hit. Broadcast at 9:00 p.m. on Thursday nights—a valuable time slot in a pre-streaming era when nearly all viewers watched programming when it first aired—*The Apprentice, *debuting January 8, 2004, was the number-five-ranked show on television for the 2003–2004 season, averaging 20.7 million viewers.*

Pivotally, Trump had stepped into a network TV publicity machine that multiplied his brand's reach. The morning after each Apprentice *episode aired, that week's fired candidate would appear for a postmortem interview on the* Today *show, the most popular morning show in America. NBC News staffers bristled at Trump's omnipresence, but Jeff Zucker, promoted in December 2003 from NBC Entertainment president to president of NBC's Entertainment, News & Cable Group,[1] had propounded a new model of doing business at NBC, where certain quarters of the news division served the entertainment division. Jonathan Wald, an NBC News executive producer who would later work at CNN, was a key intermediary between Zucker and the news side.*

A Newsweek *article about "the most addictive new show on television"—a "15-episode infomercial for Trump himself"—mooned that "not long ago, Trump, 57, was a bloviating real-estate developer with a taste for young women and the spotlight. Today he's—exactly the same" but somehow "so cool."[2] His hair, his resurgence, and sometimes even his political views became part of the national conversation.*

Darryl Silver, *co-producer of* The Apprentice: It became an overnight sensation. I'd never been involved in a hit like this, and overnight, it was like, holy shit. It was pandemonium. I got a call from Conrad [Riggs], who said, "We just got picked up for seasons 2 and 3. You've got to get back here. You've got to sign your contract. We're going right now."

Bill Pruitt, *co-producer of* The Apprentice: So many of the fired contestants were jilted beyond belief. I mean, they were borderline suicidal. They come out beating their chest, saying, I'm the one. I'm the best, and then Trump very ceremoniously fired them on national TV, 30 million people watching. Then you go away for three months. You brood on it. Maybe get over your desire to hang yourself, and you get through life, and then all of a sudden it's airing, and you're watching it all happen, and then the publicity machine is chauffeuring you over to the *Today* show, where you're going to sit at six in the morning New York time with Matt Lauer, who is chiding you about why the hell did you do such a stupid thing.

Katie Couric, *former co-host of* Today: Before *The Apprentice*, Trump would come on the *Today* show and do interviews occasionally. But after he would just come on to talk about *The Apprentice*. He was pretty relaxed, sauntering in like he owned the place. That was his M.O. I never heard that he was difficult or a prima donna, or demanding, or anything like that. I think he felt like he was a bit of a fixture, a part of the NBC family, and I think he liked that. One time, I dressed like him for Halloween when *The Apprentice* was super popular. He came by and mugged with me in the Halloween costume.

Jonathan Wald: We called it "logrolling," the promotional aspect of the *Today* show and all network broadcasts touting the network siblings. That's why he was around. It wasn't just a function of himself. You have to put them on, and then later it becomes, oh, you want them on? And then it's like, oh God, these guys again? At the beginning, Jeff [Zucker] was the architect of everybody supporting everybody else promotion-ally, and then it just became regularized.

Katie Couric: There was, at times, at least from me, some level of frus-tration that we were increasingly used as an NBC network promotional machine, which is something that grew as time went on at the *Today* show. I think, back in the day, we weren't expected to promote every time there was a new NBC show. But that started to happen more and more. People felt, well, it's just part of the deal. If *The Apprentice* does well, that helps the *Today* show and that helps NBC. I understood the economics of it all, but it felt a little excessive. But I also wanted to be a good company person too, so I tried to balance that.

Elizabeth Spiers, *media reporter, Gawker and the* New York Observer: When they started *The Apprentice,* I was at *New York* magazine. Adam Moss had taken over, and Adam assigned me to go try out for *The Apprentice,* hilariously, and of course I walked in and immediately got fired the first round. I wrote about the casting committee and how the screening works, like, "I tried out for *The Apprentice* and I got fired!"

Jim Dowd, *NBC publicity representative for* The Apprentice: Donald Trump and politics and his yearning, perhaps, to run for office, was very much alive and bright during *The Apprentice* days, to the point where every week, he did Don Imus's program, which is pretty well-known for political conversation. And he would go on supposedly for *The Apprentice,* but it ended up being a couple of minutes on *The Apprentice* and usually 30 to 40 minutes was the average. Sometimes he'd have him on for an hour, [that] was all about foreign policy, jobs, immigration, all the topics that he's speaking about now, he was talking about in 2004 with Imus and O'Reilly and others.

Darryl Silver: We went from "Does anybody want to watch this?" to "We're geniuses." I was in charge of product integration. It became that the joke was, you'd call Home Depot, "Okay, so we're going to need two executives, two stores, a couple vans, some gift cards, we're going to need some paint, a million-some-odd dollars, and we're going to need this and that." They'd be like, "What was that other thing?" And we'd be like, "Oh, the two trucks." They'd say, "No, the other thing." And we'd be like, "Oh, a million-some-odd dollars. That's the standard fee." We were just making it up, what we thought a corporation would pay. Every corporation wanted to be on the show. In season 1, the ice cream place didn't even want to give us free ice cream.

Glenn Beck, *political commentator and founder of TheBlaze:* Very first encounter was at Larry King's, I don't know, 700th birthday party? It was in New York, and we were leaving, my wife and I, and in came Melania and Donald. He had such a presence to him, the room really stopped and everybody sort of ran to greet Donald. Tania and I were by the door, because he was blocking the exit. He was talking to us, and I don't remember what he said, neither does Tania, because when he walked away, all I said was, "I don't know how that works." And she said, "Right, right?" And we realized that when he was talking to my wife she was looking him in the eye, and I was trying to figure out his hair, and when he turned and talked to me, I was looking into his eyes, and she was trying to figure out how his hair worked.

Darryl Silver: Everybody always talked about his hair. We were shooting one day, and it was outside, and it was windy. I was standing right next to him when the wind literally swirled, this 50-mile-hour wind that just hit for like two seconds, and his hair went almost into a tornado shape. I was about six inches from his hair and I did a deep dive to see what was going on in there. Because everybody thought it was a piece, and I'm like, "There's no way that's a piece." It was all hair. It was just this long, thin hair. I was six inches from it, because I actually had to back my head away.

For strivers who themselves wanted to get close to Trump, his 2004 book How to Get Rich *offered tips on getting cast on* The Apprentice, *along with shallow reflections such as, "I'm told that* The Apprentice *is the highest-rated show featuring a non-acting businessman in the history of television."*

Beneath the fluff, Trump went deep—with assistance from Trump Organization staff writer Meredith McIver,* whom he credits in the acknowledgments for doing "a remarkable job of helping me put my thoughts and experiences on paper." A three-page chapter titled "Read Carl Jung" urges would-be tycoons to delve into the writings of the influential Swiss psychoanalyst. "Carl Jung's theories fascinate me and keep my mind open to my own—and the collective—unconscious," the chapter's first paragraph informs. Trump delves into the meaning of the word "persona," noting that it comes from the Latin word meaning "mask." He cautions about the danger of becoming lost in one's own persona. "These people will end up hiding behind the false personality that works professionally. As I am very much in the public eye, this hit home and I gave it considerable thought."

Jung is also known for describing 12 classic character archetypes, from the Hero to the Jester. A classic "Hero's Journey" myth, echoed in nearly every

---

* McIver became known later as the Trump Organization staffer who penned the speech Melania Trump gave at the 2016 Republican Convention that appeared to be cribbed from Michelle Obama's 2008 Democratic Convention speech.

superhero movie, starts with someone taking charge reluctantly, forced by injustices and external events. This person then emerges as a hero by overcoming obstacles, eluding shape-shifters, and defeating villains.

If Trump or his ghostwriter was stretching the truth about his interest in Jung, you wouldn't know it from watching the developer/author/TV star operate in real life. From his earliest public musings about politics with Rona Barrett, he cast himself as this sort of hero, insisting there was one man who could turn things around in the United States—not him, he didn't need it, but, well, if things got bad enough and people seemed to want him to step up . . . This portrayal of himself as dauntlessly holding off powerful evil forces is another example of the myth-making craft he carried into the presidency. By his side would be his third wife, statuesque.

On January 22, 2005, three days before the premiere of season 3 of The Apprentice, Donald Trump married Melania Knauss. The couple wed at Bethesda-by-the-Sea Episcopal Church in Palm Beach, Florida, before moving over to Trump's Mar-a-Lago estate for an ostentatious soiree that reportedly cost $1 million.[3]

The wedding was a public performance, complete with wardrobe consultants. Knauss, 34, wore a white satin John Galliano for Christian Dior wedding gown that she had picked out in Paris with assistance from Vogue's André Leon Talley and Sally Singer and modeled for the magazine's February cover.[4] With a 13-foot train, the $100,000 embroidered gown, a dreamcoat of glittering distraction, showcased 1,500 crystal rhinestones and pearls.[5]

Trump had thrown lavish matrimonial ceremonies twice before. A guest list of 1,000 for his 1993 nuptials to Marla Maples in the Grand Ballroom of the Plaza Hotel included New York politicos, celebrities, and sports figures with East Coast pedigrees. Among the businessmen in attendance was Saudi arms dealer Adnan Khashoggi,[6] whose nephew Jamal Khashoggi was an editor and foreign correspondent at a Saudi Arabian newspaper at the time.[7] (Jamal Khashoggi, who became a regime critic as a Washington Post correspondent, was killed at the Saudi Consulate in Istanbul on October 2, 2018, a year after Adnan died from Parkinson's disease in London.)

Trump's Mar-a-Lago wedding to Melania, with a shorter but more A-list guest roster than the Maples jamboree, showed how he had grown beyond his New York tabloid roots. Mark Burnett's son Cameron was the ring bearer.[8]

The 350 guests at Mar-a-Lago included heads of state and governors (Bill and Hillary Clinton, Rudy Giuliani, Arnold Schwarzenegger, George Pataki, and Chris Christie), media and business personalities (Oprah Winfrey, Matt Lauer, Chris Matthews, Katie Couric, Mark Burnett, Kathie Lee Gifford, Regis Philbin, Barbara Walters [who arrived in a white Volvo station wagon], Anna

Wintour, Heidi Klum, Star Jones, Simon Cowell, Pat O'Brien, Stone Phillips, Gayle King, Les Moonves, Jeff Zucker, Steve Wynn, and Kelly Ripa), sports icons (Derek Jeter and Shaquille O'Neal), and musicians (Elton John, Russell Simmons, P. Diddy, Usher, Paul Anka [who complained to a reporter about being seated behind a pillar during the ceremony], Billy Joel, and Tony Bennett), who feasted upon Cristal champagne, Jean-Georges Vongerichten–catered hors d'oeuvres, and a seven-tier wedding cake.

Rick Wilson, *Republican political strategist:* It was going to be a huge event with a lot of other people that the [Clintons] know. Remember Donald Trump was not a Republican donor, heavy hitter, activist, conservative of any kind at that point in his history. Trump had supported Chuck Schumer, Nancy Pelosi, the Clintons, and Planned Parenthood. They weren't going to Jerry Falwell's house for high tea.

Andrew Stein, *Democratic Manhattan borough president:* The kids gave toasts. Melania's mother gave a toast. The Clintons were there. He thought it was prestigious, The Donald.

Conrad Black, *Canadian financier and publisher:* I had a talk with both the Clintons and Rudy Giuliani, who I knew. I didn't feel out of place. We knew Anna Wintour really well—nice talk with her and Barbara Walters.

Roger Stone, *political consultant and Trump adviser:* It was in Palm Beach at the church that's not far from Mar-a-Lago, where there was a reception afterward. I still have the invitation. I drove a 1959 Jaguar Mark 9, which is a behemoth of a four-door sedan, not terribly valuable, but I bought it off Craigslist. It overheated on the way. I have read that the [Clintons] were there, but I don't remember seeing them. I wasn't that impressed with [Bill Clinton] at the time. There were a lot of famous people there, so they didn't stand out.

Bo Dietl, *former NYPD detective:* Bill Clinton was sitting in a corner sucking on his thumb, and Hillary was running around. She came over, she gave me a big hug and kiss. "Bo, I love you." She was very nice. I hadn't met her before, but she knew me. I'm a high-profile guy. I had been doing TV.

Conrad Black: I have to say that they seemed to me to be happier there and more convivial than one would think from just reading Hillary

Clinton's description of it in her book *What Happened*. She represents that it was just sort of a curiosity to drop in, and that they left right away. They were subject to a good deal of attention, and they even worked the room. You didn't have the impression that they just showed up out of pure curiosity.

Roger Stone: The wedding was amazing. I sat in the same row with Chris Matthews. It's funny. Chris really liked Trump when I got Trump to speak at the University of Pennsylvania for a live show [in 1999]. He just doesn't like Trump so much now.

Katie Couric: I guarantee you, if I hadn't been anchoring the *Today* show, I would not have been at that wedding.

Conrad Black: By the way, if I may ask: Katie Couric, did she make any reference to the fact that she rose up and moved around the room a lot? I think after a while she went and sat somewhere else.

Katie Couric: I had a hidden camera in my purse. I took some video through the camera. We were going to do a fun thing on the *Today* show.

Conrad Black: I don't think they asked that phones be checked at the door. All they did was ask that they not be used. I took her moving around as her finding someone more interesting for her purposes as a news figure than us.

Bo Dietl: I would say that the British royalty can go fuck themselves. Donald Trump's wedding was the wedding everybody and their mother wanted an invitation to. Shaq O'Neal, everybody. Jack Welch, Jeff Immelt of General Electric. It was the who's who. What I remember, Shaq, he was so big, he was showing me his sheriff badge.*

Conrad Black: Don King sat behind us. When we were leaving the church, he complimented my wife on her appearance, which he had seen chiefly from behind at that point.

---

* According to our research, neither Jack Welch nor Jeff Immelt attended or was invited to the wedding. But Dietl's point that the big day excited many people, present and not, is taken.

13.

WOLFGANG DOES NOT HAVE ANY RECOLLECTION

Peering behind the scenes of the rarely discussed later seasons of The Apprentice *offers a view of the real person behind the Trump persona.*

The level of detail presented here is unique and for years was kept hidden by the cumbersome confidentiality agreements Apprentice *candidates signed. But with Trump in the White House facing bigger issues and Burnett having shown little indication of enforcing those agreements, many participants are now willing to discuss in detail the entire process of casting, psychological profiling, filming, and legally questionable manipulation of the contest. If there is one method of Trump's on display most prominently, it is his delegation of messy details to those with less standing. Until problems actually touch him, he turns a blind eye. But when they do, he roars.*

While no subsequent season of The Apprentice *had ratings as high as the first, the next two seasons, still broadcast on Thursdays, also landed in the top 20. It remained a valuable franchise even when season 4 sank to a number 38 average ranking, with about 11 million weekly viewers in the first half of the 2005–2006 television season. Trump's* Apprentice *was generating millions of dollars in product placement advertising with each episode. It was worth NBC continuing to invest, hoping a few tweaks and the cancellation of a Martha Stewart–hosted version would help Trump's original. But with season 5 sinking to the 51st-ranked show in the second half of the 2005–2006 season, a bigger change was made.*

Season 6 was shot in 2006 in Los Angeles with Kepcher and Ross, then 78, replaced as assistant judges by Trump's offspring Ivanka and Donald Jr. Kepcher was bounced from the show and from Trump's employ entirely. She had parlayed her Apprentice *fame into a* Saturday Night Live *appearance and a bestselling book,* Carolyn 101: Business Lessons from The Apprentice's Straight Shooter. *An August 2006 article by the* New York Post's *Richard Johnson praised Ross's egolessness and quoted an unnamed Trump insider insulting Kepcher as "a prima donna. . . . She was no longer focused on business. She was giving speeches for $25,000 and doing endorsements." The cast change raised the public profile of Trump's children, building the impression of them as integral members of the Trump team and paving the way for Ivanka to become a White House fixture with her eventual husband, Jared Kushner.*

The winners of the first challenge of that season earned a dinner at Spago with Chef Wolfgang Puck, Trump, and his wife.

Accounts of Trump's life that cover The Apprentice *generally focus on the top-10 success of the premier season and the way the show helped the struggling NBC network just as the hit sitcom* Friends *was ending. There is sometimes mention of how much money Trump made from it. In a July 2015 press statement to answer questions about his wealth, he claimed $214 million in payments from NBC related to the show. Trump hosted* The Apprentice *across 14 seasons—seven "regular" seasons and seven seasons of the spinoff* The Celebrity Apprentice.

Trump's time as the big cheese on The Apprentice *was his most public turn at a job before he was in the White House. While deciding the fates of striving entrepreneurs is not like overseeing the federal budget or negotiating with Kim Jong-un, the show revealed Trump's thinking on personnel, money, and social issues while exposing him to public feedback about his decisions. The show was an uncanny prelude to Trump's presidency—a future he never ceased planning for even in the midst of* The Apprentice's *lucrative run.*

Jim Dowd: So fast-forward to the fourth season of *The Apprentice*, which was the end of 2005, and it was New Year's Eve and usually during holidays when there's like lull time, he gets very anxious because he wants to be working, or he wants to be part of whatever's happening in the media. It so happened there was going to be a live shot at Mar-a-Lago in Florida on New Year's Eve, so we were just talking about that around 5:00 on New Year's Eve 2005. . . . We were talking about politics, and he said, "Jimmy, would you be my [White House] press secretary?" I had to sort of sit down, was like, "Well, Mr. Trump, if you're very serious about it, we should definitely have a conversation."

Jenn Hoffman, Apprentice *candidate, season 6:* We had to go to the beach. He was wearing a tie and a suit, and everyone else was wearing Trina

Turk, very beachy stuff. He had a makeup artist with him, tiny girl following him around with bronzer, but no one else besides me. He takes off his shoes and his socks, and he's balancing kind of awkwardly. Then he notices that we're watching him. Sheepish is too strong a word, but he says almost bashfully, "You can tell I'm not a beach guy." It wasn't his usual bravado, leaning into it. It was a little quieter, like he got caught being awkward, vulnerable for a second. Seeing him take his shoes and socks off, I realize he's a ginger and very fair-skinned, freckled, red-headed. It didn't occur to me this entire time we were filming, because his suit goes down past his wrists and he always has pants on, he's not a shorts kind of guy. Occasionally we saw him in like a polo and khakis when he golfed, but he was always covered up. First time I saw him I was surprised at how big he is. He's not just tall, he's big and not in an overweight way. He's got a shoulder-span and he's solid. He's just a big dude. Just his presence can be intimidating.

Poppy Carlig, Apprentice *candidate, season 10:* I had come back for the finale. The first group was doing a golf tournament, and the second group, which was my group, was hosting the after-party. I was setting something up in a back room, no cameras with me, wearing ripped jeans and a sweaty t-shirt, and my hair was in a bun. Trump walks in, and he had just finished golfing, he was sweaty, and he goes "Oh, hey, how's it going?" We had a very short, but to me, a very intimate conversation, just him being genuinely interested in how I was doing. He asked how my experience was and if I was having fun. He asked what my plans were after, and I really wasn't sure. But he told me he thought I had a bright future, and I reminded him a lot of his daughter. That really resonated with me, because I know how much respect and love he has for his family. I think he has a TV personality and a non-TV personality. When the cameras are on, he's on, and he's very good at selling himself.

Randal Pinkett, Apprentice *season 4 winner:* The day that I arrived at Trump Tower for the first day of my apprenticeship, I was escorted into his office, and Donald had a stack of magazines and newspapers. Each of them had a Post-it Note stuck inside of the magazine or newspaper. Donald was picking off the top of the pile, turning to the Post-it Note, reading something, and then putting it to the side. As we began the meeting, he did not stop this ritual. He continued as we were talking, picking up the magazine or newspaper, opening to the Post-it Note. So I kind of leaned over the desk to see, what are you looking at? He's looking at articles about himself. He's feeding his ego, like, a steady diet of vegetables and fruits. And I said, okay, I get it now. Donald loves Donald.

Derek Arteta, Apprentice *candidate, season 6:* He has zero gaydar. When we won that first task and we were at Spago, Trump went around the table asking all of us what our marital status was and boyfriends or girlfriends. To me it felt like he wanted to know which ones were going to be easier to move in on at some point. I was at the end of the table next to Melania, and he says, "How about you Derek, you got a girlfriend or what?" And I said, "No, but I have a boyfriend." He gives me a quizzical look, and I'm like, "I'm gay, Mr. Trump." He says, the first thing out of his mouth, "So my daughter Ivanka does nothing for you?" The sarcastic version of me was going to shout, "No, but your son Don does!" I don't feel he was homophobic. It kind of bonded us. At the Playboy Mansion, for example, I was in this private Jacuzzi area with two Playboy bunnies. Trump walked back there, and he sees me talking with the girls. They're like, "Hi, Mr. Trump!" They're flirting with him. He said, "Don't worry, girls, you have nothing to worry about with Derek in the Jacuzzi with you." And then he winked at me.

Jenn Hoffman: Trump started asking people about marital status, and this is where he discovers that Derek is gay, where we all discover that Derek is gay. Trump said, "I don't understand it with all these beautiful women." Then somehow we get to him talking about George Bush, president at the time. He's talking about how he can't stand how stupid W is and how his family fucked up the whole thing. He starts talking about how he was always against the war, what a waste of resources it was, how they were so selfish for making it happen. Nobody had to interact with him, he was just going off. Saying it was for their own interests and that they don't know how to run a country and that if he ran it—and that segued into "Should I run? I think I should run." He kept telling us that he'd like to run, but if he runs he'd have to win, he doesn't like to lose. And we're like, "2008?" He said, "No it's too early." Hillary Clinton in 2008 gets brought up, and he says for her, no, he doesn't think so, too early. He said, "If I run it'll probably be in 2016, versus my friend Hillary." I remember very distinctly he said "friend."

Surya Yalamanchili, Apprentice *candidate, season 6:* This was day two, and we were all so obsessed with Trump paying attention to us, we're totally caught up in this myopic world, somehow thinking it's a real job interview. It's, "Does Mr. Trump like me? How do I get him to notice me?"

Jenn Hoffman: Nobody's cameras were up, so we were just shooting the shit at this point. Wolfgang Puck is now seated with us, and Trump directly asked him, "What do you think, should I run for president?" and Wolfgang's, like, "Uhhh"—suddenly his accent's 10 times thicker, very purposefully not replying, and then Trump directly asks him again, and he says, "Do whatever you want with it." Then Trump turns to us. "What do you think? Should I run? Would I be a good president?" And, of course, everyone's like a bobblehead, "Uh-huh, uh-huh, yeah."

Tesia Kuh, *executive administrator, Wolfgang Puck Worldwide:* Wolfgang does not have any recollection of the conversations with Donald Trump at this dinner.

Derek Arteta: On my very first interview, I spoke to a junior-level casting person. She said, "Oh my God, I love you, I want to elevate you. I want you to meet the head of casting," and I went to the head of casting, and he's like, "Why do you want to be on this show?" I said, "I want to be on any show. I love reality TV." He said, "I'm going to stop you right now. I like you, you could totally be on this show, but when you get into that room with the producers, you have to 100 percent say that you love Trump, that Trump is your hero." You've got to be a super fan of Trump. If you aren't, then you should fake it because if he realizes that you're not a fan of his, he won't hire you.

Surya Yalamanchili: You're supposed to go along with the producers. When they're like, "Hey, so-and-so was moping around in the corner, don't you think he's a sulky little bitch? You're supposed to say to the camera all through this task, "So-and-so is just moping around," just repeat word for word what they tell you. You go on reality TV, you want to be seen. They say that Trump is so needy for attention. All of us that went on that show, we are also pretty needy.

Derek Arteta: They rented the house. [Trump] didn't live there at all. He was at the Beverly Hills Hotel the whole time. He had plenty of free time, because we didn't see him that often. He gives you the task on day one, and then you don't see him again until day two and day three, and when he filmed, he got in, he got out. The only thing that took a long time was the boardroom. That could take three hours.

Jenn Hoffman: The first thing that happened to me on the show was that a producer wanted me to make fun of Surya's hair. She said, "What's your first impression of Surya?" I said, "I don't do first-impression stuff." She's like, "Well, what do you think of his hair?" Surya's hair was like big and wild at the time, and she said, "Isn't it unprofessional?" And I said, "Listen, lady, I'm not going to do that."

Derek Arteta: At the Playboy Mansion, Hugh Hefner took us out to the pool area, where all the bunnies were, and then Trump rolled up.* He introduced us to Hugh, and Trump made a remark, "All the ladies here are so beautiful, I can't tell which ones are yours and which ones are mine." In reference to the women on my team.

Jenn Hoffman: Trump, Kristine [a fellow contestant], and I are standing by the pool, and Trump tells us, "Wow, your team is very beautiful, maybe better looking than the Playboy models, and natural too," looking at our chests, and I started laughing. "Ha ha ha, you think everyone on our team's breasts are natural?" He thought about it some more, looked around for a minute, and said it again, "Yeah, your team is better looking than the Playboy models." He did say stuff to Kristine that was what the fuck, like, "You're married? You're way too into your husband to win this." During the audition, he noticed she had tattoos. "Ugh, you're so beautiful, why would you do that to yourself?"

Kristine Lefebvre, Apprentice *candidate, season 6:* Once in a boardroom, he said, "I don't think I can hire you because you love your husband too much. You won't be devoted enough to the job." The producers were

---

* This is the night Playboy model Karen McDougal says she met Trump, sparking a 10-month affair she would chronicle in a *60 Minutes* interview in March 2018.

worried how they could make that work in the final cut if he did fire me then.*

In week seven of the Los Angeles season, Derek Arteta was in the boardroom defending himself to Trump over why he thought it was a good idea to promote Lexus cars by having potential buyers ride go-karts around the dealership.

Derek Arteta: I came up with, how about we do go-karts? They can do it around the dealership, that'll be fun. And then I realized, eh, that doesn't really convey luxury, let's not. And then later on Jenn said, "No, let's go with it."

Jenn Hoffman: A producer pulls me outside, tells me the other team is doing mini golf, it's not going to be that visual, "Do me a solid since you do have extra space and plenty of room in your budget, do the go-karts." I said I didn't really want to, and he said, "I can't guarantee you a win, but I will make sure that it does not come down to you being fired, because we give Trump the notes, and we can make it very clear in the notes that Derek was like 'go-karts, go-karts.'" He guaranteed me that I would not be fired. That was our deal. We shook on it.[1]

Derek Arteta: Fast-forward, you get interviewed for several hours the day of the boardroom, before going in. The producers asked why did you come up with that idea, and I'm like, "I'm from Covina," which you know is in LA, but in my mind it's a small town, very conservative and very white. "I'm white trash, I like that shit." I didn't think those words were going to come out of my mouth later, but in the boardroom it all came out, and the fun camaraderie that Trump and I had suddenly ended.

"I'm white trash," Arteta told Trump in the boardroom. "I only eat at restaurants with deep-fried appetizers."

Trump wheeled on Arteta. "What do you mean, you're white trash . . . you don't joke about that . . . that's a pretty stinking statement. . . . You know what?

---

* Lefebvre, married to the prominent chef Ludo Lefebvre, was not fired then. She was one of the final six candidates, fired in the episode prior to the finale for putting the wrong phone number in a promotional brochure. She would later appear nude in the June 2007 issue of *Playboy*. According to the Associated Press, she posed to raise awareness of cervical cancer, of which she is a survivor. (Associated Press, "Fired 'Apprentice' Contestant in Playboy," *Hollywood Reporter*, April, 21, 2007.)

Derek, you're fired. I think that is so stupid. You're fired. Go. Terrible. You shouldn't use that expression anymore either. How stupid can you be?"

Derek Arteta: The publicity people said, "We think this white trash thing is going to get added attention." Unfortunately, when the show started airing, it didn't do well in the ratings. In previous seasons, all the firees got to go on the *Today* show, and our season nobody did because it tanked.

Jenn Hoffman: I got fired three minutes later. They take you out to dinner that night, but it's to monitor you, make sure you're okay, try to cheer you up. I thought they must do this with everyone and didn't say anything at first. Then I was talking with the show's psychologist to do a decompressing-type therapy thing. I waited about a week to see her, and I tell her what happened, and she's like, "What?! I did your psychological profile, and if you say that a producer made you that promise, I'm going to believe you, and I'm going to follow up." She calls me back in her office and says, "Okay, he did this. I talked to JB [head producer Jay Bienstock]. He's going to talk to Mark Burnett about this. What do you want done? This is something they cannot just sweep under the rug unless you make it possible for them. If you make a stink about this, you're going to be back on the show." But I felt like I would look like a sore loser. I get a phone call in my room where we're staying, at the Oakwood apartments, first from the producer who pushed me. He apologized, saying, "I shouldn't have done that. It was unprofessional"—never uses the word illegal—but repeats many times it's unethical and that Burnett and Trump have no idea, but he has admitted it to Jay. Jay called me, "Ball's in your court, what do you want to do?" and I was like fuck it.* I don't accept his apology, but I just wanted away from the whole thing. It had nothing to do with Trump; he was the only person I didn't think was an asshole.

This alleged disregard of game show regulations combined with another alleged incident on the part of producers before the live finale at the Hollywood Bowl shows the fundamental shadiness of the entire Apprentice *operation. Trump, tellingly, seemed to function quite steadily in chaos—until a breach of protocol in the finale triggered rage.*

---

* Jay Bienstock did not reply to numerous requests for comment.

Jenn Hoffman: They tried not to pay us. We were in the greenroom for our walk-through rehearsal for the live finale. They come in and tell us, "You aren't going to be paid at all for this season, because the ratings weren't good."

Surya Yalamanchili: When we arrived at the Hollywood Bowl the night before for the walk-through, someone from production was telling us final details of what we needed to know. She spoke for about 15 minutes but didn't mention anything about our compensation, $1,500 an episode that we appeared on before getting fired. I raised my hand and asked when we'd be getting our checks. She seemed momentarily uncomfortable and then said that she wasn't sure where we had heard we'd be getting paid, but with the move to LA the show was over budget and that wasn't possible. I laid into her that Mark Burnett Productions had paid every prior season and the sister show, *Survivor*, and that was bullshit. She tried to throw others under the bus—NBC, the MBP casting people—but we didn't relent.

Jenn Hoffman: We go, "That's not our problem, we all showed up, and you guys make enough money." They said, "We're really sorry, it's not happening," and we're, like, "Well, we're not going onstage." They said, "You're contractually obligated," and Derek goes, "Hold on." He has a copy of the contract on him, and he says, "Well, that's true. But you can't control what we say or what we don't say because that's not in the contract. Either we get everybody to swear all over the live finale, or silence, tape over our mouths." And then we each took a role. Derek said, "I'm the attorney." I said, "I'm PR media, and I'll press release this, announce it by tonight."

Derek Arteta: Surya was a leader of the coup as well. He was pretty angry.

Surya Yalamanchili: I told her how classy I thought she was for being so ready to throw her co-workers in casting under the bus. The NBC lawyer chimed in that NBC wasn't involved. They had paid the full contractual rate to MBP with the understanding that they wouldn't have pissed-off contestants. It ended with her saying she'd get back to us since Mark Burnett was in the air. They talked to him overnight, and he green-lit the payment.

Jenn Hoffman: A producer sat in an office and cut us each a check, one by one, before we went onstage.*

Surya Yalamanchili: During the live finale, Trump paid me the respect of consulting with me last before he made his decision of who to hire. I made a joke, "You should ask Sanjaya." He was the *American Idol* candidate with long hair who was super famous at that time. Trump was so angry. He's like, "Brilliant, just brilliant." He picks the person, and then afterward onstage we find each other in the middle, and I stuck out my hand. Immediately his finger goes up to my face and he starts screaming, "What was that? That was disgusting! It wasn't funny! Terrible!"

Derek Arteta: The white trash thing never came to fruition in terms of media attention.

Surya Yalamanchili: Making us sleep in tents wasn't going to save the show. The show was just tired. It needed celebrities to revive it. To some extent even that got tired.

---

* For Mark Burnett Productions to pay all 18 candidates $1,500 per episode was about $245,000 total. MBP in 50-50 partnership with Trump was still collecting about $2 million per episode for product integrations, revenue not shared with NBC. Meanwhile, a single 30-second ad on the NBC broadcast of *The Apprentice* in 2006 went for $168,000. (Claire Atkinson, "The Ad Age 06–07 Network Price Chart," *Ad Age*, 2006.)

14.

BELOW THE BELT

There is some madness in the method as well, evident in the savageness with which Trump can level a personal attack. Taking on a fellow celebrity or world leader in the media over just about anything, from beauty pageant rules to nuclear proliferation, can pay dividends in increased attention, but even Trump has admitted there may be a "mental sickness" in it. For some audiences, though, watching one famous person insult another gives satisfaction—and Trump has long been uniquely willing to go there.

Rosie O'Donnell hosted her own Daytime Emmy–winning talk show from 1996 to 2002 and joined the cast of ABC's popular daytime show The View from 2006 to 2007. Her long-running feud with Trump is one of his most notorious, featuring what seem like unforgivable insults hurled from the world's biggest stages.

Some of the injuries Trump causes with name-calling last longer than the kind of bruises caused by sticks and stones. He would show how sticky his rally-tested insult monikers could be on debate stages in 2015 and 2016 ("Crooked Hillary," "Low-Energy Jeb").

When Trump says he loves his enemies, as he did on Donny Deutsch's CNBC show The Big Idea in 2007, there is ample proof. Getting in a public war with Trump can make someone millions of dollars, thanks to Trump's direct intercession. There's something impersonal about Trump's personal attacks. For him, it's not a person attacking a person but a persona attacking a persona. Many of his targets do not, however, take it that way.

Rosie O'Donnell: He always wanted to be booked on my TV show, but I remember watching him on other television shows, and he would lie.

He would say, "My book is the number-one book in the country," and all the producers were going, "It's not the number-one book in the country," and I'm like, "Why doesn't somebody say something then?" And they're like, "He does it all the time."

Michael J. Fox, *actor:*[1] Donald did an episode of *Spin City.* Since it was a show about New York, you had to have all the New Yorkers in it. He came in, did his stuff, did it well, he was pure Trump. Great. We enjoyed having him on the show. But every time I've seen him since then, the same thing has happened. If I walked out that door right now and he happened to be there on the sidewalk, it would happen again. He'd say [wagging his finger], "When I was on your show it was the highest rating you ever got!" I never researched it. But every time I have seen him, he has always said, "The highest-rated show you ever had was when I was on!"* Several times. Every time. And hey, it's great. I love it. As much as I despise a lot of the things he's said, and hate the way he's done things—I wouldn't vote for him at the point of a gun—he's this kind of New York animal, a habitué of restaurants, and he's got kind of a carny charm. You do gotta hand it to him. He fills up a room when he enters it.

Rosie O'Donnell: There were facts that were available to the mainstream media, but everyone seemed to have ignored them.

With NBC, Trump co-owned the Miss Universe Organization, which presided over the Miss USA and Miss Teen USA pageants. TMZ and the New York Daily News published reports in early December 2006 about the reigning Miss USA Tara Conner's underage drinking, testing positive for cocaine, bringing men from nightclubs to her Trump Place apartment, and kissing Miss Teen USA in public. TMZ claimed pageant authorities were considering stripping Conner of the crown. Then, on December 19, Trump held a press conference announcing that Conner would keep the title and that treatment would be provided. "I've always been a believer in second chances," Trump said.

Years later, Conner would credit Trump with his tolerance and for pushing her into a recovery program that got her sober. But what O'Donnell saw that day was a press conference where Trump positioned himself as a moral arbiter. She blasted him on The View *on December 20, 2006, the opening salvo of a*

---

* It wasn't. The highest-rated episode was when Michael J. Fox, having announced his Parkinson's disease diagnosis, made his departure from the series in 2000.

long war. Calling him "a snake-oil salesman," mocking his hair and voice, she said that Trump might try to take her to court, but "he'll probably be bankrupt by that time, so I won't have to worry."

Rosie O'Donnell: At the beginning, I shamed him. That was the day he decided to grant forgiveness and amnesty to an 18-year-old girl* from his Miss Universe pageant, who had the balls to kiss another girl in public and the *New York Post* got a picture of it. He had a big press conference and announced that he had forgiven her and that she was going to carry on representing the Trump name, even though she had fallen to such disgrace, by being an 18-year-old, and you know, exploring in a night at the bar. I made an analogy that it was very pimp-like, that he's like Huggy Bear on *Starsky and Hutch*. That you're the one who gets to decide what kids can do? You? Donald Trump, who's been married this many times and has all these allegations against him. You are the moral arbiter for teenagers? Well, I don't think so. Sit and spin, my friend. That's what I said, and it infuriated him coming from a woman such as me, in his book, the lowest-value player on the board, an overweight, loud-mouth lesbian.

Conrad Black, *Canadian financier and publisher:* He respects anyone who is successful unless that person does something that he finds very offensive to him personally. He thinks success is a good thing, and not just his. That's part of his charm. There's no hint, in my presence, of him being an envious person, or being destructive of anyone other than people he thought were hostile to him.

Trump struck back over the next few days across TV and print media, insulting O'Donnell's looks, her comedy act, her TV ratings, her intelligence, and her magazine, telling Access Hollywood, *"Rosie is somebody out of control who really just doesn't have it. And she ought to be careful 'cause I'll send one of my friends to pick up her girlfriend, and I think it would be very easy."*

On Extra, *Rosie called Trump a "hot bag of wind, frankly, with bad hair." Trump wheeled and fired, saying his friend Barbara Walters regretted bringing O'Donnell onto* The View. *On* Good Day LA, *he compared her to "a little clam. A disgusting thought, isn't it, when you compare Rosie to a clam?" On*

---

* Conner was actually 21. Her birthday was December 18, the day before the press conference with Trump.

Larry King Live, *he dug in with "disgraceful, a horrible human being."* *O'Donnell turned to verse, comparing Trump to a pimp on her blog: "he roughs her up a bit / shames her in front of the others/ teaches her to behave."*

On Late Night with David Letterman, *Trump called her "degenerate."*

At one point, a Trump fan bought at auction a set of lingerie O'Donnell had worn in a 1994 film, framed it, and sent it to Trump, who sent it to Walters at The View. *Trump told the* New York Post's Page Six *that he didn't want it in his office: "It was funny, except that it was really gross."*

Corynne (Steindler) Cirilli, a reporter for Page Six, had been filing scoops on backstage tensions between Walters and O'Donnell, some arising due to the tone of the attack on Trump.

Corynne (Steindler) Cirilli: Rosie had really helped *The View*'s ratings. She was hurt. This was supposed to be a women's empowerment show. This man was coming out and saying horrible and disgusting things about Rosie publicly, and Barbara Walters turned this steel cheek and this blind eye to all of it and never really defended her.

Rosie O'Donnell: Everybody was laughing along with him and thought it was funny, even David Letterman! I remember sitting at home and thinking, I can't believe the National Organization of Women, or some-one, is not standing up and saying, "This is unbelievable what he's doing to this one person."

Katie Couric: It's not as if Rosie's completely the victim. I think she's been the aggressor, hasn't she, in a lot of these cases?

Corynne (Steindler) Cirilli: It wasn't until he started doing these things like sending Rosie's lingerie, writing letters, and going on *Larry King* that it became a big deal. People were calling me for comment. He kept breathing fuel onto the fire. Fox News loved the story. It was dripping in misogyny, and she was a great punching bag. Page Six, we ran with it.

Rosie O'Donnell: I was one of the most-loved people. When he started doing this, I was not thought of in the way that I am thought of now, and he has a lot to do with that. He has changed the narrative. So, Rosie O'Donnell can't be beloved, can't have given away millions of dollars, can't have adopted five children from compromised mothers, can't have done all the things that she did, because then, it wouldn't be a funny joke. But he is able to change that whole narrative. To say that he's not good at it is a vast understatement. If you grow up in New York, and you see somebody doing three-card monte, you feel bad for the tourists from the Midwest. They think it's an honest guy playing a card game. When I was in my teens, I would feel so bad for these families, and I'd say, "Walk away now, you're not going to win. This is New York City, take your money and walk away." Well that's how I feel about Donald Trump. I was that kid, and he three-card-monte'd me.

Donny Deutsch: In the full hour-long show I did on him, I brought up Rosie. "One thing I have an issue with is the way you referred to her." And he goes, "I thought you were my friend." I said, "I am. That doesn't mean I'm going to agree with everything you do, or any other friend." And he goes, "You have to choose sides." I said, "No, I don't. I can like both of you. You can both be my friends, but I can disagree with a particular aspect." He was very taken aback by that. He goes, "Well, I guess you're playing it safe for advertisers." I said, "No, actually, being polarized would even get more attention, but I'm just telling you the truth."

On The Big Idea, *Trump also said, "I love my enemies, and I love having ene-mies to a certain extent—that's probably a mental sickness, to be honest with you. But you need it. It invigorates."[2] Other TV journalists did not come to O'Donnell's defense, piling on with comments about her body and demeanor that they didn't find ladylike. On Joe Scarborough's MSNBC show, the host scurrilously intro-duced a segment on the feud with "It's the pimp versus the pig," as he sat in front of a garish "PIMP vs. PIG" graphic.*

Soon Trump-O'Donnell escalated to war by other means. At a January 2007 World Wrestling Entertainment event, a wrestler in Trump makeup defeated one in O'Donnell garb by slamming her in the face with a Fudgie the Whale ice cream cake. "The bitter battle between the Brash Billionaire and the Left-Leaning Lesbian came to a climax on Raw," the WWE's website exulted. "And in the end, it was Donald Trump who got the last laugh."

On MSNBC's Tucker *show, correspondent Willie Geist reported, "Yester-day at the Waldorf-Astoria hotel, [Rosie O'Donnell] was at a ladies lunch, at-tended by high school girls, Barbara Walters, all these refined women. She was asked about Donald Trump, grabbed her crotch, and said, quote, 'He can eat me.' So she's really a sweet, sophisticated woman."*

The allure of pitting celebrities against each other led NBC to announce in

June 2007 that the next season of The Apprentice *would feature stars and be called* The Celebrity Apprentice. *The show would debut in January 2008.*

Not quite a year after the feud began, both Trump and O'Donnell had books out bashing each other. Trump's, written with Bill Zanker, the founder of the Learning Annex, and promoted on Larry King Live, *was titled* Think Big and Kick Ass in Business and Life.* *O'Donnell's was titled* Celebrity Detox (The Fame Game). *In it, O'Donnell, who was 10 years old when her mother died, reveals that as a child she deliberately broke her hands and fingers with a baseball bat in the hopes of winning nurturing.*

On October 15, 2007, Trump told Larry King, "People love to see feuds. They love to see fighting and they love to see celebrities fight. In a very perverse way, the fight with Rosie turned out to be a good thing. And most people think I kicked her ass, as per the title of the book."

King read a passage about Trump from O'Donnell's book: "He turned his entire being into a product with a price tag on it."

Trump replied, "Maybe I am a product to a certain extent. But who wants to read a book where her biggest, most revealing thing was she broke her hand with baseball bats? . . . Now, my book, it's like a book on success. . . . You know, Rosie's ratings were not good until she started the fight with me."[3]

Rosie O'Donnell: It started out he was attacking me, and I thought, "Oh, this will last a month or so, and then he'll get sick of it." It ended up lasting over a decade. Every so often when he wanted to, he would bring it up, not really out of cause, not out of something new that happened or that I did. A lot of times when world crises happen, my therapist says to me, this is not happening to you personally, like Columbine, or 9/11, or Katrina, but this one actually feels as though it is, because it has been so personal for so long, even though I've only said two words to him in my life.

Randal Pinkett, Apprentice *season 4 winner:* I've been in the room with Donald alone. And I've been in closed-door meetings with Donald, and there's something inside of Donald that is insecure about whether he's the richest, the smartest, the baddest person in the room. There's an overcompensation to prove that to others, like the kid in the sandbox who couldn't get along with everybody, and now he's all grown up. To fire back at Rosie O'Donnell, to have this unabashed inclination to be

---

* A later paperback version lost the "Ass": *Think Big: Make It Happen in Business and Life.*

divisive. To me, all of that is a little kid saying to the world, "I'm smart. I'm rich. I'm important. I am somebody."

Rosie O'Donnell: I don't think Donald Trump thought very much about me and my family when he threatened to take my wife away from me. The things he said about me, that everyone knows she's a horrible person, I don't care who you are, no one deserves what he did to me. Oh my God, not only did it hurt, it was relentless! It was like torture. You know I'm a comedian, I can take it, if I say something that offends you, you say something, I'm a public person, I can take it, but the relentlessness with which he did it and the viciousness and vulgarity about who I am, what I look like, what I'm worthy of, whether I'm worthy of basic human rights and human dignity and respect, it was hurtful, it was traumatic, it was reminiscent of the abuse I had as a child.

Another more telling battle was with the feminist lawyer Gloria Allred, a proven player of the media game, unafraid to make sensational statements in the service of clients, who have included those victimized by Bill Cosby, O. J. Simpson, and Scott Peterson. The Allred-Trump match started when beauty pageant officials ruled that a transgender contestant, Jenna Talackova, was not eligible to compete in the 2012 Miss Universe Canada pageant because she was not a "natural-born" woman. The rhetoric went quickly below the belt.

> **Allred,** *at press conference:* [Jenna] should not have been judged by who she was at birth but on who she is now. . . . She did not ask Mr. Trump to prove he is a natural-born man or to see the photos of his birth to view his anatomy to prove that he was male.
> **Trump,** *on TMZ:* Gloria would be very, very, very impressed with me. I think she'd have a whole brand-new image of Donald Trump. . . . I just want to know how much Gloria will pay me. If the payment is high enough, I may just do it, and boy, will she be impressed.[4]

Gloria Allred, *women's rights lawyer:* I understand that Mr. Trump only understands power. It's important to show him that persons who have been victims also have courage and power. We were not going to back down until Jenna was reinstated into the Miss Universe pageant and until they eliminated the rule, which would have barred others who were transgendered individuals from being afforded that business opportunity. We fought it in the court of public opinion with him;

however, I had a backup plan to file lawsuits, either in Canada or in New York. I don't threaten—it's not what we do. But we do persist. So during this strong conflict we had for a number of days, part of what he did with me—very similar to what we've seen him do with others—was a great deal of name-calling and trying to trash me personally. I always receive that when someone is calling me a name, whether it's Mr. Trump or anyone else, it's a sign to me that I've won my argument. If they had a good argument, they would give it. So he was calling me names, suggesting I wasn't a terrific attorney and all that I don't like to repeat. . . .

> **Trump,** *on social media:* I hope Jenna is not paying Gloria a fee other than all the free publicity that Gloria is getting for no reason. Gloria actually hurts Jenna—I do nothing for Gloria, who in my opinion is a third-rate lawyer. Is Gloria a man or a woman????—few men would know the answer to that one.
> **Trump,** *on Good Morning America:* Gloria is easy to beat.
> **Allred press release:** Last week, in response to your offer to show me your penis, I said in jest, that I would not be able to view something so small without a magnifying glass. I apologize if that offended you. I'll make you a deal. If you change your discriminatory rule I promise to tell everyone that your penis is enormous, and that the only thing bigger is your ego.

Gloria Allred: I had lawyers in place in Canada and New York. We were ready to move to the next level.

> **Allred,** *at press conference:* We need a clear answer, not a wimpy, wishy-washy type of answer, but something that we can take to the bank. Will Jenna be allowed to compete or not?
> **Trump,** *on social media:* If you take the first 3 letters from Talackova and add them to Jenna, it's Jennatal (genital?) . . . In any event, I have given the okay for her to compete in the Miss Universe Canada Pageant. It will be a wild evening with ticket sales through the roof—lots of interest![5]
> **Allred,** *on 20/20:* With all due respect to Mr. Trump, he really needs to stop being focused on genitals. His or anyone else's. This world does not revolve around his penis or anyone else's genitalia.
> **Allred,** *on Good Morning America:* We are very happy that he has

conceded that that rule does violate the laws of Canada and the United States.

Gloria Allred: So anyway, after he ended up caving in and putting her back in the pageant and eliminating the rule, then I didn't see him, I didn't speak with him. Maybe a year or two passed. I happened to be at the Fox News channel one day in New York with a client who had nothing to do with this case. I'm sitting in the greenroom with her, and I look up to the screen, and I see that he's on a program right before I was on, talking about something completely different. I thought, "Oh my goodness, he's here in the building in New York at the Fox News channel. Well, he's probably going to just rush out and jump in his car, his limo, right after his interview concludes." I didn't say anything to my client, who, my guess is, didn't know anything about this previous case involving genitals. His interview concluded, and a couple minutes later, instead of leaving, the door opened to the greenroom, and he literally ran in and over to where I was sitting with my client, and he said, "Gloria, I heard you were here in the building with a client, and I just had to come back in before I leave, and I want to say something to your client!" And I said, "Oh, okay," and introduced my client to him. He said, "Miss, I just want you to know you have the best attorney you could ever have. This woman is relentless. Gloria will fight to the death for you. She will never ever give up until she gets you the justice she thinks you deserve. So never ever fire her because you will never get anyone better." Well, needless to say, I was stunned, given the trashing. We all shook hands and I said, "Thank you very much, Mr. Trump," and he left. I thought about it for quite a bit afterward. What precipitated that? At one point I thought, well, maybe this is how he does business, and then after the deal is done he tries to repair the relationship and move on. And then I didn't know at that time that he was also thinking of running for president. After I learned that, I thought maybe it wasn't just a business deal, and maybe it was partly that as well. Maybe he was trying to repair the relationship because he made the calculation, if I run for president, it's highly likely that if there are women in my life that I wouldn't want to come forward, they would probably come to Gloria Allred, and maybe it would just be wise and be smart to have a better relationship with her. I don't know.

Trump, *on TMZ:* I certainly have gotten a tremendous amount of publicity. . . . In certain ways it's not necessarily the worst thing that could ever happen. As you know, the Miss Universe Pageant has become tremendously successful since I've bought it. . . .

The result of Trump's fight over the transgender contestant was the same as with the uproar over the Bonwit Teller facade destruction and the ratings for The View; what appeared to be bad publicity had good results from his perspective. It is not surprising that Trump would be impressed by Allred's toughness. Few can match him in the public arena, and she did.

Allred has since represented a number of women who have accused Trump of sexual misconduct, including adult film star Jessica Drake, Apprentice candidate Summer Zervos, yoga instructor Karena Virginia, and Miss USA contestant Temple Taggart.

Gloria Allred: To be strong and powerful and not back down, I would say that's a similar trait I have with him.

15.

STAYING TUNED

After season 6 of The Apprentice *floundered in Los Angeles, NBC entertainment chief Kevin Reilly canceled the series. At the time, its 7.5 million weekly viewers was considered substandard, but the industry has changed. In late 2018, those numbers would make it a top-20 broadcast show, on par with an influential hit like* This Is Us.

Soon after Reilly decided not to renew The Apprentice, *he left NBC. His replacement, Ben Silverman, was hired by Jeff Zucker, who had become the chief executive of NBC Universal. Silverman had previously worked with Mark Burnett. On his first day at NBC, Silverman called Burnett about making two more seasons of* The Apprentice. *A key business change was that this time NBC would be a one-third partner in the product integrations. But it was the format change, celebrities playing for charity instead of regular people vying for a job, that allowed Trump to project an image of power in a new way. The original, noncelebrity version was tried one more time in 2010 as a recession-themed show, where Trump was to help candidates who faced tough times, but ratings were low. The first season of the celebrity version improved viewership to 11 million weekly. With casts that included Joan Rivers, Dennis Rodman, Gary Busey, Adam Carolla, and Meatloaf, it ran for seven seasons with Trump as host. There were other celebrities whose feuds with Trump made them enticing possibilities for a medium that thrives on conflict, but not all could be wrangled. Al Sharpton declined to be on the show, and Rosie O'Donnell refused at any price.[1] When Trump's young social media director Justin McConney, unaware of the offer to O'Donnell, suggested the idea again years later, Trump dismissed it.*

It's not just that The Apprentice *made him more famous. It's also that from* The Apprentice *Trump learned methods of holding an audience's attention and of playing up his own persona that would serve him when he turned his full attention to politics. What's more, with good ratings he prospered most, and therefore had the most power when he was giving the people what they want.*

Reverend Al Sharpton: In 2006, Trump came to the National Action Network convention for the dinner I was throwing to honor James Brown, who had performed at the Taj Mahal a lot. We always do it in April because that was the month Dr. King got killed. When James died that December, I called Trump and said that I had a problem. We wanted to fly James's body to the Apollo. His kids had got this gold-plated casket, and the body was in Augusta. We couldn't get a plane. Could he get his or a friend's plane to bring the body back? He said his plane was in repair. He never sent it, of course. We ended up driving the body. Then I get a call out of nowhere, 2007, that Mr. Trump wanted me to be on *Celebrity Apprentice.* I said, "I'm not interested." I would not do *Dancing with the Stars.* I wouldn't do *Celebrity Apprentice.* Trump told them, "Let me talk to Al. I can talk him into it." He called me twice. "Come on, Al. Do you know how many people watch my show?" He gave me the whole spiel. I said, "You know, Mr. Trump, we started fighting over housing discrimination. We totally went at it over [the Central Park Five]. You would like nothing better in front of a huge audience than to fire Al Sharpton. You will never get that opportunity." He couldn't conceive that I was going to turn down being on television. I always knew how to work television, but I also knew what I wanted to be projected as, and an apprentice or having on tights doing *Dancing with the Stars* was not what I wanted to be.

Rosie O'Donnell: They offered me $2 million to be on *The Celebrity Apprentice* [around 2007]; I said, "No." And they offered me $2 million to do a Doritos commercial with him, and I said, "No." He didn't understand why I wouldn't do this and take the money. I think I confused him. He never met a woman that he couldn't buy. Even my agent was trying to convince me to do it, and I'm like, "I don't think you fully understand. Are you ready? I will never do anything with him. The darkest energy of any human I've ever met in my life."

Justin McConney, *Trump social media director:* We did a video where he was feuding with both Lawrence O'Donnell and Rosie O'Donnell [in

December 2011] and the tagline was, "Same last names, same bad ratings." I tried to convince him to get Rosie on *The Celebrity Apprentice*. I said, "She would probably do the show. Howard Stern had a huge feud with her for years. They made up. It would be a TV event. She would be a great contestant raising money for charity and the guests she would bring in." He just wouldn't go for it. "Nope, not doing it. I just can't do it."

At a certain point he cut back on feuding with people. He said, "I think there's something to what you're saying here. I'm going to stop doing this." But he went right back to it. His line was always, "I have to hit back." Because I would question sometimes, "Is there really a reason to respond to this guy?" He goes, "You don't understand. I have to hit back. You have to hit back."

Jonathan Wald: Piers [Morgan, onetime CNN host] owes his initial prominence in the U.S. to Trump because he was the first *Celebrity Apprentice* winner, and he translated that into appearing on and then signing with *America's Got Talent*. That was how Piers became known in the States. He established a relationship with Trump, and when he came to CNN, he leveraged the friendship with Trump to book him on the show numerous times. It was a crazy time at CNN, when we were doing whatever we could to prop up the already dying franchise of the nightly interview at 9:00 p.m., which had been the biggest thing on TV at one time. We had Trump on a few times, and executives asked me, "Why do you keep booking Donald Trump on Piers Morgan?" I said, "Because he's great TV, the ratings are always good, and he always says something interesting, to put it mildly."

Tucker Carlson, *Fox News:* Trump believes that television is the most democratic of the media, and by definition when a show has high ratings, its producers understand what people want. That's a lesson he learned from working in television. If you want to know what the public thinks, pay close attention to the programming. There's some truth in that. It's probably at least as accurate as public opinion polling.

Reverend Al Sharpton: He thinks that he's telegenic. He knows that you don't need heavy language on television, because you're talking to people in their living rooms, so he doesn't have to be scholarly. He's not a reader, he's a talker, so it's a natural medium for him. He didn't want to just be a businessman. He wanted to be a star, and television was a way to be a star. He created a brand that was more based on hype than anything else.

Surya Yalamanchili, Apprentice *candidate, season 6:* There's this entire universe created by the producers. You're waiting for him, and then when he arrives, you start filming.

Tucker Carlson: He's a natural television communicator. He doesn't speak like a writer speaks. Obama was a writer, and he talks like one. Trump speaks to be heard rather than to be read. There's a huge difference between the two. Trump is a television expert. You listen to him talk, you hear it, the producer in him. He literally speaks in teases. "We're going to reveal the next ambassador to the UK!"

Stuart Marques, *former producer,* A Current Affair: It's all, "I've got some good news for you, but I'm not going to tell you what it is. I'll tell you tomorrow or the next day." Then the next day he'll say, "Pretty soon I'll tell you." That's all tabloid TV. That's all reality TV. Keep 'em hanging on. Keep 'em guessing. Keep 'em anticipating. He's a master at it.

Surya Yalamanchili: *The Apprentice* playbook boiled down to its simplest form is really boiling things down to their simplest form. The producers told us how you won't recognize yourself, because it may be an exaggerated version of you. It's very easy to follow along, and there's good guys, and there's the bad guys, there's the idiot, there's the genius.

Conrad Black, *Canadian financier and publisher:* He uses a mixture of these ethnic words like "schlong" and old words like calling someone a "stiff." I haven't heard anyone call someone a stiff since the movies with Jimmy Cagney. So he's got traditional jargon mixed with New York ethnic words, and that coupled with his delivery makes the whole thing hilarious.

Tucker Carlson: I never thought Trump got credit for being as amusing as he is, because he's highly amusing. Paradoxically, he turns a lot of people completely humorless, which is sort of interesting. Most funny people make the people around them funnier, but Trump seems to zap everyone else's sense of humor completely. His defenders become kind of robotic true believers versus critics who go completely insane and try to ban humor. He's like the one funny guy at the center of all of this.

Corynne (Steindler) Cirilli, *Page Six reporter:* He was becoming more endearing to the general public. He was kind of hated in New York for a long time, by Kurt Anderson and *Spy* magazine and by these gritty leftist journalists. He was mocked by Graydon Carter. Joan Rivers, who I know at one point was not a fan of Donald, went on *Celebrity Apprentice,* and then she would be out on the scene talking about what a great guy he was and how he gave all this money to charity. Donald Trump understands the media game almost better than the media itself. He's the best bully there is, and he knows how to pick his target and how to get the narrative spun in his favor. Now that it's politics, it's gotten a little more serious, but for many years he was able to do it with a shrug and a laugh in the celebrity world, and he really honed it.

Michael Avenatti, *lawyer:* I did meet him once, in 2009, when he hit on my date. I was standing at the bar with her at the BOA Steakhouse in Los Angeles. I went to get drinks. Donald Trump walked up to her, looked her up and down, and introduced himself. He was startled that I walked up. He clearly figured out that I was with her, introduced himself, we shook hands, and he turned around and left. If you're going to go out with an attractive woman, then it's to be expected to a certain degree. She made some joke about feeling like a piece of meat hanging from the rafters.

Conrad Black: *The Apprentice* made him much more popular than he had been and much more well-known than he had been to the socioeconomic middle of America, and he came across as a competent, humane, and humorous person. It also gave him a huge amount of publicity for all these products he was selling with his name on them and some of the locations he had. A large section of the public got to think of him as a person they liked to see on television and had respect for him.

Tucker Carlson: *The Apprentice* recast him for the masses. If you spent a lot of time in New York at least, you knew Trump for many years. But it was really *The Apprentice* that created that brand, somewhat of an illusion. It's not just that *The Apprentice* brought Trump into more homes. It's that *The Apprentice,* starring on it, being the executive producer of it, trained him in a certain kind of communication, so it changed him, it didn't just change our perception of him.

If you think of The Apprentice *like a magical car wash, Trump stepped in one end a dinged-up classic luxury car with high mileage, a Rolls-Royce that had seen better days. The nozzles sprayed some bronzer, the soapy scrubbers buffed out dents, the suction pulled out dirt, and then, through the magic of TV, a polished new Trump emerged. That 1989 Rolls appeared to be a sparkling new model with its odometer rolled back. Underneath the hood may have been the same engine, but it had been tuned up, ready to race.*

Many people played their parts in this transformation: Burnett—perhaps Bethea—Riggs, Pruitt, Bienstock, Zucker, Silverman, and others. But Trump ultimately was both vehicle and driver, the person behind the persona. He was at the wheel.

And yet, although he had conquered television and books, a new form of media was emerging. In April 2009, publisher Vanguard Press, a division of Random House, was publishing yet another Trump self-help title, Think Like a Champion. *Vanguard's director of online marketing, Peter Costanzo, went to meet with Trump's team. Trump, ever eager for free publicity, expressed interest quickly when he heard about Twitter and Facebook. The only problem was an online imposter.*

Peter Costanzo, *Vanguard Press director of online marketing:* We were publishing a book by Donald Trump, and we began having meetings at Trump Tower with his core team. They kept asking, "What can we do that's different for Mr. Trump?" I strongly recommended we start a Facebook account and a Twitter account. The challenge was that there was an imposter who was already using Donald Trump's name. They were very surprised to learn of that. I contacted Facebook and informed them the actual Donald Trump wanted to start using Facebook. They transferred the account over to us, but Twitter was so new that Mr. Trump's lawyers were unable to reach anyone. The team was Rhona Graff and Meredith McIver, who was the co-writer of the book, and Amanda Miller, who, at the end of *The Celebrity Apprentice,* people would see and say goodbye to before they got on the elevator. They informed me that I would meet with Mr. Trump and it would be seven minutes long, to explain to him why social media would be very important to the successful promotion of the book.

Inside the conference room was a full-size image of Mr. Trump, one of those cutouts you could put your arm around and look like you're with the person. He came in the room very serious-looking, determined, and he sat down and said, "Okay, what do you got for me?" I explained that for social media to be effective, there has to be some level of participation by the actual person. I explained to him that initially I could be the one tweeting on his behalf. He was asking, "Why are we going to do this? Who's going to care?" I explained that the beauty of it was that you could communicate directly to your fans. I was talking about fans of *The Celebrity Apprentice*, who we were hoping to convert into buyers of the book. I wasn't thinking politically.

When I explained to him that we could use it to promote anything having to do with the Trump Organization, such as a new golf course or Ivanka's jewelry line, that's when he started to get very interested, and he became intrigued by it. He said, "I like the sound of that. I like the idea of being able to directly communicate to people." When I told him about this hurdle with the imposter, he didn't like that. "What are we going to do?" I said, "While your lawyers are trying to resolve this and get the handle @DonaldTrump, let's call you @realDonaldTrump. You're the real deal. You're the man that people want to follow. Let's let them know that it's really you." He nodded. He said, "I like the sound of that." He stood up, said, "Let's do it, make it happen," and he left.

The first known tweet from @realDonaldTrump, on May 4, 2009, a month after the book was published, said, "Be sure to tune in and watch Donald Trump on Late Night with David Letterman *as he presents the Top Ten List tonight."[2] The next couple of weeks had "Enter the* Think Like a Champion *signed book and keychain contest," and "Did you know Donald Trump is on Facebook? . . . Become a fan today!"*

Peter Costanzo: Benign and promotional. There were no political tweets. I made a request to interview Mr. Trump to create a YouTube video to promote the book. He did a very good job in giving answers that you would want him to say. He knows how to sell. After we were done, I asked him what he thought about the newly elected President Obama, and he said, "Oh, he seems like a nice family man. I really hope he does some good for the economy." But then he said, "But if he doesn't, I'm thinking of running for president." He said that to me in a way that I felt like he was telling me something in confidence, so I never mentioned it to anyone.

PART THREE

SETTLING ON A POLITICAL VOICE

2010—2013

Trump builds a political team and slowly learns
the power of social media.

16.

CREATING A
BRAIN TRUST

The first time Trump entertained a run for president, he said Americans would only elect an outsider during a severe economic downturn. When President Barack Obama was sworn into office, the country was in the midst of a debilitating recession that cost 8.8 million jobs. It even touched billionaires. Trump postponed a $300 million Philadelphia development and sued Deutsche Bank to avoid paying $40 million in guarantees on a $640 million loan for Trump International Hotel and Tower in Chicago.[1] And he complained about the "horrible state of the economy" as The Apprentice's *eighth season premiered on March 1, 2009.[2]*

But the financial crisis presented Trump with an opportunity. His NBC show, capturing 8 to 10 million viewers an episode, brought an audience that perceived Trump as a leader, and a fresh wave of political operatives began to recognize it.

Washington-based strategist David Bossie first gained notoriety as a congressional researcher in the 1990s investigating the death of Bill Clinton aide Vince Foster. He rose rapidly in conservative political circles after his media nonprofit Citizens United won a landmark ruling in January 2010 characterizing political spending as free speech, eradicating limits. Bossie crossed paths with Trump shortly after his court victory, thanks to an introduction from Las Vegas casino magnate Steve Wynn and pollster Frank Luntz.

Bossie and other conservative haymakers, including political propagandist and Breitbart board member Steve Bannon, would have a profound effect on Trump. Both men became part of an informal network Trump phoned to discuss politics—another Trump method, instant phone polls of powerful friends. If the subject was boxing or casinos, he'd call Don King or Bob Torricelli. If media, Chris Ruddy of Newsmax or Richard Johnson of the New York Post. *If business, real estate owner Richard LeFrak, private equity head Stephen Schwarzman, or investor Carl Icahn.*

Roger Stone was his political contact for decades, but Trump added new ones after Obama's election. There was Michael Cohen, an attorney who bought a unit in Trump World Tower in 2001, defended him in a dispute with his co-op board, and was working for him by 2007.[3] Joining him in 2011 was Sam Nunberg, a political junkie who learned Stone's tricks by osmosis and had an equally rocky relationship with his boss.

Trump had an instinct for finding sycophants and extracting everything he could from them. Once he questioned Cohen's worth and tried to fire him, ultimately cutting his $400,000 salary in half.[4]

When Bossie realized Trump wanted to run for office again, he scheduled a meeting and invited Bannon to tag along. Might 2012 be the right moment for a full run?

David Bossie, *deputy campaign manager of Trump 2016:* I got to know Trump through nonpolitical means. Steve Wynn was helping me raise money for a children's hospital in 2010 and introduced me to Donald Trump, because Trump bought the golf course where I held my fundraiser. During the first year of knowing him, we talked about campaigns, elections, and public policy. Once we got to know each other, he started talking about whether he should think about running one day.

Steve Bannon, *former White House chief strategist:* I met Trump on August 5, 2010. I was making films for Dave Bossie in his office on Pennsylvania Avenue. I'm a full-time propaganda documentary filmmaker. I'd made a film called *Generation Zero* in 2009 about the financial collapse and how the millennials are going to get fucked. It got to be a hit. It did an hour special on *Hannity*.[5] Bossie and I figured out that propaganda-type films would be important for the 2010 [election], so we started making them. *Fire from the Heartland*, all these Tea Party films. Bossie had met Trump through his son, who was very ill. Bossie thinks the sun rises and sets on Trump's head. A real fanboy.

David Bossie: I had known Trump before I brought Bannon to meet him. He was talking to me about these things and I would talk to him on the phone. I would see him when I would go to New York. The couple of times that he came to DC I would see him.

Steve Bannon: I was editing three films simultaneously. They were all going to be released in a fusillade, Labor Day 2010, for the run-up to the election. Bossie called me up in the middle of it and said, "Hey, what are you doing tomorrow?" "What am I doing tomorrow?" I said. "I'm fucking cutting the fucking film in the basement of your office. That's what I'm doing tomorrow." Dave said, "Can you come to New York with me?" I said, "No, I can't go to New York with you. These things have got to come out. We're way behind." He said, "You've got to come with me to see somebody." I said, "Who?" He said, "Donald Trump." I said, "I don't give a fuck. I'm not going to go see Donald Trump. What the fuck do I got to see Donald Trump about?" He said, "No, you've got to see Donald Trump. You've got to come with me." I say, "Why?" He said, "He's thinking of running for president." I said, "Of what country?" "Knock it off," he said. [*Bannon, without a beat, on a roll, fueled by two morning Red Bulls, makes an aside to us, his interviewers, making sure we are keeping up: "You know, the Tea Party? This populist bullshit. 'Cause I'm a conservative. You know this stuff. You've got to be with me."*] "David, I don't have time to waste," I said. "You're not wasting time," he said. "I'm paying for all the films."

David Bossie: The purpose of bringing Bannon was to have Trump hear different voices. I had several people with me. J. T. Mastranadi was and still is my political director, working together for 20-plus years. And I brought Rex Elsass,* he's an ad guy, strategic guy.

Steve Bannon: I was at Goldman Sachs in the '80s. A sure way to get fired was to get Donald Trump to come down to a meeting at 85 Broad [Goldman's Manhattan headquarters]. He was unclubbable. He was not financeable by white-shoe investment banks. He's a legend in the *New York Post* and *Spy* magazine, but he's not a guy that major financial institutions took seriously.

I take the train up. Bossie's all giddy. We get up to Trump Tower, the twenty-fifth floor. That huge boardroom, the conference room, which

---

* Political consultant Rex Elsass has advised Ted Cruz, Rand Paul, Michele Bachmann, and Newt Gingrich.

would become a big part of my life later. They've got food set up at the end. It's massive. This thing can seat 40 people. This is where, later, after we win, we have all the heads of tech. It's where he practiced for the inaugural address. I had 10 major moments in my life in that boardroom. You look back and you go, "What the fuck?"

David Bossie: It was Steve's first meeting with him. I had already been talking to him extensively about these things. He was showing interest in running for president.

Steve Bannon: Trump comes down. He was the old Donald Trump, thin and dynamic. Michael Cohen's with him, and Bossie's got a presentation, PowerPoint. He introduces himself, checks us out, knows Dave. We get into it, and I have never seen this ever, since then. He takes the presentation, and he's focused and engaged on the PowerPoint. Bossie's presenting how you win a Republican primary, then how you win the presidency to Trump. Literally five minutes into it, he tells Cohen, "Hey, Michael, I got it with the guys. You can take off." Cohen gives him some shit, "Oh, no, I ought to be here for this. . . ." Trump said, "Michael, I got it." Boom. Out. Gone.

David Bossie: I brought a memo that outlined extensively what he would have to look at. Here are three states, some benchmarks and dates to consider, and opposition research on yourself. He had been living on the front page of the paper for a long time, but even people who do that have things that can come up. It was a how-to-run-for-president conversation.

Steve Bannon: Bossie walked through how you win the Republican primary. Trump was engaged. He asked fabulous questions. It was good give-and-take. I got more impressed with this guy as it went on. I'm going through the history and tenets of populism, and he asked me a ton of questions. I try to explain economic nationalism, and he gets it right away. I start back with Andrew Jackson, walk through how America's gone through cycles. William Jennings Bryan and his Nail me to a Cross of Gold speech. How it was anti–Wall Street. Trump said, "Well that's what I am. I'm a Popularist." I said, "No, no, no. It's Populist." He said, "Yeah, that's what I said. Popularist." I said, "No, it's Populist." He said, "Yeah, Popularist."

David Bossie: It was a message of, if you are interested in running in the future, you can't do it overnight. You have to spend time, energy, and money in building an operation so you can put yourself in a position to run. I had looked at his financial giving in the past. He was a Manhattan real estate guy, so he had given to a lot of Democrats. To his chagrin I said, "You give to more Democrats than Republicans." He said, "How do you know that?"

Steve Bannon: The one thing that most impressed me is that Trump sat there for 20 minutes and went through China. I'd lived in China. I'd been in the Navy in Asia. This guy knew China. You could tell he had listened to Lou Dobbs. He quoted Lou Dobbs a lot. The inexorable rise of China was the second law of thermodynamics. It was just a matter of physics of the universe. Trump was questioning that. Bossie's a typical Washington guy, one of the smartest political operatives around. What he knows about China is you buy it in a store and serve tea on it.

David Bossie: I don't go around beating my chest. I don't go around telling everybody, "Me, me, me." I know what I did.

Steve Bannon: It was a two-hour presentation. Trump today wouldn't sit through a five-minute fucking meeting. We left it with two things. Bossie to test him said, "You need to write a check for every senator and every congressman, and they've got to come to New York. You've got to shake their hand, look them in the eye, and give them the $2,500 checks." Bossie said, "About $500,000 you'll cover the universe, but it's a marker. The other thing you've got to do is a policy book, because you don't know enough policy."

David Bossie: I told him, "It's hard to run for the nomination when you've donated more to the Democrats than to the Republicans." It wasn't a big deal, he said. "Send me some names."

Steve Bannon: We're walking out. Bossie says, "What do you think?" I said, "I was 10 times more impressed than I thought." This guy was very serious, very dynamic. I went in thinking, "Why the fuck are we doing this? This is a waste of time." I was genuinely impressed. He didn't know any policy. Didn't know any social conservative stuff. Didn't know any of the bullshit. But he was impressive.

David Bossie: He was totally engaged and really enjoyed the conversation. We left thinking, "Maybe he does, maybe he doesn't [run for president]," because who knows?

Steve Bannon: I said, "There's zero probability he writes a check to anybody. He will not do it." Dave said, "Come on. It's only $500,000." I said, "Dave, it is zero. Will never happen." Bossie said, "What about the book?" I said, "Donald Trump's going to do a policy book? Are you fucking kidding me? Zero chance."

In September, a month after the meeting with Bossie and Bannon, Trump was hyping season 10 of The Apprentice, *his wife Melania was hawking her jewelry on the QVC network, and Trump invited Libyan dictator Muammar Gaddafi to crash in a tent on his 113-acre Bedford, New York, estate during the United Nations' General Assembly. The town put in a stop-work order preventing it.*[6]

But a Time *magazine report about a New Hampshire telephone poll pulled him back into politics publicly.*[7] *The survey, likely financed in secret by New York City mayor Michael Bloomberg to explore his own ambitions, asked whether Trump's past campaign donations to Democrats or frequent television appearances would sour voters on him.*[8] *"It's not something I talked about or considered," Trump told CNN on October 4, 2010. "But somebody has got to do something for this country or it's not going to be a very good country for long." The next day, Trump appeared on MSNBC's* Morning Joe. *Joe Scarborough asked what the election's top issue was. Trump hammered China for manipulating its currency, claiming Chinese rulers viewed the Obama administration as "foolish."*

One of the guest analysts on Morning Joe *was Trump's former foe Pat Buchanan. Trump had repeatedly called him a "Hitler lover" back in 1999, but that was then. Now Trump was coming around to Buchanan's America First ideas. Buchanan asked what Trump would do to contain China. Trump answered that he would "get rid of the stupid diplomats that are representing us" and replace them with private sector "killers." Co-host Mika Brzezinski asked Trump about running for office.*

I am absolutely thinking about it. I don't know that I'll do it. It's probable that I won't do it, but I can tell you, I'm thinking about it. Somebody has to do something. We are losing this country. This country will not be great if something isn't done rapidly. Hello to Pat Buchanan because he's got a lot of good answers.[9]

Pat Buchanan, *presidential candidate 1992, 1996, and 2000:* While I was on *Morning Joe,* he would be on there. He was very gracious. On the immigration issue, I don't know when he picked it up, but it was a very potent issue for me. I ran in California against Bush in June 1992. I had not a dime in my pocket, just driving around with Secret Service. By hitting the immigration issue, I was rolling up almost 30 percent of the vote in San Diego, Los Angeles, and Orange Counties. It was a blazing issue. Pete Wilson used it two years later to turn a 20-point deficit into a 10-point victory [in the California governor's race]. I never understood why the Republicans didn't seize the issue. It was a vote-getter.

Erick Erickson, *conservative blogger and former editor of RedState:* This period is coming as the right was beginning to separate itself from the [Georg W.] Bush era. There were lingering bad feelings over the GM bailout, TARP, and immigration.

Newsday quoted regular New Yorkers as skeptical about a Trump presidential run: "He's not remotely qualified" and "He'd say he was running for dogcatcher if it would get his name on the front page." Undeterred, Trump added more interviews. On Election Day 2010, he speculated on the results with Fox News's Neil Cavuto, who fawned over Trump, saying, "Maybe you're the guy." The next day, Fox News's Greta Van Susteren asked whether 2012 would be Trump's year. A few weeks later, Michael Cohen launched a draft-Trump website called ShouldTrumpRun.com.

Fred Dicker, New York Post *Albany bureau chief:* Most people looked at it as, there he goes again. Not something that was real, just an opportunity for him to get some publicity and have his ideas heard. Another installment in the ongoing saga of Donald Trump's megalomania.

Talking heads cited his flirtation in 2000 as proof that this was another bluff. But Trump's statements were completely clear. Trump said he probably wouldn't run in 2012 but was absolutely thinking about it. It is not accurate to say he bluffed too many times. He didn't bluff. He explored. This raises a question. If you know what you are saying is true and much of the media says it is not, and if the media says you don't mean what you say even though you do, might you start thinking what the media says is false and biased?

Trump had for years fed hyperbole and half-truths about his finances and his personal life to newspapers that printed them as fact. As tight as his relationships were with some reporters, as much as he craved attention from his hometown papers, he knew firsthand that some news is fake because he made it so. If Trump saw that some of what was being reported was not true, he must have reasoned that others saw it too. There were weak points. Then came market forces putting increasing pressure on reporters to do more in less time, leading to mistakes in articles, which can undermine readers' trust. This too created opportunities for those who saw an advantage in dismissing all news as fake and had made long and careful study of the journalism industry's vulnerabilities.

17.

A PARTY TRUMP
LIKES THE SOUND OF

Barack Obama's 2008 election victory and the president's policies—bailing out banks whose practices sparked the recession, dispensing relief to bankrupt home-owners, and providing affordable healthcare—gave conservatives a platform to oppose. But it was CNBC journalist Rick Santelli's televised rant about the government-led housing bailout on February 19, 2009, that catalyzed the Tea Party movement.[1] "This is America!" Santelli exclaimed on the floor of the Chicago Mercantile Exchange. "How many of you people want to pay for your neighbor's mortgage that has an extra bathroom and can't pay their bills?"

Eruptions of populist rage had bubbled up in various guises for decades. This incarnation, financed by wealthy donors and amplified by conservative media outlets, sought to oust mainstream Republicans in the 2010 primaries by running far-right candidates against them. Tea Party activists resented lawmakers for allowing the national debt to balloon, supporting the costly Iraq War, and not blocking the Affordable Care Act ("Obamacare"). It mirrored Ross Perot's agenda of fiscal discipline while adding a strident anti–Wall Street message.

Tea Party candidates toppled numerous Republican incumbents in primary elections, most notably college professor David Brat's victory over House Majority Leader Eric Cantor in Virginia. In New York, Tea Party candidate Carl Paladino defeated Republican Party darling Rick Lazio in the gubernatorial primary.

The scope of the Tea Party victory on November 2, 2010, showed that populism was thriving—and that pockets of the country virulently opposed the Obama presidency. Republicans took control of the House, picking up 63 seats, and added 6 Senate seats, narrowing the Democrats' majority.[2] President Obama called the defeat a "shellacking."[3]

Pat Boone, *singer, columnist for WorldNetDaily, and conservative activist:* I wrote a column [in 2009] that it was time for a new American Tea Party.[4] The concept grew, and I became very active. I did millions of robocalls in 2010 and 2012. The Koch brothers funded an organization for this purpose.

Katrina Pierson, *Trump 2016 campaign spokesperson:* I'm one of the founders of the Tea Party movement. I started watching cable news on 9/11 and realized things were a lot worse than I thought they were. By 2009, 80 to 100 of us formed the National Tea Party Coalition and then our state Tea Party groups. In Texas, we formed groups all the way down to the zip code level.

Some figures from the Reform Party managed to stay relevant as populism took a new twist, among them Ross Perot's former campaign manager Russell Verney. He joined the conservative-leaning media not-for-profit Project Veritas as its executive director in 2011.

Russell Verney, *Reform Party chairman 1995–1999 and Project Veritas executive director:* In 1992 and 1996, Ross Perot gave a voice to the people of this country who were angry over the runaway spending and arrogance in Washington, DC. In early 2009, voters flooded local town hall meetings of members of Congress. The angry grassroots had seen Republican administrations replaced by Democrat administrations, and the answer was not just another Republican or Democrat. They wanted a change agent.

Katrina Pierson: My biggest problem was Republicans didn't fight back. W didn't defend himself on anything, and that drove me insane. The mayor in DC got caught with a hooker, smoking crack, and gets reelected. But Republicans should resign because something didn't look right.

Steve Bannon: Early on in Breitbart, in 2007, I said, "Why are [we] going after Obama? We have no ability to touch him." The guys holding us up are John Boehner, Eric Cantor, Mitch McConnell, the Kochs, Paul Singer, these dirtbags. We're going to stay batshit about the Democrats, but we have the ability to lay a glove on these guys. These guys are in our target zone.

Katrina Pierson: People think the Tea Party started because of Obama. The Tea Party started because of the bailouts. People didn't agree with the Patriot Act and civil liberties abuses—basic constitutional values. Nancy Pelosi was saying, "They had swastikas on their shirts." We were branded as racist and old white men.[5] This was truly an organic groundswell of people tired of politicians ignoring the platforms, lying to them, patting them on their heads and saying, "I know what's best for you"; at the same time people were losing their jobs.

Carl Paladino, *New York Republican gubernatorial candidate 2010:* It was the beginning of the antiestablishment nationalist populist movement that gave us Trump in 2016. They were the frustrated patriots fed up with big government intruding into their lives. They were the frontiersmen paving the way and setting the platform and agenda for Donald Trump.

Russell Verney: True conservative candidates found a source of grassroots support, but some Tea Party candidates who were not ready for prime time caused ridicule to be heaped on the Tea Party movement, and they reflected badly on the reputation of Republican candidates at large.

Katrina Pierson: By 2010 you had a lot of the Tea Party people out there in the media, because we were turning over elections. That was really when Tea Party voices were being heard. That's how Trump had seen a lot of us too.

Steve Bannon: We had this massive win in 2010 of 63 seats. There was really no Tea Party candidate in the presidential primary in 2012. Michele Bachmann starts, but she gets blown up early. The two people I try to get to run are Lou Dobbs and Sarah Palin. Palin doesn't run. I spent a ton of time with Dobbs, used to go out to the farm in New Jersey. But [the media] found out most of the people at the farm had questionable documents. Which, if you're Lou Dobbs, you can't do that.

Michael Caputo, *Carl Paladino's campaign manager 2009:* There would not be a President Trump if Rick Santelli had not ranted on CNBC in early 2009.

Katrina Pierson: Trump had seen me on Fox. I had been doing TV six years before I met him personally. One of the best-kept secrets about Trump is he had been speaking to Tea Party groups five years before the escalator ride.

An onslaught of Republicans—including future CIA director Mike Pompeo, future White House chief of staff Mick Mulvaney, Kentucky senator Rand Paul, and Florida senator Marco Rubio—arrived in Congress in January, while fellow Tea Party–blessed figures Nikki Haley and Scott Walker moved into governors' offices in South Carolina and Wisconsin. Even those who lost, including Paladino, realized they were part of a movement. The question was, what would they do with it in 2012?

Longtime Trump political adviser Roger Stone had an idea, but first he'd have to rekindle his relationship with Trump. The two had had a falling-out in August 2007 over a dirty trick. Billionaire real estate mogul Bernard Spitzer discovered a menacing voicemail threatening him with a subpoena and arrest for making "shady campaign loans" to his son, Governor Eliot Spitzer, and calling the governor a "psycho." Attorneys for Bernard traced the call back to Stone, a consultant with state senate Republicans at the time.[6] Stone adamantly denied the accusation, but state GOP leaders fired him anyway.[7]

Trump was upset with Stone for threatening the Spitzers. "Roger is a stone-cold loser. He always takes credit for things he never did," Trump told the New Yorker's *Jeffrey Toobin in June 2008. "I lost respect for Eliot Spitzer when he didn't sue Roger Stone for doing that to his father, who is a wonderful man."[8]*

While Trump met with Bossie and Bannon, Stone was working as a pro bono adviser for former madam Kristin Davis's quixotic New York gubernatorial campaign.* True to his often complicated allegiances, Stone wanted Carl Paladino to get into the race and convinced him to hire Mike Caputo and pollster Tony Fabrizio. "Guys like Roger, they tend to traffic in information," Caputo told the New York Times. *"Being connected to all these campaigns helps him inform the people he's working for."[9]*

Roger Stone, *Trump adviser and political strategist:* We were not particularly in touch during *The Apprentice* period, so I watched it from the outside. There was a period in which we were estranged, because he

---

* Kristin Davis was known as the "Manhattan Madam" because she ran a high-end prostitution ring and claimed to provide escorts for Eliot Spitzer and Dominique Strauss-Kahn. Spitzer denied he was in contact with Davis.

didn't like what he thought I did to Eliot Spitzer, which I had to claim I had nothing to do with. We're past all that. Somehow [Trump] thought Spitzer was his friend, but that all changed when Spitzer attacked him viciously on CNN.

In 2011, Spitzer joined Toobin on CNN to lambast Trump for exaggerating his net worth. "His entire life story is one of 'I am bigger than everybody else. I am better than everybody else,'" Spitzer said. "On the other hand, it's unfair of him to then turn around and say, 'Look, everybody does this,' which isn't simply the case, certainly when it comes to financials, and it also is not the case despite the public perception when it comes to politics."[10]

Tucker Carlson, *Fox News:* Roger's a very complicated person. He's a great guy actually, and honest in his own way, but Trump and Roger have this complicated relationship.

David Bossie: The last time I talked to Roger Stone was in a federal courthouse in 2007, when I sued him in federal court.* He and I were the only two witnesses during the case.[11] That's the last time I ever talked to Roger Stone. I had zero interest in talking to him about this stuff.

Tucker Carlson: Trump has this theory, which is approximately true, that when you ask a man's opinion, he may give an inspired piece of advice, but he can never factor out his own self-interest. He's always simultaneously calculating how he can benefit from whatever good fortune you have. Whereas if you ask a woman for advice, she will take herself completely out of the picture, if she's on your side. The second a man upstages him in any way, even physically, he beats the guy off the stage for trying to belittle him. You saw it when [then New Jersey governor] Chris Christie endorsed him. It was the tail end of the primaries, and they get onstage, and the first thing Trump says is, "Hey, Chris, lay off the Oreos." That's why he has few enduring male friendships. Women are a totally different thing. He does have a constellation of women around him who he trusts and listens to. Roger is, of course, a

---

* Stone had filed paperwork with the IRS to form a political group to attack Hillary Clinton. Its name was to be Citizens United Not Timid—C.U.N.T. This led Bossie, who led the influential political group Citizens United, to bring a trademark infringement case. Stone changed the name to Citizens Uniformly Not Timid.

man, and that is the problem. Roger is also a promoter of himself, and that can never stand, so they have this really rocky relationship.

Rick Wilson, *Republican political strategist:* Roger is the master troll at the center of so much of Trump's bullshit and the force you'll see popping up over and over again. For Roger it's never been about Trump. It's always been about Roger. It's this colorful, bombastic, big swaggering-dick attitude. Roger is sui generis. There's not really another Roger.

Now that the governor's race was over, Stone needed a new job. He published an essay in his StoneZone blog in December 2010 saying that Trump "must run for president in 2012" because he "is probably the toughest business negotiator in the country, understands more about capital formation and job creation" and "has broader experience and greater credibility than any of the prospective candidates considering a White House bid." Stone noted Trump's talent for attracting press coverage and that he is "happily married to a wonderful wife and has a son in his formative years," implying Trump's dalliances with women were over.

Roger Stone: I don't know whether he called or whether he had one of the girls forward me a note or he sent me a note where he wrote in the margins, "Very Nice!"

Stone introduced Trump to someone familiar with modern tools of the political trade, a 30-year-old lawyer named Sam Nunberg, who had made a mark in populist circles. Nunberg got his start in politics in 2008 volunteering for Romney in Iowa. There he met Jay Sekulow, chief counsel at the conservative values–promoting American Center for Law and Justice. Sekulow hired Nunberg to work as his deputy political director in New York.

One of Nunberg's tasks was opposing an Islamic community center proposed for Lower Manhattan. Anti-Muslim bloggers Pamela Geller and Robert Spencer coined the term "Ground Zero mosque," and like-minded opponents called it a "victory monument to terrorists."

Nunberg would have a tumultuous but influential four years working with Trump as his main political scheduler and aide. He encouraged Trump to court voters through alt-right websites and radio shows, helped him refine his message on Twitter, and accompanied him to right-wing conferences. Trump would fire and rehire him multiple times.

David Cay Johnston, *author of* The Making of Donald Trump: Donald is always surrounded by sketchy folks. There are very smart people who have some sort of flaw that doesn't allow them to sort of fit into the mainstream culture out there, people who want to be associated with what they think of as the glamour of the place.

Sam Nunberg, *Trump campaign aide:* There are three types of people in New York. People who thought about Donald Trump as someone who is not a billionaire, full of shit, and not a good businessman. The business class—bankers and lawyers. Another is the average New Yorker who reads the tabloids and thinks he's an idiot. And there are people like me. My relationship with Trump goes over years. If you read the beginning of *The Art of the Deal*, he says in the first couple pages, "I'm on the phone with my attorney Jerry Schrager of Dreyer & Traub" [where Nunberg's father, Noah, was a senior partner]. He owed my father's firm money, so I have no delusions about who he is.

I was continually interested in what he was doing. Were there hits? Were there misses? It was always funny watching him on the news. I would come home from Yeshiva, and this was something interesting to watch. His whole life and the Marla–Ivana saga. When Drudge Report started, I was following Trump. His tax proposal was always on Drudge because Roger had this relationship with Drudge very early on.

Next I do the Ground Zero mosque case in July 2010. I testify at the Landmark Commission hearing, and I do a sound bite that's repeatedly played everywhere. I say, "It would be a travesty to tear this building down. It would be like taking a sunken ship from Pearl Harbor to erect a memorial for the Japanese kamikazes killed in the attack."[12] That's how I become close with Roger, because Roger and I had met that summer.

In addition to Sam Nunberg, Trump pulled another tech-savvy millennial into his orbit. He had admitted he knew little of the internet in 2000. But in February 2011, still behind the times, he took a leap to catch up, hiring 24-year-old video editor Justin McConney to become his social media manager. McConney would soon run Trump's Twitter account, taking over duties from Peter Costanzo.

Justin McConney, *Trump Organization social media manager:* There were two executives dealing with a meeting at Mar-a-Lago for all the golf club managers and they needed a video quickly put together to get people psyched at the meeting. They had known I was a video editor. I decided to cut together a video about Mr. Trump with hard rock music. They said, "I'm not sure this is what we're looking for, but we only have a day left. Let's just go with it." I didn't think anything of it. I get a phone call. Trump apparently loved the video. He had a show on the Golf Channel called, I believe, *Donald J. Trump's Fabulous World of Golf*. When they showed this video he thought the Golf Channel had put it together. They explained, no, this kid had done it. They told me, "If you could stop by the office he'd like to talk to you." I'm not even dressed in a suit. They said, "It doesn't matter. Just come by."

I walk into his office, and he had this MacBook on his desk. The MacBook was just used to show him videos and stills. He never actually used it himself. And he was watching the intro they had sent him for the upcoming season of *The Apprentice*. He said, "What do you think of this?" And I gave him my opinion. He started asking me what I do. I said I'm into editing. At that point, I'm thinking I have an opportunity here to pitch him. I had realized when putting together the golf video that they had no YouTube channel, they had very little of a media catalogue for such a huge brand. His Twitter presence was very bland for someone who was such an outspoken character. I mean, he would go on Howard Stern, Larry King, he was really a great interview. But you look at his feed, it felt like it was ghostwritten. It felt bland. It didn't feel like him. So, very quickly I pitched him on, "I could really do this, build out new media for you, social media. It's like earned media," I said. "You could put out a Tweet, you could put out a video, and it will get on the news." I believe he was familiar with the names Twitter and Facebook, but not exactly how he could maximize them to his best effect. I think he liked that it would end up on TV, and the fact that it would be relatively cheap. So he said, "Alright, let's work on this together."

I walk out of there and the other executive said, "You just got yourself a job." I said, "Really?" He goes, "No, he hired you." I was hired pretty much on the spot. They didn't even know where to put me. I was operating out of the lunchroom in the beginning. My first thought was, "How do I explain Twitter to a guy who's in his mid-60s, and to the best of my knowledge doesn't use computers?"

Trump had begun speaking publicly about his interest in a presidential run— which led to the familiar pattern of writers doubting him. Molly Ball led a Po-

litico article with, "Donald Trump says he's thinking about running for president. But of course, that's what he said last time. And the time before that. And the time before that."

The idea that he would think and then actually run seemed impossible to some, but not to Roger Stone, who insisted, "He tells me he's more serious than he's ever been."[13]

Stone recommended Trump attend the Conservative Political Action Conference in Washington on February 10, 2011. The event attracts thousands of fervent activists, along with presidential hopefuls eager for approval in a climactic straw poll. That year 11,000 people heard former Massachusetts governor Mitt Romney, former Texas congressman Ron Paul, Minnesota congresswoman Michele Bachmann, Newt Gingrich, Rick Santorum, and Donald Trump orate.

Striding into the Washington Marriott ballroom to the tune of the O'Jays' "For the Love of Money," The Apprentice *theme song, Trump pointed to an audience member and said, "You're hired." In his speech, Trump listed countries "taking advantage" of the United States in trade by "ripping us" off with cheap consumer goods and expensive oil. He declared he was pro-life, against gun control, and anti-Obamacare. And he touted his résumé as a "competitive businessperson" who is "very successful" while contrasting himself with President Obama, who "came out of nowhere." "Wonderful guy, he's a nice man, but there was no record, nothing to criticize," he continued. "Nobody knew who the hell he was. He's now our president."*[14]

Before leaving, Trump turned on Ron Paul, saying, "[He] has zero chance of getting elected," generating a chorus of boos because the libertarian was a favorite of the elite-disdaining CPAC crowd. Paul trounced Trump in the straw poll; Trump couldn't even get 5 percent.[15]

Sam Nunberg: I see Trump speak at CPAC. I feel the way people felt seeing Obama in 2004. This guy's a star. He has "it." Now, if you want to define what "it" is, I can't. But he has "it." He has a stride. He can get people excited. Part of it is his cavalier attitude—this is me, you either accept it or not, or go fuck yourself. It's confidence. He's a celebrity. Barack Obama was a celebrity. McCain, the moron, attacked him for being that. It was the dumbest thing. Who doesn't want to elect a celebrity as president?

Steve Bannon: Trump's a marketing guy. He came to CPAC in 2011, and that's where we interviewed him. All the themes of the campaign later, talking populism, he's talking Tea Party.

David Bossie: That's where Trump did Steve's radio show for the first time. Steve Bannon had been on the radio, and we had Mr. Trump do a live segment with him. That became a regular thing for Steve's radio show over the next year and a half.

Sam Nunberg: Trump is a leader. He's obviously had it since '88, because he was invited to New Hampshire then. He's cultivated that over the years with *Apprentice*, and he doesn't give a shit. And he's outside of the whole system. They were talking about nominating Newt Gingrich, Rick Santorum, Mike Huckabee's going to run again, and Mitt Romney.

Stone was not only a provocateur of the media and his political foes—he also prodded his friends. In a February 25 interview with Politico's Maggie Haber-man, Stone said Trump could "write a check for $200 million if he wanted to" self-fund a presidential campaign.[16] Several hours later, Trump called up Haber-man complaining that Stone "does not represent me, and he is not an adviser to my potential campaign."[17]

Michael Cohen had become more prominent in the Trump sphere. In an ABC News profile of Cohen, headlined, in part, "Donald Trump's Political Pit Bull," he said, "It means that if somebody does something Mr. Trump doesn't like, I do everything in my power to resolve it to Mr. Trump's benefit."

Cohen took Trump's private jet on March 7 to Iowa's Faith and Freedom Conference to meet with Iowa Republican Party chairman Matt Strawn and state GOP donors.[18] He told reporters that the mogul would be making a "big personal sacrifice"[19] if he were to run and that "hopefully he decides in June," sparking another round of Trump-teasing headlines.[20]

Trump wanted to run, but his path was unclear. He had tested arguments that Obama was a weak leader, the country was being ripped off through trade, and Obamacare was ineffective. He needed to channel some conservatives' disgust. He chose to challenge the president's identity.

18.

BORN IN THE USA

In the 1990s, far-right media personalities had espoused theories accusing the Clintons of murdering dozens of people, including their friend Vince Foster; most of the American public dismissed such rhetoric as hatred-fed lies.

But the September 11, 2001, attacks unleashed a deluge of conspiracy theories not seen since the Kennedy assassination. The 9/11 Truthers believed the Bush administration was complicit in the attacks. Others propagated falsehoods that the mass shooting at Sandy Hook Elementary School in 2012 was a hoax by anti-gun liberals, the Federal Emergency Management Agency built concentration camps, and the Obama administration contrived attacks on two U.S. government facilities in Benghazi, Libya, in 2012. They also trafficked in older hate-filled tropes, such as denying that millions of Jews died in the Holocaust.

Misinformation spread more quickly in the new millennium, while trust in government fell steadily, from 54 percent in 2001 to only 25 percent by 2008, a Pew Research Center study found.[1] Distrust in the media among Americans rose slightly from 49 percent to 56 percent over the same period. By September 2012 it would reach 60 percent.[2]

What was dangerous for the mainstream media had become profitable for the alternative-right media. A gaggle of fringe-right media personalities led by WorldNetDaily's Joe Farah and Jerome Corsi, Savage Nation radio host Michael Savage, and InfoWars host Alex Jones fanned falsehoods to compete for an audience of evangelical values voters, libertarians, Tea Partiers, and Perot-loving populists—often the same pool. Other outlets, including Breitbart News, Newsmax, and Project Veritas, produced documentaries and published stories under the rubric of journalism.

Breitbart News, founded in 2007, broke the story that Democratic congress-man Anthony Weiner was sexting photos of himself in 2011.[3] Founder Andrew Breitbart died in 2012, and the website began courting white nationalist views under the leadership of former board member Steve Bannon, who described it as the "platform of the alt-right."[4]

This loose collection of media entities comprised the alt-right juggernaut that Hillary Clinton once called a "vast right-wing conspiracy."

Melinda Arons, *former ABC news producer and television booker for Hillary Clinton's 2016 campaign:* The politics of personal destruction came about during the Clinton/Gingrich era. The Clinton conspiracy stuff was deeply personal too. Vince Foster was their best friend, and they're getting accused of murdering the guy. As wacky as that was, you didn't have mainstream Republicans going on national television and accusing Bill Clinton, or Hillary, of murdering Vince Foster. It still remained in the fringe.

Erick Erickson, *conservative pundit:* I caution anyone who uses the [phrase] "the vast right-wing conspiracy." These groups certainly are there, and they're all buddy-buddy, but the level of competition and lack of collaboration between them is staggering to behold when you go to their meetings.

Russell Verney, *Project Veritas executive director:* When Fox News started in '95, '96, it wasn't necessarily in a conservative advocacy position. Even Hannity was Hannity and Colmes back then, sort of a balance. It gradually grew more and more conservative over the years. They set the tone for our next generation of conservative media. Breitbart took the lead from Fox and tried to include a segment of the conservative voice, and then Newsmax and others developed. They all found that there was money to be made in expanding that viewpoint.

Katrina Pierson: I knew Andrew Breitbart. He had spoken at several of our events. The Tea Party and Breitbart are definitely in lockstep. The alt-right comes in far later than that. When the media starts talking about it, I'm thinking, "alt-right," what is that?

Sam Nunberg: Newsmax is not alt-right. Breitbart is. The Gateway Pundits. The Blaze. There was more than Fox News. These were people that were willing to cover him.

Tucker Carlson: I never understood what that meant, I still don't understand. I'm not being disingenuous, I don't know what qualifies as alt-right.

David Bossie: Let's get to that for a second. I've been in this business a long time, and I've heard bullshit terms made up and created for their own purposes, but Donald Trump had never heard of, I had never heard of, the alt-right. It is what the mainstream media narrative wants to create. This whole argument about his use of the word "nationalist"—Webster's Dictionary is quite clear on what a nationalist is. It's somebody who loves their country and is loyal to their country. It is not a pejorative.

Steve Bannon: Trump said we always criticize [the political class] as being the elites. "They're not the elites. We're really the elites. We have better cars and better things." He used to tell me, "You can't keep calling them elites because people aspire to be elite. If you make them elites, make them better, they're always the best, and we can't be the best." I said, "No, no, no. That's not how it works. In populism, it's always anger at this contingent of elites keeping the people from fulfilling their destiny as the rule of people. The underlying grievance is always the elites against them. They have to be called elite, because they haven't gotten it through their own hard work and labor, because the hard work and labor of the virtuous plebeians is what the populists are." He said, "No, no, no. Because people want to be elite."

If there is any episode in Trump's political career that answers the question whether there really is a method to his madness, it is his questioning of Barack Obama's birthplace. "Birtherism" looked like madness to many, even some close to him.

Birthers asserted during the 2008 presidential campaign that the Hawaiian-born candidate was born in Kenya and his American birth certificate was a forgery. In June 2008, a National Review writer called for Obama to release his birth certificate, and when Obama complied, birthers continued to argue that the document was a fake. At a Minnesota town hall in October 2008, Republican senator John McCain honorably tried to kill the argument once and for all, saying, when a voter raised the issue, that Obama was a citizen. But two months into Obama's first term, Florida representative Bill Posey wrote a bill requiring presidential candidates to send their birth certificate to the Federal Election Commission.

Birthers found a home to propound their theories on Fox News, as well as in fringe media outlets starting to build their audience of disaffected Tea Party voters, including Breitbart and WorldNetDaily. When Trump discussed his political aspirations and addressed devotees at CPAC in February 2011, he did not question Obama's origins. But he quietly reached out to prominent birthers, including WorldNetDaily's Joe Farah, author Jerome Corsi, and entertainer Pat Boone.[5]

Backing a conspiracy theory would signal to alt-right news outlets that Trump might be their man. Did Trump believe Obama might have been born in Africa? Did he worry about the societal side effects of birther rumor-mongering? Immaterial. But the political question of how to woo a certain constituency—he thought this through. As he would tell the Reverend Al Sharpton about his birther stance, "I got to do what I got to do."

Carl Paladino: There's pretty clear evidence it was true [Obama wasn't born in America]. Also true he never attended Columbia, whose largest donor is George Soros.* I always thought he was a Manchurian candidate. He came close to destroying the fabric of America.

Jesse Ventura, *Minnesota governor 1998–2002:* Nonsense. That's how I felt about it. I have my feelings on Obama, where he came from. I get the feeling he comes from the intelligence community. He had weird jobs around the world. And they call him a community organizer. What the hell's that? Then you learn that the YMCA is a major CIA operational unit.†

Pat Boone: [Birtherism] was a general thought amongst conservatives. I did my own investigations. I was attuned to the questioning and lack of legitimate answers. In my articles I was making the same demand [for Obama to release his birth certificate]. When he was running for the nomination, on his website he produced what was not a birth certificate, though it was presented as one. It was a certificate of live birth, which in Hawaii, anybody that wanted to could get if they could produce a passport, social security, and say the dog ate my birth certificate.

Steve Bannon: In February of 2010, the opening speaker of the Tea Party Convention is Joe Farah of WorldNetDaily, king of the birthers. Sarah

---

* Both "true" assertions are false.
† Ventura's outspoken views earned him a reality TV series, *Conspiracy Theory with Jesse Ventura,* which ran on TruTV from 2009 to 2012.

Palin's going to speak the next night. Joe Farah gets up. It's this massive ballroom. People all over the place. All the world's media is there. He starts with the Gospel of Matthew. "Adam begat Cain and Cain begat Zoab, and Zoab begat that and this guy begat that . . ." A hundred begats. He's doing all of them. David. Boom. Abraham. Boom. "This begat Joseph, who begat our lord and savior Jesus Christ." It takes five minutes to read it. He stops and says, "This shows that even the only son of God needs a birth certificate." The place explodes and goes crazy. They're standing on the fucking tables high-fiving. The BBC, NHK, *New York Times*, they're all writing it down. They started the Tea Party Convention with the fucking birther thing. Andrew [Breitbart] is standing back with me in the wing. He says, "I'm going to go up and punch that motherfucker out." Breitbart's the guy to do it. "Do you understand what he just did?" he said. "He just labeled us a racist organization." Andrew pulls Farah out into the lobby, about to punch him out, and [journalist] Dave Weigel's sitting there. The next day it's the lead story on his website.[6]

Pat Boone: Trump had become aware. It was all over the internet. Conservatives were well aware of all the questions. I was sharing some of that with Trump by phone and letter, and he was picking up the cause and running with it, because he believed the president was not legitimately born in the States.

Neera Tanden, *president, Center for American Progress:* With Bill Clinton they went after his personal life, and with Barack Obama they tried to other-ize him by making him seem like he was born in another country. Donald Trump was the latest hard-right conspiracist trying to undermine support in the country for a Democratic president.

Steve Bannon: [When we first met Trump], no birther shit. He was maniacally focused on Obama. Obama clearly was under his skin. But no crazy talk on birtherism. Trump never heard one mention of birther, ever, from us. Breitbart is anti-birther. Andrew and I were absolutely anti-birther guys.

Robert Torricelli, *Democratic U.S. senator from New Jersey 1997–2003:* That was not a high point of the Trump political ambitions. That was not Roger. Roger knew that was hurtful. I don't know where that came from.

Sam Nunberg: Roger has said that Trump called him about it, and Roger said he thinks it's a very good idea. I don't know who Trump first heard about it from. I had nothing to do with that.

Roger Stone: Someone gave him Jerry Corsi's book and he reached out to Corsi. I was neither a progenitor or an advocate of making birtherism the centerpiece of a 2012 presidential campaign.

Pat Boone: We had some correspondence about it, letters, and if I'm not mistaken, his lawyer then was Michael Cohen. I'm not saying that I, by all means, please, I don't represent myself as having convinced him of anything.

Trump first floated the birther theory in an interview with ABC's Ashleigh Banfield that would air on Good Morning America *on March 17, 2011. She spent five hours with him on his private 727 airplane for the interview, during which Trump sounded like a candidate. He suggested a "surgical strike" on Libyan dictator Muammar Gaddafi, pledged to spend $600 million on a campaign, and ridiculed half the Republican field.[7] Mitt Romney "doesn't seem to resonate," Tim Pawlenty can't captivate the voters, and Jon Huntsman is "very disloyal," he said. Trump liked Mike Huckabee, Newt Gingrich, and Sarah Palin, but he compared House Speaker John Boehner to Meatloaf "sobbing uncontrollably" on* Celebrity Apprentice.*

It was scintillating for a news segment, but, given Trump's history, unlikely to get major attention. Then he unleashed his birther barbs at President Obama. Here was a well-known businessman moving this subject from alt-right websites and online chat rooms to the airwaves of morning network television. Trump larded on a string of factually incorrect statements—while praising birthers:

Everybody that even gives a hint of being a birther . . . even a little bit of a hint, like, gee, you know, maybe, just maybe this much of a chance, they label them as an idiot. Let me tell you, I'm a really smart guy. . . . The reason I have a little doubt, just a little, was because he grew up, and nobody knew him. You know? When you interview people, if ever I got the nomination, if I ever decide to run, you may go back and interview people from my kindergarten. They'll remember me. Nobody ever comes forward. Nobody knows who he is until later in his life. It's very strange.[8]

Melinda Arons: There was a period when George Stephanopoulos was anchoring *Good Morning America* and there was a conversation about interviewing Trump. I absolutely refused to do it. I felt very, very strongly that he served as nothing more than a ratings ploy. You did not put someone on the Sunday shows to do an entertainment angle the way you might with a morning show. The Sunday show was such a serious political interview, and he was not a serious political person. He had been playing this kind of dance with the political media for years. He always said he was going to run and never did. That was part of it and there was this other feeling that the media is sort of in on it, but also kind of turned off by it, but also kind of in on it.

Trump's birther claims drew widespread condemnation from business leaders and policymakers across the country. Former New York City mayor Rudy Giuliani said there was no question that Obama was born in the United States and any doubts were "too late and futile."[9] The New York Post *mocked Trump's "fake run for president" and "weird embrace of birthers."[10]*

But Trump knew the power of the lie would resonate with voters who despised Obama. An April 2011 CNN poll found that 43 percent of Republicans believed Obama was born outside the United States.[11]

Trump made increasingly outlandish claims about President Obama's origins, and television and radio producers were eager to book him. On ABC's The View—*Rosie O'Donnell was long gone from the show—on March 23, he asked, "Why doesn't he show his birth certificate? There's something on that birth certificate that he doesn't like."[12] Trump had been invited by Fox News founder Roger Ailes in 2011 to make weekly appearances on the channel's morning show.[13] And at the end of March he appeared on* Fox and Friends, *saying, Obama was spending "millions of dollars in legal fees trying to get away from the issue."[14] He called in to Laura Ingraham's radio show on March 30 and said that some "so-called birthers"—he said he didn't like the term because it demeaned the "great American people . . . hard working, unbelievable salt of the earth people" who were raising this issue—were speculating that Obama was hiding his birth certificate because he didn't want it known that it was marked "Muslim" under religious affiliation. Trump said he believed it was more likely there was no American birth certificate.[15] By April 7, Trump was suggesting on the* Today *show that "I have people that have been studying [Obama's birth certificate] and they cannot believe what they're finding" and proclaiming on MSNBC's* Morning Joe *that he had obtained a video confirming the president's Kenyan heritage.[16]*

Trump's message resonated among Republican primary voters. In a Wall Street Journal/NBC *April 2011 poll of a nine-candidate field, he had tied Mike Huckabee with 17 percent, trailing Mitt Romney's 21 percent.*[17]

But Trump seemed concerned with maintaining moderate and Democratic friends. Michael Cohen spun to CBS that his boss is "not part of this birther movement, he's just an individual that is questioning."[18] *Seven years later,* Morning Joe *co-host Mika Brzezinski revealed that she had challenged Trump on his birther views at the time. She said that Trump confessed off-camera, "I know it's bad but it works."*[19] *It was a method that had come across as madness to some political journalists, but Trump was courting a different audience, playing to Americans he called "salt of the earth people."*

Donny Deutsch, *CNBC host:* His birther thing. That was like, "What?" I went on whatever show I was on and said, "It's racist. There's no other way to look at it." Michael Cohen called me up and said, "Donald's really hurt. He really is hurt. Because we thought you were his friend." I said, "I've got to tell you, I'm shocked." He said, "Will you get on the phone with him and talk to him?" I got on the phone with him and I said, "I've never known you to be a racist, but that is a racist thing you are saying. You can't slice it any other way." Back and forth. Somehow we got out of the phone conversation. That was a very seminal, striking, public, non-gray area to put a stake in the ground.

Kwame Jackson, Apprentice *season 1 runner-up:* My relationship with Trump was great up until the birther movement. I met Melania at events and stayed affiliated with NBC and the *Apprentice* family. Then it was, "Who the hell is this guy?" The Dr. Jekyll and Mr. Hyde moment where I thought, wow, you have totally changed your tune.

Sam Nunberg: Trump does the birth certificate. I think it's politically genius.

Eleanor Clift, *political reporter for* Newsweek *and the Daily Beast:* Donald Trump spread lies about Obama because it rallied a segment of voters to his side. Trump tapped into their grievances and made them believe he would upend the system. He appealed to their baser instincts, demonizing political correctness and encouraging people to say what they think no matter how harmful or hurtful to others.

Erick Erickson: It certainly struck a chord. I ran a website, RedState, that banned the so-called birthers. Anyone who came in and started questioning the legitimacy of Barack Obama's parentage and lineage we banned from the site. We got some blowback over it.

Melinda Arons: Birtherism is the first conspiracy that took grip in such a way that mainstream outlets felt they had to cover it. It clearly was the first one that took root in such a way that the White House felt they had to respond to it.

Jefrey Pollock, *Democratic pollster:* The birther thing had made it clear he wanted to be a player in the debate in some way.

Katrina Pierson: I wasn't thinking about Trump politically at that time. This is something he was concerned with, and a lot of people were concerned with it too.

Ed Rendell, *Democratic governor of Pennsylvania 2003–2011:* I figured if he was doing [the birther stories], he was going to move to the Republican Party, but I never thought he would run for anything.

Anthony Scaramucci, *Romney national finance co-chair:* I accepted from day one that the president was born in the United States and born in Hawaii. Why President Trump was saying that, I don't know. I was working for Romney. We were trying to help Romney get the nomination and raise money.

Katie Couric: That was the first glimpse of the darker side of Donald Trump and the lengths he would go to destroy his enemies. Very Roy Cohn.

Erick Erickson: The underlying racism of it was dragging the right back into the conspiracy theories of the Clinton age. The "Who killed Vince Foster" nonsense. There were people who, because of Bush's victory, had been silent on those issues. The crazies we thought we had set aside and moved beyond were suddenly resurgent.

Donald Trump's son-in-law, Jared Kushner, who helped run his father's real estate firm, Kushner Companies, bought the New York Observer *in 2006 to gain cultural currency in New York City. After clashing with several editors, Kushner hired Gawker founding editor Elizabeth Spiers to run the paper in February 2011. The two argued over what stories were newsworthy and how to cover Trump's politicking objectively. Eighteen months later, Spiers would leave the paper.*

Elizabeth Spiers, New York Observer *editor 2011–2012:* Trump informally ran in every cycle since the '90s. He was running for the first three months I was there, and it became a source of conflict between me and Jared Kushner. There was no way for the *Observer* to cover Trump the way it would've covered Trump before Jared bought the paper because Ivanka was the partial owner. At the very least, any time you mentioned him, you had to have a disclaimer that the Trumps technically own a piece of the paper. Trump was getting trashed elsewhere, and he was very visible. I told Jared, "We can't pretend that he doesn't exist."

Even if you're just aggregating pieces, Trump was getting himself into the news, and all the pieces were negative. Jared and I were getting in fights about what we were aggregating. There would be a front-page [*New York*] *Times* story, and he would say, "Why did you pick that negative one?" I said, "It's not that we're picking the negative ones. We're picking the ones that are most relevant. Your father-in-law happens to be doing insane things." He said it speaks to editorial choice to pick the negative ones. By that standard, it's an editorial choice to pick anything. I said, "We've got to aggregate straight down the line because otherwise we're not reflecting what's happening." He started moving in the direction of "You guys have to write positively about Trump," and I said, "That was not an option. Don't tell my reporters what to report." That's just not how journalism works. He walked up to the line of threatening to fire me if I didn't.

Erick Erickson: I found it deeply funny, but also very problematic. So many of us on the right worked very hard to marginalize the nuts peddling this conspiracy. Suddenly, here comes Donald Trump, who has this show on national television who is willing to fan the flames of this. I don't know that he even believed it, but it was a convenient way for him to beat up Barack Obama and get some attention, so he did it.

Pat Boone: When Trump began demanding that Obama produce a birth certificate, that's when the groundswell for him as a potential presidential candidate began to grow. It seemed preposterous right then, but because he was demanding the president prove he had really been born in the States and produce a birth certificate, it started the groundswell. "Wow. We'd like a guy like this—fearless and outspoken and daring." The Tea Party took to him right away.

Glenn Beck: He spotted the anger, and he wanted to play into it. The birther thing was ridiculous from the beginning. The left played some of the kooks on the right who were into the birther thing to keep that alive. Those are useful idiots. When Donald Trump picked that up, you're either crazy or you're trying to build a coalition.

Reverend Al Sharpton: Trump starts becoming the face of birtherism. I'm really livid with him now, and I back away from any communication with him. In 2011, I start *PoliticsNation* on MSNBC, and every night I go after Trump on birtherism, calling it racist and calling it for what I saw it as: race bait.

Tucker Carlson: I've always thought the race angle was the wrong way to understand Trump. A lot of people who accuse Trump of being racist are obviously themselves actual racists. They're race-obsessed people. The birther thing comes from another impulse Trump has, which is not all good by the way, it's bad. Trump believes the story everyone else believes is bullshit. Trump is innately, natively skeptical of whatever the story is. Trump always thinks that there's a story behind the story. That made him perfectly suited for the moment because the whole election was about how rigged the American economy and the American ladder to success are.

Reverend Al Sharpton: He saw people who wanted to buy into it on the right, and he kept feeding it. I never thought he was crazy. He would overestimate himself, but he would have had to have been psychotic to think there was evidence he didn't have—and he didn't have it because it's not true.

Elizabeth Spiers: Jared kept saying to me that we were being unfair to Trump. He said, "You should really spend some time with him, if you spend some time with him, you'd really like him." I said, "Jared, liking him has nothing to do with coverage. There are things that your father-in-law is doing that are appalling me. The birther stuff. It's incredibly racist." He rolled his eyes and said, "Oh, he doesn't believe that stuff, he's just saying it because he thinks Republicans are dumb, and they'll buy it."

I was trying to process that response. In Jared's mind, he thought that would be a more acceptable response than "my father-in-law's a racist." Jared thought I would be sympathetic to a cynical point where Trump is manipulating people. Because Trump is racist, he doesn't give a shit about the consequences of what he's doing to black people in America. I was thinking, either way Jared, your father-in-law is racist, but your response says something about you.*

Anthony Scaramucci: Lee Atwater, he was the guy who developed the Willie Horton ad. George Herbert Walker Bush, who was a patrician and viewed a certain way, launched that racist ad. Did George Herbert Walker Bush believe in that ad? Is he a full-blown racist, or did he do that ad to incite people and to attract certain voters to his community? That's politics.

Donny Deutsch: If you go back to early interviews with Trump, he would try to drift into issues to show gravitas. To become part of a bigger discussion mattered more to him versus how he was going to make money and what his next reality TV show [was going to be]. But now he was doubling and tripling down. "I have proof. You're not going to believe. I've got people working on it now and they have found . . ." Absolute insanity. We didn't talk much after that. I started to see what this guy was turning into and stayed away.

Erick Erickson: It looked like he was willing to fight more aggressively and dirtier than any of the Republicans against Barack Obama. Here comes this guy not only willing to do that but forces a response from the Obama administration on it. A lot of people in the comment sections at RedState were cheering. This topic was a big deal when people called in to my radio show and when I filled in on other shows. Donald Trump was willing to throw the punches the Republicans wouldn't. It highlighted the contempt the base had with the Republican establishment.

Reverend Al Sharpton: As it heats up, a guy named Kedar Massenburg, who was the former president of Motown Records, called me and

---

* Jared Kushner declined to comment on the record.

said that his friend Michael Cohen wanted me to meet with Trump, that Trump resents and is hurt that I'm on TV every night calling him a racist. I told the guy, "I did not call him a racist. I said what he says is racist and race-based. I've gotten out of name-calling." He said, "Would you do me a favor? My friend really wants to try to get you all at least lukewarm. Would you meet with him?" I said, "Yeah, but I'm not going to say to him what I don't say on TV every night."

I went up to Trump Tower, and it was Michael Cohen, Donald Trump, Kedar, and I, and his kids were there, and they were looking at these architectural drawings. That was supposed to impress me, and I said, "Yeah, but we're not getting a minority contract." We sat and we argued for 45 minutes on how it was racial and it was race-based. He did say in the peace meeting he really believed he was going to prove Obama was born in Kenya. I told him, "That's a lot of hogwash." "Al, I've got big people on this," he said. "Big people." Finally we agreed to disagree. "I don't call people racist anymore unless they absolutely give me no choice, but it's racial and it's disgraceful and you shouldn't do it. I want to tell people we met and I clarified my position." Got in the elevator. I walked back to 30 Rock and Kedar says, "You're going to mention this tonight? Why don't you just let it go?" I said, "Oh no. I don't trust Donald Trump. Donald Trump will lie." I got on TV that night and said, "I met with Donald Trump. This is what I said." Sure enough, before morning he tweeted out, "Reverend Al came to see me and apologized for calling me a racist." A little while after that I ran into him somewhere and said, "I knew you were going to distort it." He said, "I've got to do what I've got to do. We're both New Yorkers."

19.

ROASTED

Trump kept plotting a 2012 presidential bid while fanning birther rumors. He regularly spoke with strategists Dick Morris and David Bossie and pollster John McLaughlin. He interviewed campaign manager candidates and tried to hire other consultants. And he continued to lean heavily on advisers inside his company, such as Michael Cohen, and outside, including Roger Stone, to promote his candidacy.[1] His meetings with Morris and McLaughlin were especially fruitful because they created a campaign plan on spec, laying out how he could run in Iowa, New Hampshire, and South Carolina and which key personnel he could tap in each state. One of the names McLaughlin suggested was a New Hampshire operative named Corey Lewandowski, who would become Trump's campaign manager in 2015.

David Bossie: As the Romney campaign was going, he and I were talking about taking on Romney. That's why I decided to put together some people to have him hear more voices about what that would be like.

Dick Morris, *political consultant:* I got to meet him again when he was looking at running for president in 2012. I volunteered to come in, and I met with him three or four times [in 2011] in the company of John McLaughlin, a Republican pollster. The purpose was to brief him on public policy issues preparatory to a presidential campaign. There was no money involved, as often happens with Donald. Michael Cohen sat in and would take notes. He would clarify points so Donald could get it and participate in the conversation. Back then, I gave him what I thought should be his slogan in 2012: "Barack Obama, you're fired," taking advantage of his line on *The Apprentice*.

John McLaughlin, *Republican pollster:* Dick asked if I wanted to help out with Donald Trump. He was going to run for president and we needed to put together a campaign plan. We spent about a month doing it. The only one who took it seriously in the media was [*Time* magazine's] Mark Halperin. We gave him a campaign plan of what he needed to spend, what he needed to do, how to structure the campaign. A lot of the people that we would recommend and put him in contact with then became parts of his later campaign. Jason Miller was going to be the campaign manager and Corey Lewandowski, a friend of mine from when he managed some of Bob Smith's campaigns in New Hampshire, was going to be the New Hampshire person.

Dick Morris: Many of the bios I've read about Trump suggest he has the attention span of a hummingbird, and that's totally not true. He would sit there for two hours taking notes, listening, asking intelligent questions, occasionally interrupted by a phone call by his secretary. I found him very retentive and very focused. Those issue preparations probably served him well throughout the presidential race. I would make each briefing on a different topic. Defense was one. Education was another. Immigration and trade.

John McLaughlin: We were going to launch polls in these states at the time. I had media buyers, too. There was a real media plan. We weren't going to take the matching funds. They were going to spend the money. We also had to do vulnerability research on him. We hired Gary Maloney, who used to do that for Lee Atwater and Bush. We weren't quite sure Trump was a registered Republican. One of the first places these other Republicans would shoot at you was that you weren't always a Republican. There were times in the '90s he was a Democrat. He was also registered as an Independent. I asked him and he said, "Oh, Roger Stone suggested I do that."

Dick Morris: When he was thinking of running for president, I asked him, "Are you liquid enough? Do you have enough money?" He said, "I have $4 billion." I said, "How would you like to have $3.7 billion?"

John McLaughlin: You could see that he would vertically control information and deal with people directly. He might tell us one thing, Dick Morris and myself, about his plans to run and how he started planning but then at the same time he might be talking to Roger Stone separately. He controls information that way so that he keeps control of things, everybody reports to him, and he's the one making the decision. That's how he operated in his business and that's how he was going to operate in politics. Mr. Trump often doublechecks things on his own.

President Obama brushed off requests for his birth certificate, but by mid-April 2011, just five and a half weeks after Trump had started his attack, they had become a distraction when reporters besieged him with questions about Trump's demands during a budget address. The White House scheduled a news conference for April 27, at which Obama's long-form birth certificate was released and the president warned,[2] "We're not going to be able to solve our problems if we get distracted by sideshows and carnival barkers," without mentioning Trump by name.[3]

On the same day, Trump made a jaunt to Portsmouth, New Hampshire, to meet Republican activists and donors. Obama's move forced Trump to hold an impromptu Q&A with reporters while standing in front of his Trump helicopter, a Sikorsky S-76B, at the airport. He said he wasn't done with the birther issue and hinted at future questions about the president's Ivy League academic record.[4] By getting Obama to meet his demands so quickly, Trump claimed a victory.

John McLaughlin: I saw the president was going to hold a press conference at the same time that Donald Trump was going to land in Manchester. I called him and said, "You realize that when you get off the plane to hold your press conference that President Obama is going to hold a press conference and he's going to release his birth certificate. You've just got to be aware of that because you're going to get asked about it. He's obviously concerned about you that he's going to do this while you're on the ground." Right as they were landing, Obama was on CNN and Fox News releasing his birth certificate, so that was eclipsing any press we were going to get. But it was a sure signal that President Obama sure took us seriously as a challenger.

Neera Tanden, *president, Center for American Progress:* The fact that the president of the United States had to respond is a sign of the power of the conspiracy.

John McLaughlin: We had a lot of people who were ready to move into New York to start the campaign. We were thinking of who was going to run different parts of the country for us, like the Super Tuesday states and Trump would just call these people. I knew Joel McElhannon, the consultant for [Georgia Governor] Brian Kemp in 2018, from working in Georgia. He was going to handle the south for us. Joel told me, "I got this call, it was a message from Donald Trump. I thought it was a joke." I said, "No, you've got to call the guy back. That's Donald Trump. He wants you to run the south for him. We need to move on Super Tuesday." Jason Miller was ready to come into New York and run the campaign. Corey was ready to run New Hampshire. Trump called him up. We had people all over the country in the early states. We were discussing that everybody was ready and all we needed was a go from him and we were going to start with the lawyers and forming the committee, and bringing people in to work for us. It was going to be an instant campaign.

Before he'd begun his birther attacks on national television, Trump had taped the freewheeling Comedy Central Roast of Donald Trump. *Family Guy creator Seth MacFarlane and a cohort of entertainers including Snoop Dogg and Larry King spent at least 90 minutes mocking Trump about the poor quality of his erections, the "gaudy, tacky, monstrosit[ies]" he builds, and his "big and bloated" face. His wealth was the only off-limits subject.*[5]

> **Seth MacFarlane:** As long as I have you here, it's pronounced "huge," not "uge." And here's another one, it's pronounced "I am fucking delusional," not "I am running for president."

> **Snoop Dogg:** Donald says he wants to run for president and move on into the White House. Why not? It wouldn't be the first time you pushed a black family out of their home.

Through it all, Trump laughed and exhibited every outward sign of being a great sport. He could take a ribbing in this context. The special was broadcast on March 15, 2011.

Trump had reason to be in an even better mood the last week of April. Obama produced his birth certificate on a Wednesday, and Trump attended his friend Steve Wynn's Las Vegas wedding on Friday. He flew to Washington the next night to attend the White House Correspondents' Association dinner as a guest of the Washington Post's *Lally Weymouth. It was an occasion when, generally, the president delivers a stand-up comedy set before solemnly noting the importance of a free press. When asked before the event started whether he expected any jokes at his expense, Trump told reporters he was "fine with this stuff."[6]*

Just as typical narratives about Trump's life treat his presidential explorations over the years as ego- and branding-driven jukes, a neat little story about this night has become a piece of pop history. It goes that Trump was so humiliated over the jokes Obama made at his expense at the dinner that, driven by rage, he decided then and there he would run for president. This simplistic version of events is wrong because, first, it incorrectly supposes Trump was not serious about running for president before that tuxedoed evening. Second, some of those close to Trump portray him as not being bothered much by the roughly one minute of jokes Obama fired at him. Maybe that stone face Trump held as the president fricasseed him was the look of a man with wheels turning, inwardly pleased his attacks had stung so much that Obama felt the need to hit back.

Perhaps Obama's insults did spur Trump to run four years later, but for the opposite reason most people believe; Obama's jibes, intended to cut the cartoonish real estate developer down to size, instead elevated Trump to special gadfly status. The president threw some quick humorous putdowns at Republicans Paul Ryan, Michele Bachmann, Jon Huntsman, Tim Pawlenty, and Mitt Romney, but Trump received roughly seven times more words than any of them. Like in the Republican debates on the 2016 campaign trail, Trump's outrageousness earned him that most valuable asset—camera time.

David Plouffe, *senior adviser to President Obama 2011–2013:* Knowing Trump would be at the dinner and all the controversy over the birth certificate, it would just be a nice way to have a little fun with him. You need a lot of humorous content for the dinner, and it's harder than it looks. It was not strategic so much as, "We're now going to define him as the face of the Republican Party."

Melinda Arons: Each network and print organization throws their own pre-party. Then there's the dinner. Then there are these after-parties, the biggest of which for a long time was the Bloomberg–*Vanity Fair* after-party, which was at the French ambassador's residence. Even if you didn't get invited to the dinner itself, people would still attend all the events surrounding the dinner because it was fun. Some people bring celebrities. That became a big thing, especially during the Obama years, because celebrities wanted to go.

Ed Rendell: I was there at the MSNBC table, and Donald was in the audience. He had already started the birther movement attacking Obama, but Obama spoke that night and ripped the shreds out of Donald.

Anthony Scaramucci: My first awareness of the birther story was in May of 2011 when I was at the White House Correspondents' dinner, and President Obama was making jokes about the birther situation, showing animation from *The Lion King*. Then he proceeded to rip into Mr. Trump.

David Plouffe: I was a few tables away. Everyone was uproariously laughing. That's the first test. Are people having a good time? And is he landing his material well? Trump was, even back then, a bigger-than-life figure. To have fun made of him was a noticeable thing.

Neera Tanden: There was a lot of laughter in the room, and obviously Obama was pissed off he had to produce his birth certificate for this asshole, and he was not going to let that go. The room was really with Obama, even though a lot of Democrats and Republicans go.

Anthony Scaramucci: President Obama is a great public speaker. He's got a comedic sense for timing. The jokes were written by some of Hollywood's best comedy writers. Judd Apatow helped him write that speech.

David Plouffe: I wouldn't say Obama was excited. He generally just wanted to make sure they'd be funny. I'm sure part of him loved giving a little bit back to Trump, given all the hot air that'd blown in his direction.

> **Barack Obama:** Donald Trump is here tonight! Now, I know that he's taken some flak lately, but no one is happier, no one is prouder to put this birth certificate matter to rest than The Donald. And that's because he can finally get back to focusing on the issues that matter—like, did we fake the moon landing? What really happened in Roswell? And where are Biggie and Tupac?
>
> But all kidding aside, obviously, we all know about your credentials and breadth of experience. For example, no, seriously, just recently, in an episode of *Celebrity Apprentice* at the steakhouse, the men's cooking team's cooking did not impress the judges from Omaha Steaks. And there was a lot of blame to go around. But you, Mr. Trump, recognized that the real problem was a lack of leadership.

And so ultimately, you didn't blame Lil' Jon or Meatloaf. You fired Gary Busey.[7] And these are the kind of decisions that would keep me up at night.

Well-handled, sir. Well-handled. Say what you will about Mr. Trump, he certainly would bring some change to the White House. Let's see what we've got up there. (Screens show "Trump White House Resort and Casino.")[8]

Anthony Scaramucci: I was at the table next to him. He didn't look happy about the jokes. He wasn't rolling in self-laughter. He was roasted by Seth MacFarlane on Comedy Central, and he was enjoying that more than the jokes that were pointed at him from President Obama. He wasn't happy about it. Fairly expressionless on his face. Not displaying any emotion one way or another, but that's typically a sign that someone's not happy about a situation. People were laughing and he wasn't.

Ed Rendell: Trump was getting red in the face, he didn't take it well. I said hello but I didn't talk to him after Obama ripped him.

Washington Post *style correspondent Roxanne Roberts, sitting behind Trump at the* Washington Post's *table, had a view nearly as close as Trump's wife Melania. Trump waved at the crowd and smiled meekly during Obama's routine. He later told Roberts, "The president was making jokes about me. I was having a great time. I was so honored. I was actually so honored. And honestly, he delivered them well."[9]*

The next morning's papers would focus on Obama's authorization of a successful raid to kill terrorist Osama bin Laden and noted that Trump was "humiliated." Trump disagreed with that assessment, telling Fox and Friends *the next morning, "I didn't know that I'd be virtually the sole focus, and I guess when you're leading in most of the polls, that tends to happen."[10]*

Roger Stone: I talked to him afterward and he said, "It's amazing, isn't it? The president spent the whole time talking about me." He got it, immediately.

Sam Nunberg: He was upset. I never spoke about it with him. I didn't need to. He felt it was too much what Obama did. With that said, he won that issue. Obama doing that to him may have given him a little dip in the Republican primary polls at that point but was eventually going to help him.

Jerrold Nadler, *Democratic congressman from New York city:* The only talk [in Congress] was, "Boy, Obama really got him. He was good. He was funny." He's been doing all this nonsense and Obama got him good.

Eleanor Clift: It was only later people began to focus on Trump. The more we learn about Trump and how thin-skinned he is, some people have attributed his desire to be president to that evening. But he had wanted to be president for a long time.

Roger Stone: It's a seminal event. It's a throwdown. It's a challenge. He takes up the challenges and he wins. The dinner was a major factor even though he would still maintain that it didn't bother him and it had no significance, but I don't agree with that analysis.

Neera Tanden: It's overstated. It's ridiculous. There was a mythic nature about this. The New York guy who's trafficking with the hard right way before this moment.

Roger Stone: Being attacked by the leading Democrat only raises your stature. In 1967, Nixon was launching his comeback, and he was relentlessly, articulately taunting Lyndon Johnson on the Vietnam War, and Johnson finally erupted and attacked him. Johnson says the vice president didn't know what was going on in government when he was in it, doesn't know what's going on now. It elevated him. It was galvanizing. Same thing when Obama attacks Trump, it only increases the intensity of his support.

David Bossie: I saw what happened that night when I was home, and then I talked to him after that. He got more into it. Look, certain things bring clarity. That event was a moment of clarity for him that he said, "Let's see if these people can take what they like to dish out." And that's part of how he started to get a little more forward-leaning. Not one event did it, but it's a culmination over the years. It's part of the tapestry, it's just one leaf on the tree. That's all it is.

Roger Stone: I think it was a mistake on their part. They taunted him beyond good humor and that would backfire. All it did was strengthen his resolve to run and win, the only way to prove them all wrong.

David Plouffe: No regrets because Trump had danced around with running before. The notion that he'd only run because of that night I find not to be credible. The amazing thing about politics, let's say it's 2004 and you had said, "Seven years from now, Barack Obama, state senator from Illinois, is going to be president and he's going to be having fun at Donald Trump's expense, who's at this dinner, and then will be president in 2016." You would have gotten a-billion-to-one odds on that. It's an amazing story.

In the short term, the numbers said that being the brunt of jokes was not helping Trump. He tumbled into a fifth-place tie with Ron Paul with only 8 percent of the vote in a May 10 Public Policy Polling survey.[11]

Trump dropped birther talk from his stump speech the next day in Nashua, New Hampshire. Instead he touted his business savvy and teased a presidential decision after wrapping up Celebrity Apprentice *later that month.[12]*

John McLaughlin: The next day [May 12], we met in Trump's office— Dick Morris, myself, Trump. We'd mapped out a schedule for the summer and fall. He said, "Do I really have to go to Iowa and New Hampshire every weekend?" I said, "Yes, you have to go. Michele Bachmann's living there and other candidates are living there. People will want to see you." "I like to play golf every weekend," he said. "Well, we'll find you a golf course in Iowa and New Hampshire," I said. After we go through the whole plan, he said, "NBC's offering me $10 million an episode instead of $5 million to continue to do *Celebrity Apprentice*." I said, "If you're not sure you're going to do this, take the money because there's a hundred senators in Washington that would want to run for president. But if they could become you, I think most of them would."

Frank Luntz: The first time I had a long conversation with him was at Steve Wynn's wedding. Romney was already a candidate and Trump was fooling around about running. I said to Trump, I bet he wasn't going to run in 2012. Publicly. I placed a $10,000 bet challenging him. He looked me straight in the eye and said, "You need to get your money back. I am going to run. I don't want you to look foolish, so you should say on the air that you were wrong." Two [weeks] later he announced he wasn't running.

Elizabeth Spiers: [Jared Kushner and I] had a nasty fight on the phone on a Friday in May. We agreed to stay the issue until Monday. I called a mutual friend of ours that weekend and said, "I don't know what to do here.

He's asking me to do something that is unethical. He might be able to find an editor to do it, which is to commission a piece that's intentionally positive about Trump and false by virtue of that. Even if I were willing to do it, which I'm not, my entire politics desk would resign because they're real journalists. This isn't a PR publication." A PR guy said to me, "I feel bad for you because you are between a rock and a hard place. There are conflicting value systems. He views this as an issue of family loyalty, you view this as an issue of journalistic integrity." I said, "That's all well and good, but Jared can stand to get yelled at by his father-in-law. I can't throw my professional integrity out the door." He backed me into this corner. He was going to have to fire me and nobody's going to be sympathetic to it. That Monday morning, the PR guy said, "Your problem is solved." Immediately after, I got an alert Trump had dropped out of the race.

John McLaughlin: If he could have announced for president at the time and not give up *The Apprentice,* I think he might have done that. When he realized he would have to give up the show, it forced a gut check about whether he really wanted to do this right now. He said he was going to think about it over the weekend. Over the weekend I got a call that he wasn't going to run. Then I had to let a lot of people know.

On May 16, 2011, Trump sent reporters a statement he would not be a candidate in 2012.

> After considerable deliberation and reflection, I have decided not to pursue the office of the presidency. This decision does not come easily or without regret, especially when my potential candidacy continues to be validated by ranking at the top of the Republican contenders in polls across the country. I maintain the strong conviction that if I were to run, I would be able to win the primary and, ultimately, the general election. I have spent the past several months unofficially campaigning and recognize that running for public office cannot be done half-heartedly. Ultimately, however, business is my greatest passion and I am not ready to leave the private sector.[13]

It couldn't have helped that Michael Cohen warned him that Mitt Romney had too much of a head start. Or that Republican voters didn't see Trump as a political figure—7 out of 10 voters thought Trump had no chance of becoming president, a May 2011 Politico/George Washington University poll showed.[14]

Most importantly, NBC executives pressured him to make a decision before they released their fall 2011 schedule, which would contain another season of Trump's Celebrity Apprentice.[15]

David Bossie: He had an incredibly hectic schedule running Trump Organization but also the TV show. He didn't have a lot of time to sit around, ponder, and build a campaign structure. Time slips through your fingers. It's one of those natural progressions if you're not completely dedicated or serious about it.

Dick Morris: When Trump decided not to run for president, I was very disappointed. I had invested a lot of time, and he was not running, in part maybe to drive up the price of his TV show. I wrote him off at that point and figured he would not run.

Anthony Scaramucci: Some people say [Obama's White House Correspondents' dinner speech] spurred him to run for president. I do not believe that because then why didn't he run in 2012? Why did he wait until 2016? There was ample time to announce his candidacy. The debates didn't start until August.

Rick Wilson: Even he realized you can't beat Barack Obama, so he didn't run in 2012. Obama had pretty decent numbers, and he had killed Bin Laden the day after the Correspondents' dinner. The fact that Bin Laden was dead and the economy was alive was a major sticking point for anyone who wanted to run against Obama.

Dick Morris: To thank me for my work he gave me a membership to Mar-a-Lago for free and told me it was a $125,000 gift. I would meet him at Mar-a-Lago three or four times a year, when I was having dinner with my wife and guests. He would stop by the table and we would chat.

It looked like the same Trump fake out. He raised his media profile and dove back into The Apprentice. But this waltz with politics was his most serious yet. With his well-calculated birther attacks, Trump aroused a powerful populist constituency. He alienated friends, not for the first time or the last, but he'd gained a following.

One more thing. He hadn't entirely given up on 2012, despite proclaiming he had.

20.

THE TWITTERER

After Trump announced he was passing on a presidential run, he questioned whether he had made the right choice. That summer he continued giving speeches to friendly conservative audiences and met with far-right political personalities, including Sarah Palin, without the scrutiny or pressure afforded a candidate-in-waiting.

Roger Stone sensed Trump's restlessness and that he might want to jump back into the 2012 race, possibly as an independent, even though the Reform Party run more than a decade earlier had shown how difficult that path would be. Stone recommended Trump bring Sam Nunberg on full time to handle day-to-day political activities. Nunberg would introduce him to radio programs and alt-right websites where he could connect with conservative voters outside Washington.

Sometimes intersecting with the political operatives, Trump's social media manager Justin McConney sought to rehabilitate Trump's celebrity image after the White House Correspondents' dinner. McConney began filming short candid videos of Trump in his office talking off the cuff, which he would upload to Trump's social media accounts. His advisers taught Trump how to use Twitter to transmit his provocative musings. Nunberg and Stone focused on political remarks, while McConney and Meredith McIver concentrated on Trump's businesses and entertainment news. With their help, Trump's Twitter account would become a weaponized distillation of his voice.

Roger Stone: As soon as he did not run in the 2012 election, he had immediate seller's remorse. I stayed on for a month or two after he decided not to run because he wanted to preserve his options.

Sam Nunberg: He hired Roger and Roger paid me a portion of his fee. Roger was the senior partner and I was the day-to-day associate, managing the account. Part of it was to keep him relevant and make news, and keep him involved in this political process. How do we do this? We started doing Twitter. He already had a Twitter account. He started tweeting. Obama was already using Twitter. Others were using it.

Roger Stone: Sam would get up very early, go online, look at Drudge Report and other headlines, suggest some tweets, and send them to me. I would add some, take some out, pass them out. Sometimes Trump would use some of them, but most of the time not. Most of the time he would come up with his own tweets or he would do some combination..

Sam Nunberg: One of the things I talked with him about was you really pissed off a lot of people by being a tease. He regretted not running. With that said, he was in the midst of real estate deals, such as Trump Hotel DC, and he had *The Apprentice.*

Justin McConney: *The Apprentice* was filming that fall. He's a celebrity, he decided not to run, and my focus was keeping him relevant in PR and having him talk about anything and everything. The idea was translating the Donald Trump who was very interesting in the New York papers throughout the '80s and '90s to social media. I started doing these video blogs with a little Panasonic point-and-shoot camera, because I wanted to give it that purposefully webcam-like, low-budget look. I'd walk around with a small camera on my suit jacket, and I would get him to answer tweets and speak about current events. If I get him to say something that goes viral he'll see it on TV or in a newspaper article and understand the value of social media. It was a way to put him in more of a positive, comical light after what was negative PR from the Correspondents' dinner and the birth certificate.

His desk was always messy. And that was an interesting thing to video blog. Because when we started doing them, the late-night comedians would make fun of the stuff on his desk. Trump said to me, "Should we clean it up?" I said, "No. If anything, let's leave it a mess because it makes you more relatable to people. Let's do a video explaining why your desk is a mess." And he actually did a video explaining why his desk was a mess. He had so much stuff, it got to the point where he would have framed photos on the floor lined up not only in his office but going around the reception area. He actually has a closet that I found one day. He had all these old photos from the '80s and '90s that all the old paparazzi would send to him. I started using them for Instagram, for Throwback Thursday.

On May 31, 2011, Sarah Palin rolled into New York on her "One Nation" bus tour to gin up attention for her own White House bid. Trump agreed to meet with her, and the two split a pizza at a Manhattan branch of Famous Famiglia. Palin told CNN the pair gabbed about "specific candidates and potential candidates, and kind of just what our perception was of each of these folks."[1] Journalists and comedians focused not on the politics of the meeting but on how Trump ate his pizza slice with a knife and fork instead of the classic New York way of picking it up and folding it in half.[2] That gave McConney an idea to spoof the coverage and show Trump the power of social media.

Justin McConney: There was a meeting that was arranged for Sarah Palin and Trump to go for pizza. All the coverage was centered on him using a fork and knife. I wanted to be the first guy to get a response out of him on this. If he's willing to do it and he's wanting to have a sense of humor about this, it would be a turnaround for him.

I went in the next day and said, "Mr. Trump, would you want to answer why you used a fork and knife to eat pizza?" Surprisingly he said, "Sure." We filmed this video blog at his desk, we put it on YouTube, we linked it on Twitter. It gets picked up by the media, it's on *The Daily Show*, it's written up in various major outlets. The next morning I get called into his office. "That was amazing," he said. "You don't understand, years ago I'd have to do 20 different interviews to get that amount of TV coverage. Are you telling me that this social media stuff with videos, that this could happen again?" That's what started to sell him on tweeting more and vlogging more.

Sam Nunberg: He gives a speech at Ralph Reed's Faith and Freedom Conference [on June 3]. He blows the roof off. Great speech. Amazing. Everything was good. Roger then calls up Trump, and says we have an idea: you running as a third-party candidate, and you control the Electoral College, and then you can pick who runs. We sent him a memo. Roger said social media can run this campaign from Trump Tower. All we had to do was get into the debates.

Justin McConney: It was very analog back then because he did not use a computer and he was still on a flip phone. I would print out his Twitter mentions, bring them to him, and he would take a Sharpie and mark which ones he'd want to retweet, and then he'd write down his responses on them. I would have to go back and type out his response and do the retweets.

When it got to the point of him dictating tweets, the way the process would work is that it was almost like an editorial meeting. First thing in the morning I'd show up at his office, I'd pitch him topics to talk about. I would check out what was in the news and what was trending. Or he would pitch me what he would want to speak about. Then Meredith [McIver] would usually come in, jot the notes down, and sometimes we would have to edit the tweets down because Trump would just talk. Then I'd figure out which hashtags to put in, who to tag.

Meredith was outside his office, so it wasn't uncommon for him to shout out a tweet to Meredith. She would come in, write it down, and then put the tweet out. If I was in his office and he came up with a tweet or I pitched a tweet to him, I would put it out. Meredith and I would split the job of posting the tweets. If he wanted to write a letter to someone or he wrote a speech, she would be involved with that aspect.

At the beginning he did not really understand social media as much as he understood PR. He understood news cycles. We would sit and discuss the timing of tweets, and he understood perfectly. I would say, "Friday afternoon really doesn't work." He's like, "You're right. Friday is terrible for news cycles. We'll save that one for Monday."

Sam Nunberg: I used to send him updates to see where his tweets could get covered. Earn media on the tweets. When he tweeted about immigration, that was the equivalent of our focus group. We'd get a lot of retweets from it and it was a good issue. He instinctively talked about the issue in 2013 when he said, "These people [meaning immigrants] are never going to be Republicans. Not a single one of them."

Justin McConney: I met Sam a few times during that period. Sam was involved in the political aspect. We would coordinate whatever material Sam was suggesting Trump should post. Everything would be approved by Trump. He would mark down which tweets he would want to send out. If Sam sent him something and, for instance, we had hotel openings to promote that day, we had to push it off. There was coordination of timing of the release of his tweets. His Twitter very quickly grew. When I started it had 300,000 followers. Organically, with no spending, we got to over a million followers. The videos would consistently air on TV. The tweets started being read on newscasts. Every once in a while, Ivanka would give input. She'd say, "You should have Dad tweet about this." Or, "I liked the tweet he put out about that yesterday." Sometimes when he would put out something insulting someone she was friends with, she'd go in and say, "Why'd you do that? I'm friends with this person."

David Bossie: Sam became the person I would talk to regularly because I didn't want to bother Mr. Trump. The idea was to have a political person. I told him, "You need somebody who's going to help you with scheduling and deal with invitations and make sure you can put stuff together. That's got to be a building block." Sam performed in that role, and he did a good job.

Steve Bannon: I knew Nunberg, and Nunberg is a genius. Roger Stone is a merry prankster and talks a big game.

Roger Stone: One of the things Sam Nunberg was adept at helping him do, which I wholeheartedly agreed with, was full use of conservative alternative media—alt-radio and in print. We were getting aggressive coverage in Breitbart, Daily Caller, WorldNetDaily, and yes, dare we say it, InfoWars. He was talking to Rush Limbaugh, Michael Savage, Sean Hannity, the big names of conservative talk radio.

Sam Nunberg: He liked radio because it was popular and he grew up listening to it. His father listened to radio. He would be interviewed by John Gambling. Imus. He would listen to conservative radio. Mark Levin and Rush Limbaugh. He'd leave it on. He's not cerebral, he's not academic. He's a very smart man. He's very underrated for that. These were people who were willing to cover him. He agreed with them on the issues. He knew Breitbart in 2011.

Roger Stone: Trump was listening as much as he was aggressively calling in. It was a very important part of his strategy. Back in 2000, conservative radio was not the powerhouse that it would become. We did some of it, but we were going after a different constituency. We were running more as a centrist for the Reform Party nomination, hoping to have a candidate to our right and a candidate to our left, whereas in 2012 and in the run-up to 2016 he repositioned himself to the right.

Russell Verney: In 2000 you barely had websites, and limited email. We've come a long way since then. You can now do your campaigning on social media and a couple of news cable stations. Even Fox News in 2000 was only in its fourth or fifth year, still in its infancy. I don't think MSNBC had much of an audience then either, but they were all going. You got a whole different communications world today to campaign as opposed to 2000. Trump is a very confident man, he expresses confident viewpoints. It's appreciated by people. There's nothing wishy-washy about Donald Trump.

Sam Nunberg: He'll tell you, "I don't work hard. I work smart." I used to think he was the only one who said that. One thing he had taught me that I'm grateful for is how to condense things, make them so Americans can understand. Not get too esoteric or in the weeds. Communicate.

Justin McConney: There was a certain point where we reserved the name @DonaldTrump and we had a discussion with the kids and with Trump about whether we wanted to switch it. I said, "Why don't we just keep it @realDonaldTrump?" We reasoned on staying with @realDonaldTrump because it was really Donald Trump. He already had 300,000 followers, and Trump liked the sound of it. He just liked saying @realDonaldTrump.

Regnery Press president Marji Ross approached Trump in the spring of 2011 about writing a new book. David Bossie had suggested in 2010 that Trump write a policy book if he wanted to run for president someday. Trump's previous titles were with publishing companies and imprints that marketed books for a mass audience. Regnery cultivated a conservative intellectual audience with influential volumes, including William F. Buckley's God and Man at Yale, *Russell Kirk's* The Conservative Mind, *and Whittaker Chambers's* Witness. *Regnery also published dozens of books by twenty-first-century conservative writers like Ann Coulter, Michelle Malkin, Newt Gingrich, David Limbaugh, Laura Ingraham, and Barbara Olson. Putting Donald Trump on that roster legitimized him with Regnery's influential audience.*

Marji Ross, *president, Regnery Publishing:* For most of Trump's life and career he's been a businessman, and the books he's written have been all business books. Trump had been talking a lot about China. He had been repeating a line many times, "Take back the oil." He had been talking about economic issues and about America not being a good negotiator anymore, not being strong anymore, and getting taken advantage of. He had also been talking at big conservative events in front of groups that lean to the right and gotten really good responses for somebody who that audience approached with wariness. "Is he really a conservative? Are we going to like what he has to say?"

We thought he's starting to have a pretty good following, especially among people on the right, for his political views and economic conservatism. That sounded like a book that would make sense for us and for him. We approached him and said, "What do you think? Would you like to do this?" Negotiated it directly with him and his team.

Dave Shiflett, *author of* The America We Deserve: I was asked around that time if I were interested in writing another Trump book. The people handling that one were associated with Regnery. I wasn't interested.

Tucker Carlson, *Fox News:* Trump had zero interest in conservative orthodoxy and was probably ignorant of a lot of it. He didn't know anything about conservatism, and that deeply offended the guardians of conservatism. But conservatism as an orthodoxy was played out. Supply-side economics didn't work and our trade and immigration policies were a disaster for a lot of the country.

He feels the trade stuff is totally real. He gets more animated on that than any topic. There's no organized conservative constituency for tariffs against China. Nobody was talking about it. I've been in the conservative media business for 25 years and "We're getting screwed by China" was not even on the list of the top 100 issues. That's him. He drove that. Immigration, same thing. There was a small group mad about immigration, but the *Wall Street Journal* editorial page, the U.S. Chamber of Commerce, and the Kochs were not on board. There was no large group of racists who were secretly running the party. Everyone knows that trade and immigration aren't good issues. Trump says, "I don't care. I'm bringing it up anyway." He was absolutely right, not everyone is benefiting from free trade and open borders. No one acknowledged it except him. In real life you don't need to be right on everything. You need to be right on one or two big things nobody else is.

Marji Ross: I attended a few of those speeches to get a feel. One speech he gave in front of a Christian conservative group, the Faith and Freedom Coalition. Thousands of people in the audience. He got a really good response.

Even though Trump was no longer publicly running, Ross went through with the deal. She drafted Breitbart managing editor Wynton Hall, who had ghost-written several books, to work with Trump. Together, they composed a Tea Party–aligned vision of America's future with a chapter assailing China and OPEC for extending the country's trade deficit, and others advocating for sharply cutting taxes, reducing welfare, repealing Obamacare, and curtailing immigration. Although ghostwriter Tony Schwartz has said he wrote nearly all of Trump's most famous book, The Art of the Deal, *Ross insists that Trump was heavily involved in the creation of* Time to Get Tough: Making America #1 Again, *which would be published on December 5.*

Steve Bannon: Wynton came to me and said, "Hey, do you have any problem with me ghosting a book for Donald Trump?" He's a huge ghostwriter. He'll write a book a year. I said, "What kind of book?" He said, "A policy book." I said, "Are you fucking kidding me? What fucking publisher is doing that?" He said, "It's very interesting you ask. All his publishers turned him down. In fact, his agent said, 'This is ridiculous.' Everything he's had is a bestseller. They said they thought it was going to be a diatribe against Obama and they didn't want to see that."* I said, "Well, who's doing it?" He said, "Regnery." "Regnery?" I said, "Regnery's never put up an advance in its life. It gets these books free from Malkin and from Coulter, and they do rev shares. Donald Trump doesn't do a rev share." He said, "No, it's better. Regnery put up a million-dollar advance." "Regnery?" I said. "They've never put up a million dollars in a cumulative 50-year history of the company."

Marji Ross: We were pretty excited to publish the book. We've been doing conservative books for 70 years. It's very significant when we publish a book because it says a lot to our market and it says a lot to

---

* Hall, likely operating under a confidentiality agreement, declined interview requests.

other people who are watching in publishing and media. We talk to conservative readers about issues and events and people they care about from a perspective they share and understand.

Steve Bannon: Wynton Hall is one of the smartest guys in the country, and he said during the writing of it, "This guy's really smart." I said, "Come on." "No, he's smart," he said. "Once he gets focused on some-thing he's really smart and he asks great questions." Wynton tells me in writing the book, "Here's what's really amazing about the guy. He is the number-one applied Jungian psychologist in the country." I said, "Wyn-ton, you're talking to me, dude. Knock the bullshit. What are you talk-ing about?" "Yeah, archetypes, all that," he said. "It's actually a chapter in his third book." Google it right now. Top 10 Trump's favorite books. The fourth is *Memories, Dreams, Reflections* by Carl Jung.

Roger Stone, *Republican political consultant:* No, honestly I don't know who Carl Jung is. I'm not familiar with his work. I doubt that he learned from Mr. Jung's books. He just learned on the playgrounds in Queens. Or in military school. I've read some of the books. He's a natural com-municative genius. He's a showman. He understands a good turn of phrase and memorability. He understands the importance of repetition. Something Al Gore never figured out. Perhaps Bannon is finding deeper meaning than I am.

Marji Ross: Donald Trump was very, very involved. Not only did he spend a lot of time talking and meeting with Wynton, but he went over every single chapter and section, and made notes throughout. He made a lot of personal edits to the book. Because he's so frank and informal, maybe people assume that means he's not careful with details, but that's an incorrect assessment. Another thing people misperceive and cer-tainly gets misrepresented is that he is not particularly interested in working hard. When people ask me what was it like to work with Don-ald Trump on a book, the first thing I say is he was one of the hardest-working authors I've ever published. He was extremely accessible and very proactive and responsive on all elements of the marketing strategy, publicity, and events. There was never a book signing, interview, or a book-related event we asked him to do that he wouldn't do. I've worked with celebrity authors who only want to do network TV or big prime-time shows. People who won't do, for instance, local radio or bookstore book signings. He was game for everything. He was very, very determined. He likes everything he's involved in to be done well and successful. The other half of that is he's willing to do the work to make that true.

Steve Bannon: It's a brilliant policy book. As soon as I took over his campaign I went right back to it. The book is really good. A lot of the Trump administration is based off that book.

Marji Ross: He had this big decision to make about whether he was going to renew his contract with NBC for *Celebrity Apprentice*. In the end he did and that's why he didn't run, or one of the reasons. It would have sold better if he had run for president, but it sold very nicely. We've actually sold over 100,000 copies of the book by now.

Erick Erickson: My website at the time, RedState, was owned by Eagle Publishing, which also owned Regnery, and they published Donald Trump's book. They decided to have me go to New York and interview him in his office about his book and why he wrote it. He seemed very interested in trying to run for president or at least laying groundwork for a future run. He was beginning the outreach to evangelicals. We started talking about his plane—he had just traded in the 727 for the 757—and got into golf and Mar-a-Lago. He wanted me to come play golf. His staff reached out to see if I wanted to go down there. I said, "Yeah, sure, I'd be glad to go." My wife was very insistent that I wasn't allowed to go. She thought he didn't want me to go play golf, he wanted me to come so he could have my soul.

Trump kept busy. A month before the book was released, Trump welcomed an unusual guest to Trump Tower. Director Christopher Nolan received permission to shoot a scene there with Christian Bale for The Dark Knight Rises. *When he realized what was happening, Trump's social media manager Justin McConney grabbed his camera for a photo op.*

Justin McConney: I show up to work and I was actually not even supposed to be in the office that day. I walk up to Trump Tower and it says "Wayne Enterprises" out front. I knew they were filming the movie in New York, and I saw Christopher Nolan out front. I heard from someone they were going to bring Christian Bale up once they wrap shooting. I said, "We need to get a picture of Trump and Christian Bale because once the movie's released, we have to post it on social media."

Christian Bale comes up and he's dressed as Bruce Wayne. I'm not sure Trump was familiar with Christian Bale's work outside of Batman. Trump says, "My wife loves your movies, Christian." He puts Melania on speakerphone and says, "Melania, you'll never believe who I have in my office. The Batman." Christian Bale starts laughing. Then Trump starts plugging *The Apprentice.* "We have a great season coming up, great cast." Christian Bale said his wife was a fan of the show, and then Trump started having people in the office take pictures with Christian Bale. "Get a picture with Batman."

He kept bringing it up after that moment. "Batman filmed in my office. It's going to be a huge movie." But I don't think he understood that it was not supposed to be Trump Tower because he was upset when *Dark Knight Rises* came out that the building said Wayne Enterprises. When *Wolf of Wall Street* filmed there next year, he wanted to make sure that they got a shot where it said Trump Tower.

21.

REMAINING A PLAYER

Donald Trump hadn't fully ruled out running in 2012, but his window was closing and the presidential primary was continuing without him. He kept up his speaking engagements even if he didn't get attention from a press corps that moved on to Rick Perry, Herman Cain, Newt Gingrich, Rick Santorum, and Mitt Romney. David Bossie reminded Trump to donate money to Republican politicians, and candidates visited Trump Tower to seek the mogul's endorsement.

Trump wanted to stay a player in the primary process. On December 2, 2011, he agreed to moderate a GOP candidates forum hosted by Newsmax and Ion Television in Iowa later that month. Only two candidates, Newt Gingrich and Rick Santorum, agreed to participate. Various GOP officials, indicating that they still thought of Trump's political forays as a sideshow, predicted the debate would be "a circus."[1]

By December 9, Trump backed out, saying other candidates would not agree to come unless he guaranteed he wouldn't become an independent candidate. In a statement distributed to the press by his increasingly prominent lawyer, Michael Cohen, Trump for the first time used a phrase that would become his campaign rallying cry.[2]

It is very important to me that the right Republican candidate be chosen to defeat the failed and very destructive Obama administration, but if that Republican, in my opinion, is not the right candidate, I am not willing to give up my right to run as an independent candidate. . . . I must leave all of my options open because, above all else, we must make America great again!

Although the slogan Make America Great Again had been around at least since candidate Ronald Reagan issued buttons saying "Let's Make America Great Again" during his 1980 run, and Bill Clinton used it in his campaign launch speech in 1991, it seemed dormant over the next two decades. Journalist Peter Beinart's 2006 book was The Good Fight: Why Liberals and Only Liberals Can Win the War on Terror and Make America Great Again. *But perhaps most relevant for Trump, the phrase was part of the subtitle of a 2011 book by 2010 Tea Party Senate candidate Christine O'Donnell,* Trouble-maker: What It Takes to Make America Great Again. *O'Donnell received media attention for her phenomenal rise in politics and then, in the last days of her unsuccessful campaign, for the release of a clip showing her saying that in college she had "dabbled in witchcraft."[3] O'Donnell's book landed her an interview on Sean Hannity's Fox show in August 2011, four months before the phrase became part of Trump's lexicon.[4] The way the slogan entered Trump's consciousness might be a mashup of all of the above plus the fact that in introducing Trump for an interview on December 6, 2011, three days before the phrase appeared in the Trump press release, Fox News host Greta Van Susteren said he "just wrote a new book spelling out his ideas to make America great. It's called* Time to Get Tough."[5]

Before Christmas 2011, Michael Cohen announced that Trump had switched his party affiliation from Republican to independent "to preserve his right to run [for president] as an independent after the finale of The Apprentice *in May."[6] Then, on December 30, paperwork was filed with the Texas secretary of state's office to create the "Make America Great Again Party," reportedly to allow Trump to run as an independent presidential candidate in the state.[7]*

Via a telephone call to the morning show Fox and Friends *on January 2, 2012, Trump denied that he had orchestrated the Texas registration but said, "Frankly I think it's a great name . . . because that's what it's all about, making America great."*

He would sign a trademark application for "Make America Great Again" with the U.S. Patent and Trademark Office for the purpose of "promoting public awareness of political issues and fundraising in the field of politics" on November 12, 2012, six days after the election.[8]

Members of Trump's political circle recall the phrase arising at different times. In their campaign memoir, David Bossie and Corey Lewandowski report hearing it at a New Hampshire rally in 2014, "the first time he had used the words as a rallying cry," and Trump wearing it on a white baseball cap at a Laredo, Texas, rally in July 2015.[9]

Sam Nunberg: Trump told me he was going to be using that as early as I can recall, as early as 2013. I'm talking January, February was when I first heard about it. He said he was going to say it. I said, "Fine, great."

John McLaughlin: At one of our meetings at his office [in May 2016], it was just he and I, and I gave him an old Reagan/Bush "Let's Make America Great" button and he says, "Oh, but you see, this is different. It says 'Let's Make America Great Again.' I just say, 'Make America Great Again.'" He thought the "Let's" was too passive. He said "Make America Great Again" is the right way to do it.

In January 2012, as the phrase was percolating and Trump was finally letting go of the idea of running for president that cycle, Mitt Romney surged ahead of the GOP field in the polls as his rivals began fading.[10] Trump's poll numbers remained low—47 percent of independents had an unfavorable opinion of him, while only 41 percent liked him in a December 2011 Washington Post/ABC News poll.[11] Trump still wanted to remain a player in the election. That meant endorsing a candidate and speaking at the Republican National Convention, where he could strengthen his standing as a conservative leader. His aides were split on strategy. Michael Cohen wanted him to back Romney, while Roger Stone and Sam Nunberg advised against it, fearing his association with a moderate.

Sam Nunberg: All these presidential candidates start visiting Trump in 2011. They want his endorsement.

David Bossie: One of the things I did during the '12 and '14 cycles was make recommendations to Mr. Trump for campaigns and organizations to donate to, and he did every single gift I came up with. He did dozens and dozens of gifts over that time to Republicans across the country running for Congress, Senate, and governor.

Steve Bannon: I would tease Bossie. Every week I'd say, "Hey, are you going up there for the check signings? How's that going for you?"

David Bossie: At the end of every quarter I would give a list of names and he would send the checks.

Sam Nunberg: By December [2011], he decides he's not going to do the registration. He doesn't want to put up the money for the states. We're done there but he keeps us around to do his public relations and interviews to keep him involved.

Roger Stone: Michael Cohen was a major factor in his conclusion that Romney couldn't be stopped for the nomination and was likely to win the presidency. I never agreed with that. It's hard to know [why Cohen convinced Trump] because I wasn't in the room when he was pitching this.

Sam Nunberg: The one Roger and I had nothing to do with was Mitt Romney. Mitt Romney was all Michael Cohen. Romney was not his friend. We explained that to Trump.

John McLaughlin: I was encouraging Trump to endorse Romney. It would help his Republican credentials for the future. Romney was not seen as an outsider to the Republicans. This is the nominee, we should get behind him. I was not in favor of running as an independent. Trump was more in touch with the grassroots Republican primary voters than the Republican establishment.

On February 2, 2012, Donald Trump endorsed Mitt Romney at Trump International Hotel in Las Vegas. The presidential hopeful seemed almost embarrassed to be there, clutching his wife Ann Romney's hand and telling reporters, "There are some things that you can't imagine happening in your life and this is one of them."[12]

In a taut seven-minute speech, Trump promised he would not mount an independent presidential campaign. "It's my honor, real honor and privilege, to endorse Mitt Romney," he said. "Mitt is tough. He's smart. He's sharp. He's not going to allow bad things to continue to this country that we love."[13] Michael Cohen, who later raised $500,000 in four hours for Romney, looked on.[14]

Anthony Scaramucci: I was working for Governor Romney as part of his fundraising team. Mr. Trump was always flirting with the run for the presidency. None of us took it that seriously. I assumed it was a publicity stunt, that he was talking about being a bride but was really going to be a bridesmaid. I saw the endorsement on the news. They looked awkward together.

Roger Stone: I was not in favor of his endorsement of Romney. He knew that. But he's his own man. It was his decision, not mine, and then we had that weird press conference in Las Vegas in which Romney doesn't know what to do.

Anthony Scaramucci: In fairness to President Trump, he was very help-ful to Governor Romney. He did a lot of robocalls. We did two fundrais-ers in his beautiful apartment at Trump Tower.

Steve Bannon: After Romney won the nomination, Andrew [Breitbart] went to CPAC. Andrew gave this massive speech about unity with Romney, and then Andrew drops dead three weeks later [on March 1]. I take over Breitbart full time. One of the first things I do is I get Herman Cain into Breitbart Embassy.* I get all 40 Tea Party heads who are all su-ing each other. Tea Party Nation. Tea Party Express. Tea Party Patriots. All the guys. They're all suing each other. Everybody thinks the Tea Party is going to be a billion-dollar brand. They're all grifters to begin with. It's the only time they ever sat in one room. I said, "You've got to lay your weapons down." Herman Cain sits there, and we spend four hours talking about all the Tea Party issues. Herman Cain's going to be the emissary to go to the Romney campaign.

Reince Priebus, first time I meet him, comes to Breitbart Embassy and gives a sales pitch for the Republican National Committee and how we've got to all work together to win.

Herman Cain never gets a meeting. Matt Rhoades and those guys who ran the Romney campaign completely blew him off. "Go fuck yourself." Couldn't care less. Tea Party's a bunch of white trash. Rom-ney's not interested.

My partners, particularly Bob Mercer, were so gung-ho on Romney. There's a Hannity panel in May 2012. It's Bossie, myself, and seven other smart guys—typical *National Review* and *Weekly Standard* guys. Hannity said, "Who thinks Romney's going to win?" Seven hands go up. Mine

---

* Breitbart Embassy is a town house in Washington, DC, where Breitbart News is head-quartered and where Steve Bannon reportedly sometimes lives.

doesn't. He said, "You're the only one who doesn't think Romney's going to win?" "Romney's going to get crushed," I said. "Obama's that good. He's got no theme. He's not drawing in the working class. It's not even close." Bob Mercer said, "Why'd you say that on TV? It's the exact opposite. Romney's going to win." They all thought that.

Trump recorded phone calls encouraging GOP voters to pick Romney over former senator Rick Santorum but continued to bully Barack Obama over his birth certificate and college records, which concerned the Romney campaign. "I wonder if @BarackObama ever applied to Occidental, Columbia or Harvard as a foreign student. When can we see his applications? What do they say about his place of birth," Trump tweeted on May 22. "@BarackObama is practically begging @Mitt-Romney to disavow the place of birth movement, he is afraid of it and for good reason," he wrote a week later. A campaign spokeswoman assured the Washington Post *that Romney believes Obama was born in the United States.*[15]

Romney used Trump as a surrogate sparingly over the summer. Trump continued to pick fights with political leaders and Beltway insiders regardless of their affiliation, and flooded his Twitter feed with birther references.

Roger Stone: The Romney people were not so much afraid of Trump, although they should have been. Trump was a wild card within the larger question of getting nominated. Nobody knew if he would really run. Nobody knew if he would support one of the other candidates. They just wanted him off the battlefield.

Justin McConney: His tweeting is becoming more and more rampant. He started calling me on weekends and weeknights and asking me to tweet things—all hours. The first time this had happened was Memorial Day weekend [May 27, 2012]. I thought it was a prank call at first because I see this number pop up and someone gets on the phone. "Hi, it's Melania," she said. "Mr. Trump wants to speak to you." I'm thinking, "This has got to be a joke." Trump gets on. "George Will just hit me on TV. I have to hit him back. Put this out immediately."

There were a few other times Melania would call because I don't think Trump saved my number at that point. He would just start giving me tweets. I'd have to pull over into a parking lot and he'd be on the phone for 15 minutes saying, "What else should we tweet about?" I would make the mistake of sometimes bringing up more things in the news or people that referenced him, giving myself more work to do.

Roger Stone: Michael Cohen once showed up at a Romney rally and he got stopped by the Secret Service because he's carrying a firearm. I'm sure he had a permit, but who brings a gun into a presidential campaign rally?

Sam Nunberg: The Romney campaign used Trump during the primary when they needed him. They used him in Michigan and they used him in Ohio to beat Rick Santorum. Then we started leaking out that Trump should speak at the convention. He wanted to speak.

Trump desperately wanted to speak at the Republican National Convention in August, but Romney didn't want him on the stage.

Trump dropped hints, tweeting, "Hmmm . . . Can you imagine me speaking at the RNC Convention in Tampa? That's a speech everyone would watch." The Romney campaign compromised, agreeing to allow Trump to show a video on the convention's first day.[16] Michael Cohen hyped the appearance, telling ABC News, "One would not be shocked to see Donald Trump" at the convention. But Hurricane Isaac barreled into South Florida on August 27, forcing the RNC to cancel the first day of programming.[17] Romney would not give Trump another time slot or air the video, which Trump operatives said cost $100,000 to make. Trump flew home disappointed and stewing.[18]

Justin McConney: I watched them shoot the video. They brought in this guy that was a known Obama impersonator. It was a whole parody of *The Apprentice*. Trump fires him and he goes back out to the limo.

Sean Spicer, *White House communications director January–July 2017:* We had to cut short the convention in Tampa because of the weather. There was a hurricane that came through. We cut the programming and that decision was made right there. He was the collateral damage. He and Romney had discussed it. Romney had gone in search of his endorsement, Trump had given it to him, then wanted to speak at the convention.

Sam Nunberg: Romney fucks him on the convention. Romney doesn't campaign with him during the general. They couldn't find four fucking minutes to play the video.

Justin McConney: He started talking about more of a variety of topics, which is what I was aiming for to begin with. I had him talking about celebrities and musicians. That's why his social media took off. He had something to say about anything and everything, and he expanded his audience to a much younger base of people that might not have been as familiar with him. Later on that year he's tweeting about Robert Pattinson and Kristen Stewart. He talked about Anthony Weiner, but instead of having Trump do a tweet about this—because he wanted to tweet about it—I said, "What if you do a Vine?" He goes, "What's Vine?" I said, "It's like those videos we do at the desk, but it's only six seconds." He did it. He kept telling everyone, "Justin got me a Vine. It's amazing. He's really innovative. He has me ahead of the curve." The news coverage was, "Donald Trump signs up to join Vine to tell Anthony Weiner to stay off Vine."

Sam Nunberg: He continually got coverage. Obama even mentioned Trump in the first debate against Romney [on October 4].* Trump loved that. Obama did that because he thought the association with Trump was bad for Romney. They had a campaign ad showing Trump's plane. We were happy either way.

Justin McConney: When Obama mentioned him, the idea pops in my head that we should live-tweet the second debate because he's a part of this now. I pitched it to him and he said, "Alright, how exactly are we going to do this?" I said, "I guess we can do this on the phone." We had to call each other back and forth and I would put the tweets out.

He went along with the idea, but I don't think he imagined how much interest there would be in it. I called him a few times and said, "Mr. Trump, I need another comment from you." When you live-tweet something, you kind of got to be tweeting every three minutes. He thought it was very funny that we were getting all these tweets from people. "Where are you Trump? Where'd you go?" We gained a lot of followers in a single night. Then we live-tweeted the third debate by phone. He kept calling me more and more wanting to tweet all hours. He wanted to see more of the mentions to see what people were saying.

---

* Obama said, "Under Governor Romney's definition, there are a whole bunch of millionaires and billionaires who are small businesses. Donald Trump is a small business and I know Donald Trump doesn't like to think of himself as small anything."

On October 24, Trump made one last attempt to goad Obama by tweeting a video of himself offering $5 million to a charity of the president's choice if he coughed up his college and passport records.[19] Obama spokesman David Plouffe sarcastically referred all questions about the announcement to the Romney campaign.[20]

Justin McConney: I actively discouraged the version he shot. I tried to convince him to reshoot it. He wouldn't move past the horrible idea, which I didn't like to begin with, and told him it was terrible. I didn't like anything to do with the birth certificate. I don't know why he was still talking about it. I thought it was horrendous. I did not like the idea that it was at his desk because I didn't want it associated with the "From the Desk of Donald Trump" videos.

Sam Nunberg: We explained to him the issue, Trump saw it, and Trump made an offer to buy it. That's where he saw that commonsense, gonzo, hard-right American politics works. He makes an offer to buy it and gets himself in the news.

Lloyd Grove, *gossip reporter, New York* Daily News *and the Daily Beast:* He went on *Fox and Friends* and said he was going to make a major announcement at noon. He or his people, Michael Cohen, uploaded a video of him saying he would give five million dollars to the charity of Obama's choice if Obama would simply provide him with his birth certificate, his academic transcript, and travel records "to my satisfaction," then he would happily give this money. With my great ability to tap into the zeitgeist and predict events of the future, I said, "That's it, you're done. We're no longer interested in you, you're a loser." I wrote a piece about it and suggested the Daily Beast would no longer pay attention to him.

Justin McConney: The birther stuff was a topic I would frequently tell him to stop talking about. Trump would always say, "You're not a fan of this." I told him, "No, it's enough already. Stop bringing it up. It's stupid." I tried to get him to stay away from it as much as possible, but the thing with Trump and Twitter was you couldn't stop him. If I didn't want to put out a tweet with him he would call in someone else and have them put up the tweet. I could tell him as much as I wanted to stay away from that subject or others, but it wasn't going to change anything.

On November 6, 2012, Barack Obama beat Mitt Romney 51 to 47 percent and trounced him in the Electoral College, winning 332 votes to Romney's 226. In a flurry of midnight tweets, Trump lamented, "This election is a total sham and a travesty. We are not a democracy!" and warned, "Our country is now in serious and unprecedented trouble . . . like never before." He called the Electoral College a "disaster for democracy."

The next day Trump tweeted, "We have to make America great again." He told Newsmax that Romney was too "mean-spirited" and that "[Romney] had a crazy policy of self-deportation which was maniacal. It sounded as bad as it was, and he lost all of the Latino vote. He lost the Asian vote. He lost everybody who is inspired to come into this country."[21]

Sam Nunberg: I knew Romney was going to lose. Trump hedged. I told him Romney was going to lose. He said it'll be close. Romney loses. All he ran on was the issues instead of beating the shit out of Obama. Americans will vote for the guy or the girl who's more likable. Who has more charisma? The 9 out of 10 other fucking issues Romney won on. He lost on that one. He acted like a child in that last debate. Plus, Joe Biden destroyed Paul Ryan.

David Bossie: We were observing Romney's incredibly disastrous third debate where he had the thing won and he mailed it in and lost. We looked at how he was ineffectual on policy and how he lost a race he should have won. Observing that election defeat sparked an interest in Trump, which catapulted us into 2013 and 2014, when we started to move things along.

Steve Bannon: [Bob Mercer and his Republican donors] all go up to the Ritz-Carlton in Boston on the night of the victory. The defeat of Romney is a crushing blow to the establishment. They all put the money on the guy because that guy is them. He's better than Obama but it would have been terrible for the populist movement. We had to show they couldn't win without us. Donald Trump would have never been around if Romney had won. Romney was the last stand.

Sean Spicer: We went up to New York. The [Republican National Committee] chairman [Reince Priebus] was doing a series of donor meetings, and I was doing a series of meetings, and on the schedule it said he was going to meet with Donald Trump. I said, "Do you mind if I sit in on the meeting?"

Reince said sure, come along. I had seen him on television and I was intrigued by what he was like in person. I went up to his office, walked in, and Reince is giving his standard pitch of why we need to give to the RNC and what we're going to do with the money and how we're going to rebuild the party. Trump goes into an entire analysis of what Romney had done wrong, why the convention wasn't as successful as it could've been, and how he could've been used more to rally support for Romney.

Justin McConney: We had gone down to Doral [Resort & Spa in Miami] in November to film a video. I'm on the plane and Trump comes on and starts looking at the iPhone and asks, "What do you prefer, the iPhone or Android?" I said, "I prefer the iPhone." "You know, I'm thinking of upgrading but the screen is much bigger on Android," he said. "I'm going to go with the Android. The screen's bigger."

I went to sleep and all of a sudden I hear his voice. "Justin. Justin." I wake up. It's Trump. "Justin, great news. Melania just told me the WiFi's working on the plane. You can tweet for me." Soon after that I hear from people who were on the plane, "He got this Android now and he has Twitter on it, and he's been playing around with it in his office." I said, "There's no way he's teaching himself how to use Twitter." They said, "No, he's sitting there and he's using it."

Roger Stone: On New Year's Day 2013, I called Donald, as I have on every New Year's Day for 40 years, 39 years at that point, to wish him happy New Year. And we were just bullshitting, talking politics, and he said, "I'm definitely running in 2016." I said, "Run this time. Romney was a terrible candidate. The guy has no instinct for the jugular." He said, "Well, a lot can happen between now and 2016, but I'm really going to do it this time. In fact," he said, "I've trademarked my campaign slogan." And I said, "Really? What is it?" And he said, "Make America Great Again." Now, whether or not he knew that Reagan had used that as one of several slogans—Reagan's slogan in 1980 kept changing. Reagan had used it, but he had used "The Time Is Now" too.

Justin McConney: On [February 5, 2013], a tweet went out at night.* Unless he had called me there wouldn't be a reason for a tweet to go out

---

* It was at 8:53 p.m.: "Thanks @SherriEShepherd 4 your nice comments today on The View. U were terrific!"

at night. The next morning I check with Meredith [McIver] and a few other people who had the password, and they said, "We didn't put this out." I checked with Trump and he said, "Oh yeah. I did it." I was like, "Oh God." I felt like Dr. Grant in *Jurassic Park* when he learned the velociraptors can open doors. "This isn't going to be good."

The Republican National Committee put together a 97-page campaign autopsy in early 2013 called the Growth and Opportunity Project. It made scores of recommendations to expand the party beyond its conservative base by passing immigration reform, reaching out to gays and people of color, and looking to Republican governors in Democratic states for leadership.

Sean Spicer: The bottom line is any party wants to figure how to grow as opposed to shrink. One of the issues was the party wasn't going to neighborhoods where there was potential growth. You've got to bring conservative values and ideas to communities where we don't traditionally go. The recommendation of the Growth and Opportunity Project said we need to address immigration as an issue. A lot of immigration hardliners took that as saying there was no policy prescription at the time. It said, "This is a barrier to entry in this community." A lot of people tried to say the party was advocating a particular policy prescription. It was very clear that it was not.

Erick Erickson: The Republican National Committee put out its audit in 2013, and they're headed in the trajectory of, "All of you people who hate immigration reform, you're to blame." There was at the base level real lingering resentment of that. Trump is beginning to tap into that. He taps into the birther stuff with the birth certificate. The Breitbart guys and others started shaping his thinking on immigration, which really wasn't hard to do.

Steve Bannon: RNC does the autopsy. How did we lose? I see in RealClearPolitics a four-part series by a guy named Sean Trende, who's a lawyer in Richmond, that's the most sophisticated analysis of the data. He goes through how the working class didn't show up. That's the key difference.[22]

Glenn Beck, *political commentator, author, and founder of TheBlaze:* I was down in Florida, and he called me out of the blue and said, "Hey, I understand you're going to be playing at such and such theater, why don't you come down to Mar-a-Lago and stay the night?" I said, "Wow that's really gracious of you, thank you." My wife and I got there late, and there's this really creepy painting in a big old paneled room, very dark, gothic, this giant painting of him in white tennis shorts and a sweater tied around his neck and a tennis racket. And you're like, "Oh, dear God, man," and he looked like he was 20. I mean, who has that painted? Well, Donald Trump does. The next morning we're getting ready to leave, and one of the people came and said, "Donald would like to say hi," and I said, "Oh, is he here?" And they said, "Yes, just go to your suite." He called me on the phone and said, "You know, you have quite a following." And I said, "Uh-huh," and he said, "You could really help unite the Republicans and the right around a candidate." Not thinking that this guy's thinking about running for president, I said, "Well, I don't know, it would depend on who the candidate is." And he said, "It was great to have you here." He was like in the next room! I don't know why we were communicating like Howard Hughes.

Steve Bannon: The autopsy says, "Here's why we lost. We didn't hug the Hispanic vote. You're anti-amnesty. The millennial Hispanics didn't turn out. Yada, yada, yada."

I call up Jeff Sessions and his young charge from the Bachmann campaign, one Stephen Miller, and have them over to the Breitbart Embassy. It's a five-hour dinner and I'm there to convince Jeff Sessions to run for president of the United States. I tell him, "You're not going to win the Republican nomination, but we've got two issues: trade, which is number 100, and immigration, which is number three. We're going to make them number one and two following Sean Trende's model. We're going to take over the Republican Party, and you are going to be our instrument to do that."

Trade and illegal immigration, they're two sides of the same coin. It's suppression of labor. But the donors are all into suppressing labor. I said, "This is going to be a war. But now we've got to go to war because if we go down the Romney path, this thing's going to be smaller and smaller. They're going to win the House, the Senate, Supreme Court, the whole deal. The whole thing's over and everything we won in 2010 is going to be thrown away." Sessions says, "This is brilliant. We're going to do this. But I'm not the guy. But our guy will come along."

PART FOUR

THE RACE
BEFORE
THE RACE
2013—2014

A productive detour onto the gubernatorial
trail in New York.

22.

SITTING ON THE HOOD
OF A CAR

Trump was peeved at Romney and the Republican Party and more resolved than ever to run for president in the next cycle. He kept his political advisers employed and sought ways to stay in the national mix. But 2016 was still distant.

New York State Republicans had even more challenging problems than the national party. Democrat Andrew Cuomo had swamped Buffalo billionaire Carl Paladino, a Tea Party favorite, by a 40-point margin in the governor's race in 2010. After legalizing gay marriage and capping property taxes, Governor Cuomo's approval rating topped 70 percent in a 2012 Quinnipiac poll.[1]

But he infuriated Republicans after pushing gun-control measures, known as the SAFE Act, through the legislature in January without public hearings.[2] And he vexed progressives when he dithered over allowing natural gas drilling known as fracking in the state's Southern Tier.[3] Still, his approval numbers stood at 62 percent in November 2013,[4] and the campaign treasury was up to $28 million.[5]

It would take a monumental effort to match Cuomo's war chest. Republicans, primarily clustered on Long Island and spread across rural swaths of upstate and western New York, had difficulty competing in statewide races. Westchester County Executive Rob Astorino, a former radio producer who won reelection in November 2013, wanted to try, and was encouraged by the state's Republican Party chairman, Ed Cox, a descendant of prominent East Coast families, married to Richard Nixon's eldest daughter.

Two western New York lawmakers had other ideas. David DiPietro, a former mayor of East Aurora who owned a dry-cleaning business, and Bill Nojay, a conservative talk radio host who would commit suicide two months before the

2016 election,[6] *won assembly seats in 2012 and were plotting how to shift the state party rightward.*

In October 2013, DiPietro and Nojay brainstormed whom to draft for governor, but the list of conservatives who could bankroll their own campaigns was not a large one. By enticing Trump to seriously consider running, they wound up connecting him more closely to the kind of ground-level activists and disaffected voters who would prove crucial in his ultimate rise.

David DiPietro, *Erie County state assemblyman:* Bill Nojay had this radio show. I was the mayor in this little village. I was running for a state senate seat, and he put me on his show and we hit it off. He said, "You're great on the radio." We both ran for the State Assembly in 2012. I hadn't seen Bill in about two years, he was totally off my radar screen. I got elected to the assembly in January 2013. I go up to the state capitol into my conference and there's seven new members, and Bill's one of them. We looked at each other and said, "What are you doing here?" He said, "I got elected." I go, "So did I!"

In October 2013, Bill and I were at a SCOPE* banquet at Lucarelli's in Lackawanna on Abbott Road, around the corner from my house. Afterward, we were sitting on the hood of my 2003 Ford Explorer at 10 o'clock talking about who to get to run for governor. We started going through names and debating if they had a chance, and we came up with Donald Trump. Both our eyes lit up. We thought he would be a great candidate, self-funded, highest name recognition of anyone in the country, would make it a marquee race. We had to decide how to get in front of him. I called a friend of mine, Mike Caputo, right there from the hood of the car and told him what we were interested in. He said he would call Roger Stone.

Michael Caputo, *Republican consultant and former Carl Paladino campaign manager:* DiPietro said that he and Nojay were having conversations, and they were looking for a Republican candidate who could beat Andrew Cuomo. One of the parameters included being able to self-fund a campaign. It would have to be someone in the business world who could raise or spend enough and somebody from the downstate New York City area because of the importance of that area in the electoral

---

* The Shooters Committee on Political Education is a not-for-profit group dedicated to preserving Second Amendment rights.

landscape of New York. We triangulated Trump. I called Roger Stone and Sam Nunberg. Roger told me that there would be no interest because Trump is shooting to run for president.

Sam Nunberg, *Trump campaign adviser 2011–2015:* I don't think they took it seriously that he was going to run but they took him seriously because he was tweeting, he was on Fox News, and he was speaking out. He told me he was running that summer in 2013. He said, "Look, I think I'm going to run for president."

Roger Stone, *Trump adviser and political consultant:* He didn't have any interest in running for governor. I also thought the race would be, ironically, a more difficult one than the presidential race, but I agreed to help facilitate a meeting on the theory that these were friends he would need down the road if he ran for president. Frankly, the job was too small for him. He would hate living in Albany. This is the bluest of blue states. This is a state without a single conservative newspaper—I would argue the *New York Post* has a more populist editorial viewpoint. Andrew Cuomo is a very tough, very mean, extremely well-funded opponent.

Michael Caputo: Roger said, "He'll tell you no but if you want a meeting, we can do it." He said Trump was going to run for president and running for governor would ruin his ability to run for president.

Sam Nunberg: He would obviously win the Republican primary but it wasn't realistic he would win as governor of New York. It's a very unwinnable race for Republicans, and essentially he'd be a smarter, classier, more refined Carl Paladino, but he'd still be a Carl Paladino.

Carl Paladino, *Republican New York gubernatorial candidate 2010:* I'd met Roger Stone during my 2010 campaign. He knew me as a very honest, straight-up person who wasn't afraid of anything. When I first got together with him in New York, he made it a point to take his shirt off and show me his tattoo, which is a face of Richard Nixon on his back, and I said, "Fucking cool, man," and he said, "Cool? This is what it's all about, man. You go all out when there's a challenge."

On October 12, 2013, Bill Nojay composed a memo titled "2014 NY Governor Race Analysis" explaining that Trump would be an attractive candidate because he doesn't have to spend as much money to tell voters who he is and can pull voters regardless of party affiliation. "In many respects, Trump is not considered a Republican—he is his own brand, an almost iconic figure of Rockefellerian proportions," the memo said.[7] Nojay leaked it to the dean of the state capitol press corps, Fred Dicker.

Fred Dicker, New York Post *Albany bureau chief:* Nojay was a very smart guy, and he was close with Carl Paladino. Guys like Caputo or Stone had a financial interest in [a Trump campaign for governor], and Bill Nojay may have had a financial interest, but he also had a genuine belief, as did Carl Paladino. He laid out a scenario, which made some sense. It was certainly a possibility putting together disparate coalitions that would back Trump. There's a downstate Republican Party and an upstate Republican Party. Downstate is dominated by Long Island Republicans. They tend to be affluent, may be better educated, but they're New York City–oriented. They may be conservative on some social issues like abortion, but that's about it. When it comes to spending, they're no different than the Democrats, and they tend to favor restrictions, say on natural gas fracking, as the Democrats do. Whereas upstaters, much poorer, are focused on trying to get jobs. It's almost a sine qua non that you're a strong Second Amendment supporter in upstate, where gun clubs, recreational shooting, hunting, and self-protection are very important. It's a fundamental divide. Trump is not a Manhattan Republican. In his policies, he's much more like an upstate Republican than a New York City Republican.

The article got Trump's attention. He called Dicker and said he was "very flattered" that Republicans wanted him, but it was "not something that I've ever even thought about." Then, a few hours later, Trump called Dicker back and argued, "Taxes are way too high, and people are fleeing New York," and "We should become the energy capital of the East." And he called Cuomo's father, former governor Mario Cuomo, "one of the worst governors in the history of the state . . . otherwise, I like [Andrew Cuomo] very much."[8]

Three days later, Trump tweeted mixed messages. "Thanks for all of the great support but I just don't see myself wanting to run for Governor of New York-I have something else in mind!" and "By the way, New York State MUST LOWER TAXES (and fast) and must start going after all of the 'energy' that lies just below our feet (now)!" He was referring to fracking.

The Cuomo campaign responded with a shrug, but the publication of the memo led to a sit-down. On November 13, 2013, DiPietro, Nojay, and Caputo flew from Buffalo to meet with Trump and his political team, including his lawyer Michael Cohen. Cohen, who lost a city council race in 2003 to Upper East Side Eva Moskowitz, had his own political ambitions.[9]

David Bossie, *Citizens United founder and political consultant:* In November 2013, I called him up and said, "Mr. Trump, I'm going to do some big events in the first three states. I'm going to put together an event in New Hampshire for early next year, would you come?" And he immediately said yes, which made me think, "Hmm, he's getting more serious."

Matt Wing, *Cuomo campaign aide:* My take was always pretty much the same. There's no way he's running. He's been the guy who cried "I'll run for office" over and over, and he's never actually done it. Donald Trump is notorious for not writing checks. We certainly didn't take seriously any concept that he would actually self-fund in any seriously competitive way. We had $30 million at that point. Donald Trump, at the most, would maybe put a million dollars in. It's all a sham. It's all a show. When you make a big deal about the fact that you live in an apartment with a gold-plated toilet that means that, actually, you're full of shit.

Sam Nunberg: We accepted the premise of the meeting. Trump would be happy people are talking about recruiting him for governor, which would then show he's a solid candidate with the potential to run for president. I had [Manhattan Republican chairman] Dan Isaacs come.

Dan Isaacs, *Manhattan Republican Party chairman 2011–2014:* Rob Astorino had been an old friend of mine from my Young Republican days. Bill Nojay said, "We're trying to convince Trump to run for governor, and would you join us?" I said, "Absolutely."

David DiPietro: I'll never forget in the cab all the way from JFK, which is about a half-hour ride to Trump Tower. Me, Mike [Caputo], and Bill [Nojay] are in the backseat, and we're talking about why Trump was going to win. He connects with the average voter. They don't know him as a political politician. They know him as a multibillionaire, from his casinos, and his USFL football team the New Jersey Generals. They know Donald Trump from everything but politics. When we get out of the car, the cab driver, who is Ukrainian, gets out and says, "I'd vote for him!" I looked at Bill and said, "That's exactly what I'm talking about. The average voter likes this guy. That's why he's going to win the governor's race."

Sam Nunberg: Right before the meeting happened, we talked. Trump didn't seem that enthusiastic about it. I explained to him who's going to be in this meeting. He said, "Okay, fine, I'll go." Before he entered, Trump was thinking about it more. He started talking about the fiscal state of the state, Cuomo, and other Republicans who ran in the past like Mayor John Lindsay. He said it would be great if the state had a Republican governor.

Michael Caputo: I had been in Trump Tower before, but Dave and Nojay had not. In Buffalo we don't have atriums seven stories high lined with Italian marble. We went up to a secured floor, got off, and we were met at the door by [Trump bodyguard] Keith Schiller, who signed us in with another security guy. They escorted us into a big conference room.

David DiPietro: They took us into the boardroom and they had a little luncheon set up for us. We were there about five minutes, and Trump came in with a couple of his people. We sat down and he said, "What do you got?"

Michael Caputo: I led the meeting, but then Trump put it into Q&A pretty quickly. We were warned by Stone that it was going to be a short meeting, that he was going to say no, and that he was going to ask a lot of questions. So we tried to give him encouraging answers, and it kept going on and on and on.

David DiPietro: Trump was taking notes and asking all sorts of questions about our analysis. Why are we going to win? What's the strategy? How do you plan on getting the vote out? We wanted a campaign that wasn't media heavy but was grassroots at the county level, and he seemed to like that. He asked, "How much will that cost?" We said, "About $5 million." He said, "No problem." He asked where we were going to put that money, and we went county by county, setting up the chairs and how to get the people registered. Our goal was to register 250,000 new voters. We would get the gun-owner list and go door-to-door.

Michael Caputo: Trump asked how this would hurt or help his run for the presidency and how much it would cost. He asked the actual chances of him winning. And he asked us about the State Republican Party chairman [Ed Cox], who he said he had a relationship with and if we thought he would be supportive. We knew that the state chairman was being very supportive of Westchester County Executive Rob Astorino, so we told him he would not likely be supportive, that Astorino was his man, and that he doesn't react well when he's challenged with his picks.

David DiPietro: He just said, "I'll take care of Rob. I know him personally. I've supported Rob in the past. Rob's come and visited me many times. I know him." A couple of times during the meeting he would say, "Clear my schedule for now, clear my schedule," when someone came in to get him.

Michael Caputo: Sam started being interested in it as well even though he was on the presidential beat. And Cohen got interested in it.

Sam Nunberg: I'm thinking this was all bullshit that he could win. He would not have got one fucking vote in New York City. He would've got 20 percent, 15 percent at the most, and Cuomo would've spent a lot of money. But all these people started telling him he could win. Flattery always works with him.

Michael Caputo: It was very clearly interesting to him. Nojay talked about how the governorship was a stairway to the presidency for so many men. That if you're governor of New York, there's nothing out of your reach politically. It was a contrast between going from businessman to president and from businessman to governor to president.

David DiPietro: He had been looking at politics but he had never cut his teeth on it. It's one thing for someone who's a doctor to say, "I'm going to run for politics." It's another thing to get out there and learn what it takes. "You flirted with the presidency," we told him. "You're the one guy that could buck history. No one's ever been president of the United States as an ordinary citizen." He said, "Really, is that true?"

Dan Isaacs: He'd be the presumptive front-runner for the GOP presidential nomination.

David DiPietro: After three and a half hours he goes, "Boys, I thought this was going to be a three-minute meeting and I was going to tell you thanks a lot but not interested. Let's set up another meeting. I'm interested."

Michael Caputo: The fact that he invited us back again was very exciting to all of us. He went from "I'm just not interested" to saying, "Okay, I'm open-minded."

Sam Nunberg: Meeting's over. We say goodbye to everyone, go upstairs, and he says, "So guys, what do you think?" He was excited about it and I said, "I think it's a mistake, I don't think you should do it, I don't think it's realistic." Michael [Cohen] is very excited about it. Michael says, "You should do it." Michael was thinking he was going to use this as a platform to try to run for mayor. Michael thought it was realistic that Trump could win. I said, "Cuomo's a very strong candidate in the state. That's the first issue. The second issue is it's a very hard race for a Republican to win, and you're very conservative." I told Roger what was going on. Roger said, "This is a big mistake."

David Bossie: He had people around him who were giving him bad advice, like Michael Cohen, who were telling him to think about running for governor of New York. And I thought, "That's the dumbest thing I've ever heard." You'd have to spend as much time and money and possibly work harder than running for president, with a greater chance to be president as opposed to getting elected governor of New York.

Sam Nunberg: Cohen has delusions of grandeur. He even mentioned trying to be Trump's lieutenant governor. He met with Ed Cox sometime early 2014 and mentioned he was interested in running for mayor.

Hank Sheinkopf, *New York political consultant:* When I first met [Cohen], he wanted to run for city council. And then he wanted to run for state senate. And then in 2013 he wanted to run for mayor. I said, "Everybody who wants to run has got to have something to say. What are you going to say?" He said, "Well, Mr. Trump's going to win the presidency and I'm going to be in position—" I said, "That's okay. That means you might be able to get the money. But what are you going to say? What's the message here?" I said, "You have to bring a check next time for one million dollars and we can talk." He talked about other people that would be happy to work with him. I said, "Okay, me too. But come back with a check." He ain't been back with a check.

Roger Stone: Nojay said he had a revelation from Christ that if Trump ran, he would win governor. Generally speaking I prefer polling data to revelations. But it's very hard to tell Donald Trump he can't win something. He's a winner by nature, and he doesn't necessarily believe you.

Ed Cox: Roger Stone gave me a call early in the process. I always thought he was a political genius. He often sees things other people don't see. He had called me and said, "Donald should run directly for the presidency." Now clearly the way it was going is Trump thought he needed to have a stepping-stone to the presidency so he had to run for governor.

Trump asked Bossie for a poll about his prospects in a gubernatorial race. Trump's interest perplexed Bossie, but he hired Kellyanne Conway, a pollster who advised Newt Gingrich on his 2012 campaign.[10] Although the raw results of the December 2013 poll showed that Cuomo would beat Trump by 35 points, Conway's summary spun it differently:

> NY loves its celebrity politicians and families: the Kennedys, Moynihans, Buckleys, Clintons, and even the Cuomos. Donald Trump fits that (loose) bill, and he has the money and moxie to compete.... When offered a choice between offices, New Yorkers are more than twice as likely to urge Trump to run for Governor of New York (27%) than President of the United States (12%). A plurality a third option: run for neither.[11]

David Bossie: Kellyanne and her husband had owned an apartment in one of his buildings, but Kellyanne was my pollster, so when Trump was asking for recommendations I said yes, she should be somebody that he brings in to help him. I commissioned that. We did a two-night poll. One of the questions in the first night we asked [if he should run for governor]. And Trump asked me to change the question to whether he should run for governor or president for the second night.

Roger Stone: Trump was well aware of my opinion. He would say, "I can beat Cuomo. He'd be easy to beat. Everybody I know hates him. He's done nothing as governor." Donald seemed to believe that he would easily defeat Cuomo. David Bossie financed a poll and the poll did not show that, but I did think the poll results, at least in the executive summary, were somewhat manipulated to highlight a more favorable number and hide the more problematic numbers. He knew both [Bossie and Conway] at the time, and they both wanted him to run for governor. The problem of course was twofold: Trump always had this issue of people not believing he was really running for anything. Another professed interest in running for governor would only exacerbate that if he didn't really run. If he ran for governor and lost, it would preclude a run for president a few years later. It never made any sense to me.

23.

SELLING TRUMP
TO TRUMP

Bill Nojay, David DiPietro, and Michael Caputo wanted to make the case that the State Republican Party needed Trump, that it was possible to defeat a Democratic incumbent, and that the governorship would vault him over a slew of Republican rivals into the White House. These state party activists were taking seriously what most in the national party never had, that Trump could be a formidable candidate for executive office. They didn't need to be sold on Trump. They were the ones selling a candidacy to him.

Although Trump showed continued interest by staying in touch with them, there was still work to do to convince him to take the plunge. They returned to Trump Tower on December 4, 2013. This time they brought several conservatives in their early 30s, including Staten Island assemblyman Joe Borelli, who would become one of Trump's most enthusiastic supporters, radio host Frank Morano, and Assemblywoman Nicole Malliotakis, a Staten Island conservative. Trump would show again his willingness to work the telephone, an especially powerful technique when the call comes directly from a famous person.

Michael Caputo, *Republican consultant and former Carl Paladino campaign manager:* Trump started calling me on a regular basis. He would call me two and three times in a day, four or five times a week. They were always very brief conversations. "I was just thinking this. I was just talking about that. What do you think of this guy? I had just had a meeting, they say this, what do you think about that?"

David DiPietro, *Erie and Wyoming Counties Republican state assemblyman:* One thing we told him was, "Mr. Trump, if you're serious you've got a lot of phone calls to make. You've got to call these people because they don't want to get a press secretary. They want you to call them. If you're the governor, you've got to be hands-on." He said, "I understand that. I can do that." We gave him a list and said call these people. He didn't wait a week. He was on the phone that night and the next day. I'm getting calls from [GOP county] chairs. They were flabbergasted. They were dumbfounded. "Donald Trump called me. I'm going to go to New York." He was on the phone, and he was masterful at it.

Joe Borelli, *Staten Island Republican assemblyman:* Bill Nojay and Dave DiPietro called me aside in Albany, and we had this conversation about who we could invite. Bill had connections to a lot of the upstate elected officials, and he lacked people downstate. He was coming to understand how very few Republicans there are in New York City. Nojay said Trump had a real chance, and I said I thought he did too, especially if he's willing to spend the money that he has. The worst-case scenario is we get to take a picture with someone who's an extremely interesting person to meet and hopefully he'll sign his book.

Frank Morano, *talk radio host AM 970 and state Reform Party spokesman:* I spoke to Trump many times as a radio producer, booking him over the years. I met him in 1999 when I was first getting involved in the state Independence Party and Trump became a member of the Independence Party with an eye towards running as the Reform Party candidate for president. When I was seven years old, I got his autograph at a show and talked with him for a few minutes. He was dating Marla Maples, and she was in *Will Rogers Follies* on Broadway. A number of the people urging him to run for governor, including Joe Borelli and Michael Caputo, were very close friends and political associates of mine. I told Sam Nunberg that I'd like to attend this meeting, and he said that "we'd love to have you." Sam had asked me if there were any other people who should be there. I invited Assemblywoman Nicole Malliotakis. She had applied to be on *The Apprentice*. She was a great admirer of Donald Trump, and I knew Nicole would get a kick out of meeting him. In retrospect, I probably shouldn't have invited her when her colleagues didn't.

Joe Borelli: Tourists were looking in the atrium and taking pictures. Keith Schiller met us downstairs and took the elevator upstairs with us. We were seated in a boardroom. There was a big granite table. It's a glass wall on two sides. One side is the entrance to the rest of the office suite, and then the back wall is a bookcase with various plaques and awards and pictures. There were crudités for the taking and some Donald Trump water bottles from his water line.

Frank Morano: Then into the meeting room walks Donald Trump, Michael Cohen, and Sam Nunberg. We met for about three hours. It was supposed to go for 20 minutes. People would pop in and out. Ivanka would walk by, he would have her come in, and he'd say, "These are all the leading Republicans in New York State. They want me to run for governor. They say that I'm the only one that can win." People would give their feedback and they'd leave.

Joe Borelli: He certainly has command of the room. He's a large-statured man, so he's physically a larger presence than most people in the room. With his trademark hair, it kind of only increases the optical presence of his dimensions. I asked, "How do we convince the party that you're in this for real when you're talking about doing other things?" He would look at me when answering questions, but then he would also look at everyone around the table. He would go around the table with his eyes.

Frank Morano: He was very interested in the fracking issue. He was very interested in talking about Staten Island. Very interested in tolls.

Joe Borelli: He was talking about the Tysens Park Apartments, which are a block of housing apartments on Staten Island. His father would stop the car. He'd have to carry a bag of coins. He said, "I spent my summers off from school traveling around with my dad emptying the laundromat coins from buildings."

Frank Morano: He was sitting to my left. Nicole Malliotakis was sitting to my right, and Trump fell, not sexually or anything, but intellectually and personality-wise in love with Nicole. It got to the point where even though I was sitting next to Trump, he didn't even see me. He only saw me as a barrier to what Nicole was saying. If I said something and Nicole repeated what I said, he would not hear that I said it and fall over himself to agree with whatever Nicole was saying. I said, "Mr. Trump, she applied to be on *The Apprentice.*" And Nicole said, "Yeah, that's right and you didn't pick me." Trump says, "That was a big mistake. I really should have."

Joe Borelli: He talked about how amending the way government contracts are awarded and rolling back regulations would be beneficial. He told us that he himself wasn't a hunter or a shooter. He made it known that he was a golfer, but he said his sons were big into hunting, shooting, and traveled the world, and his sons were spurring political conversations around the dinner table about New York's gun laws over the past year.

Sam Nunberg: I had always thought that Don was going to be the biggest asset. Don being a sportsman, Don being a real NRA-type guy, that was good. It wasn't like Trump was going to go shoot guns. Don Jr. had hunted with the governor of Iowa, who is now the Chinese ambassador.

Frank Morano: Then Eric Trump popped in. Nicole made a reference to how handsome he is and how he's single and she's single and how she'd like to date Eric Trump. This was before he was married. If you thought he loved Nicole before, he's ready to put her on Mount Olympus after she flirts through him with Eric Trump.

Nicole Malliotakis, *Brooklyn and Staten Island assemblywoman:* He was very funny and made good small talk conversation. He was very charming in terms of personality, and you would expect that from someone with his celebrity status and success. He did seem to genuinely care about the state and our nation. He was very professional, very business-like. Very different than what you saw on TV during the campaign when he finally decided to run for president.

Michael Caputo: When he said, "Does everybody think I should run?," everybody in the room, including Nicole, said yes. And when he said, "Do you think I shouldn't run?," nobody said no.

Nicole Malliotakis: The issue of president did come up. He was more interested in running for governor in order to become president, as opposed to actually being governor. As if governor was not a large enough role for someone of his celebrity status and name brand.

Frank Morano: He asked everybody's opinion about a bunch of different figures in New York politics and in the media. Someone's name came up, let's say it was Fred Dicker. People went around the room and said, "I'm not crazy about him." Nicole says, "I actually like him." And After Nicole says that, Trump says, "Isn't that funny, so do I. Isn't that funny that you and I are on the same page again." Nicole was making the most elementary observations you can imagine. "Oh, the sky is blue." Trump would stop the room to get everybody to take note of what a profound statement Nicole had just made. After one of these moments of agreement with the two of them on everything, he says to Nicole, "I really may need you to run my campaign." The only one happier than her is me, because I brought her to this meeting.

Nicole Malliotakis: Trump was definitely receptive to my ideas.

Frank Morano: He got books for all of us and signed them and he took a picture with everybody. For Nicole, two pictures. One with her and Joe Borelli, one with just her. I took both of these pictures, and so he says to me, "Wait a minute, let me see that. Let me make sure it's okay." He didn't do this for anybody else. He looks at the phone and says, "I think that looks alright." Shows it to her. "Do you think that looks okay?" She says, "Yeah, I think it looks okay." He says to her, "Would you do me a favor? Would you tweet this please? This picture of the two of us?" Nicole says, "Sure, I'll tweet it."[1]

Joe Borelli: The conversation ended by him saying, "I heard you guys out and I will consider running. I don't want to get in a situation where there's a primary. I think I could beat Andrew Cuomo, and I want to focus all my attention on Andrew Cuomo if I decide to run."

Frank Morano: Sam told me when they met privately afterward, Ivanka told Trump in front of Sam, "Oh, this would be so great, Daddy. At least you wouldn't have to leave New York." At that point nobody was angry. The subsequent meeting was a different story.

The Trump boosters would soon encounter another challenge. Rob Astorino[2] was readying his bid for statewide office after he won reelection in November 2013, and he eyed a December campaign announcement. Cox viewed Astorino as a charismatic rising star who appealed to suburban voters in Westchester and on Long Island and could compete with Cuomo in the city.

Cox was careful not to pick sides publicly. He respected Trump and knew him socially but never thought he would actually run for state office. When news of the December meeting leaked, Cox told Gannett newspapers that Trump was a "very astute observer of politics" who is "very effective in public relations."[3] Cox also called Astorino a "very special political leader" in an interview with The Capitol Pressroom *and waved off Nojay and DiPietro as "just some people who want to talk to Donald Trump."[4]*

The state party's executive director, Michael Lawler, and its skeptical spokesman, David Laska, kept Cox abreast of the Draft Trump movement.

Michael Lawler, *New York Republican State Committee executive director 2011–2014 and Astorino campaign manager:* Bill Nojay had reached out to Ed pretty quickly that they wanted to do a Draft Trump movement. It was a friendly conversation but it was a respectful disagreement about who would be best positioned. Those who were most enthusiastic about Trump were enthusiastic because of name ID—who didn't know who Donald Trump was? And the financial resources he said he would put in. It was $10 million that he would put in a bank account and maybe spend up to $50 million on the campaign for governor.

Michael Caputo: It was very exciting because Republicans would finally have a governor candidate who could win. I was campaign manager for the previous Republican governor candidate [Carl Paladino], and I saw the shortcomings. It was money and name identification.

David Laska, *State Republican Party spokesman:* I did read Nojay's memo. We treated it as a subject of derision because Donald Trump has been making head fakes toward running for office for 25 years. The thought he would ever seriously consider running never even entered our minds. From the beginning it was pretty clear that Rob Astorino would be the candidate. There was a lot of support for him among the county chairs. He had won a big victory in Westchester County in 2013, and he was seen as someone who could be a future leader of the party. Ed had a number of goals when he became state party chair, and first and foremost was taking back a statewide office. He has been very successful as a party chairman helping grow our congressional delegation from a low of two after the 2008 cycle to nine [in 2018].

Michael Caputo: Our biggest concern was that the state party leadership, especially Ed Cox, was completely unsupportive of Trump and would be sandbagging him every step of the way.

Michael Lawler: Michael [Caputo] felt that in 2014 you needed somebody who was a disrupter, an outsider in the truest sense. He, along with Bill Nojay and Dave DiPietro, sincerely believed that Trump was the best candidate to run.

On December 16, 2013, Trump spoke with Conservative Party chairman Michael Long to discuss running on his ballot line—a signal to the party's Republican establishment that Trump was serious about the race. New York State has several smaller political parties, such as the Reform, Working Families, and Conservative parties, which have earned space on the ballot because of their robust membership. That gives them tremendous power because they can run candidates to the major party's right or left, influencing the outcome of the election. Even if they list the same candidate as on a major party's ballot line, it puts a candidate's name in front of voters twice, attracting extra votes.

Michael Long, *Conservative Party chairman:* I spoke with Michael Cohen for about 15 minutes, and he said, "Mr. Trump couldn't be here, but he wanted to talk with you. Could I get him on the phone?" I said sure. Mr. Trump and I had a lengthy conversation about the potential of the governor's race. He felt very strongly the state was moving in the wrong direction. Taxes were too high, it was unfriendly for business, no real job growth, and upstate was suffering and dying. He said he was seriously considering the possibility of running for governor and asked would I be open to discussing it if he decided to run. I indicated I would be. He did say, if he was going to run, he didn't want to have a primary and the deck had to be cleared. I said to him and Mr. Cohen, if he were to announce for governor, he would most likely clear the deck himself, but I couldn't guarantee nor was in a position to guarantee to get Rob Astorino out. And Ed Cox wasn't in a position to get Astorino out. The only person who could get Astorino out is Mr. Trump himself if he made a decision to run. He said he needed until January 31 when he'd have an answer.

24.

LIKE A HURRICANE

As he'd done in his previous political explorations, Trump was using various methods to test the viability of a run for governor. This time around, he had Twitter as a tool, along with phone calls to reporters, political aides close at hand, public taunts, and the imposing force of his fame, money, and personality—and the glitz of Trump Tower itself.

Bill Nojay composed another memo for Trump in December titled "Springboards to the Presidency," which showed the historical path of the prior 43 presidents to Washington. "The most common path to the presidency is through a governor's office (19 out of 43) and the most common governor's office to hold is New York," the memo said.[1]

Trump had donated to Rob Astorino's 2013 reelection campaign. Now he, along with state Republican chair Ed Cox and Democratic governor Andrew Cuomo, needed to be sized up. On December 19, 2013, Trump tweeted, "I like Rob Astorino. He's a friend and really good guy. Sadly, he has ZERO chance of beating Cuomo and the 2 to 1 Dems for governor!" Then Trump added forebodingly, "New York Republican leader @EdwardFCox is pushing my friend @RobAstorino into political suicide. Results won't be pleasant!"

Trump told the New York Post's Andrea Peyser on December 23 that Cuomo was "being controlled by Robert F. Kennedy Jr." on fracking and environmental policy decisions.[2] He told Albany's WGDJ-AM the same day, "I think I'd win if I decide to do it because I don't have to raise money. I'd use my own money."[3]

Cox found himself defending Astorino in his end-of-year tours to newspaper editorial boards while trying to placate Trump. Trump had a "smart political mind,"

Cox told the New York Post.[4] *But then Cox seemed to dismiss Trump in a December 24* New York Times *profile of Astorino. Cox told the paper that Astorino "understands the huge positive impact that a fiscal conservative, pro-growth Republican can have on New York State." In the piece, Astorino said publicly for the first time he was "considering" a candidacy. That article did not mention Trump.[5]*

Having landed some blows on state Republicans who had not anticipated the attacks, Trump was ready to suggest a path to peace. What if they teamed up and Astorino agreed to run as Trump's lieutenant governor? Trump's advisers scheduled a meeting at Trump Tower on January 9, 2014, with Astorino and his aide Jessica Proud.

In case that approach didn't work, a second front was opened. David DiPietro, Michael Caputo, and Bill Nojay were pressing state Republican officials to attend another gathering with Trump.

David Laska: We, the state party, were working very hard on being the statewide campaign before Rob announced, staffed up, and had an infrastructure in place. We rolled out an economic platform called the Jobs Agenda, which essentially became Rob's economic platform. Rob was the presumptive nominee. All of a sudden in comes Donald Trump sucking up all the air. Every question I'm getting from a reporter for 10 weeks is about Donald Trump. I didn't want to answer questions about Donald Trump. I wanted to talk about Rob Astorino and Andrew Cuomo. That was a really big thorn in our side because it was so obvious he wasn't going to run for office. The folks who were trying to get him in, chiefly Caputo and Nojay, were very good. Not that it takes a lot of political ability to be good at getting Donald Trump free media. He probably deserves the credit for that himself.

Jessica Proud, *aide to Westchester County Executive Rob Astorino:* I started working with Rob in 2009, when he was first elected county executive. He began seriously thinking about running for governor in 2014 because he won reelection in 2013 by 13 points in a heavily Democratic county. Rob had a relationship with Trump because he has a golf course in Westchester, so Trump had donated to Rob's campaign. Some Republicans were skeptical of Rob as a downstate county executive. Trump had that common touch with a lot of people even though he's known for everything being gilded and fancy and gaudy. People that lived more simple lives never held that against him.

Carl Paladino: Westchester is nothing but the bedroom community of Manhattan, and Astorino talks and looks and chirps like a New Yorker. Didn't have the twang in his accent, but all he thought about was New York City. He couldn't relate to where the real Republicans were, in upstate New York. Ed Cox knew that Trump, given his name recognition, would kick the shit out of Astorino in a primary.

Jessica Proud: So the three of us met in Trump Tower. Trump was very nice and very charming. He was talking a lot about the photos on his wall and the business projects he was involved in. He had just done another golf course. He was talking about Serena or Venus Williams, who had just appeared at one of his courses for the opening. He was really pleased with that. He thought they were just amazing tennis players. He had Tom Brady's helmet, and he wanted to show us that. "He's a good friend of mine, an amazing football player."

He talked about Mayor Bill de Blasio. "I can't believe he got elected. How does this guy get in? He's a bumbling idiot. I can't believe after Bloomberg and Rudy that we would get someone like de Blasio as mayor." He was critical of Cuomo. "He's not as gifted as a politician as his father." Then he said, "Everyone's asking me to run, and if I run I'm going to win. I can just drop in on my helicopter, and what are you going to do?"

Sam Nunberg: I knew that the New York State Republican Party was going to want Astorino to be the nominee, but it didn't matter. Trump had high name recognition. We wouldn't have agreed to a debate. We would've knocked Astorino for not having any real private sector experience and his record of accomplishments, and it would've been very simple and easy.

Jessica Proud: It didn't feel tense at all. It felt a little surreal because it was intimate, very laid-back. He clearly had a high opinion of what he thought his electoral chances were. He said, "I could write a check for however many millions of dollars." He had an arrogant opinion about the political process, and he wanted a clear shot to the nomination. He was adamant that he did not want a primary. He felt it would be giving an advantage to Cuomo. He would have to spend time and money, and he didn't want the fight. He said he was doing us all a favor if he chose to run. Then Trump told Rob to run as his lieutenant governor and that he would be gone the following year running for president. "You can be the governor. Just come on my ticket. I'll bring the money."

David Laska: I don't know that anyone ever really thought of that offer as a serious possibility because we never really seriously thought Donald Trump would run for office. We had 30 years of evidence telling us he was never going to run. No one on the state party apparatus ever really seriously considered it a possibility. We saw this as posturing ahead of the next season of *Celebrity Apprentice*. You want to do that? Fine. But you're shitting in our backyard and getting in the way of our ability to run a good campaign.

David DiPietro: Rob had no money, no name recognition outside of Westchester, so we figured he would be glad to jump on with Mr. Trump because in two years Rob would, by default, take over the governorship if Mr. Trump ran and won for president. But Rob thought, "If I beat Donald Trump in the primary, I'm a giant killer. I'll be known around the country." That was his ego talking. He had this delusion of grandeur.

Jessica Proud: We said, "No. Thank you, but no." I don't remember Trump being upset. I don't know if Rob was even that emphatic about it. Rob's a gracious guy but made it clear that lieutenant governor was probably something he wasn't interested in. Rob's attitude was a lot of people were encouraging him to run, and he wanted to give it a serious look. He was getting closer to making the decision that he was in, and he felt, not in a negative way, but if Trump really wanted to do this, let's have a primary and whoever's the nominee is the nominee. We'll compete for it.[6]

If he was going to run, Trump wanted to avoid a primary. Since Astorino wouldn't bow out directly, Trump continued to pursue a parallel path, trying to sway a majority of the over 450 Republican county and district leaders across the state to support him. If enough of them favored Trump, Astorino might back out of the race. Or Cox might sense the erosion under him and switch his allegiance to Trump. If more than 75 percent of the GOP committee chose Trump at a state convention, they could force Astorino off the ballot.

It would be unflashy work, but Trump was showing a willingness to do it. DiPietro concentrated on selling Erie County Republican Committee chairman

Nick Langworthy, who represented the largest Republican county in the state. Caputo, meanwhile, asked Republican chairs to hold off on any endorsements.[7]

Michael Caputo: We were getting reports from county chairs who were interested in the movement. Ed Cox was calling around and telling chairmen to forget about it, Trump would never run. He'd take you to the altar and leave you there. That he wouldn't spend the money.

David DiPietro: I called Nick Langworthy on a Friday and said, "We're going to go down and see Mr. Trump next week." He said, "No, I'm not interested, Dave. Movie star type of guy. Not in my wheelhouse." "Come on, Nick," I said. "Have lunch with the guy." Nope. Called him up on Saturday. "Nick, let's have lunch with Trump." "No, I am not interested, Dave," he said. "I have no desire to see him." Same thing Monday, I call him up. "No, Dave, I'm not interested." I kept bugging him. "Nick, fly down to New York City and meet Trump." On Tuesday night I called him again.

Michael Caputo: It was very important that Nick Langworthy became supportive of Trump. We knew Staten Island would come along because it was conservative. We knew Long Island would play footsie all the way to the end. They always do. The most important chairman outside of those two was Nick. Me calling a county chairman and telling him "Support Donald Trump" is not nearly as effective as one of the top four county chairmen calling and saying "Support Donald Trump. I am."

Nick Langworthy, *Erie County Republican Committee chairman:* I was in the eye-rolling stage. I figured this was a publicity stunt at best. Eventually it came down to, the election's over this year, what have you got to lose? It's a quick trip. I book a flight and come down. I'm going to have an opportunity to tell my kids I had a meeting with Donald Trump, one of the most famous men in the world.

With Nick Langworthy aboard, four dozen Republican power brokers also showed up at Trump Tower on January 10, 2014, the day after Trump tried to woo Astorino. Melania, Ivanka, and Eric flanked Trump around the conference table, as did Jeffrey Lord, a political commentator who had worked as an associate political director in the Reagan administration. Kellyanne Conway gave a

*presentation about her poll. Neither State Republican Party chairman Ed Cox
nor his top staffer Michael Lawler was invited, but Cox's people texted county
chairmen throughout the meeting to find out what Trump was saying.*

David DiPietro: We flew down to New York. Mr. Trump had me sitting
right next to him, as I did at the first meeting because I was his main
guy. I let Nick sit there. I said, "This is my chairman, Nick Langworthy."

Nick Langworthy: It was a very opulent building. It's gorgeous. It's a
testament to his ideal. He has a vision to make things bigger and better
than other people do. I was right next to the family members. He was at
the head of the table. You saw someone who was genuinely listening to
people. You come in with an expectation of here's the character you see
on *The Apprentice*. This tough businessperson, the way he's portrayed in
the media, but he really listened. When I got there and I looked him in
the eye and I had a conversation with him, I saw him interacting with
people like this could happen.

Joe Borelli: It was exciting because we had a big coalition of people
around the state who wanted to see a Trump gubernatorial candidacy.

Frank Morano: Kellyanne Conway was there. Jeffrey Lord was there. A
sheriff from Putnam was there. John Antoniello, the former Staten Island county chairperson. A lot of county chairs. O'Brien Murray, who is
a Republican political consultant. The rule became if you were an
elected official or a county chairman, you could sit at the table. Everyone else had to stand somewhere in the background.

David DiPietro: When everybody was there, his staff had a couple of
boxes of books. He autographed them for everybody and took pictures
with them so it was fluff to begin with. He learns people's names very
quickly and he remembers what you said. The food was deli sandwiches
with all the fixings, chips, juice, pop, water, pickles, relish-type trays. He
said, "Good thing I'm not buying dinner for everybody."

Frank Morano: He said, "My wife is my best pollster, she's almost as
good as Kellyanne. My wife always says that a lot of people don't think
I'm really going to run for anything, and the minute I actually announce
I'm going to run, whether it be for president or governor, my poll numbers

will go up significantly because people will realize that I'm serious and that it's not a publicity stunt."

Sam Nunberg: It was really stupid. It was really a waste of time. It got us off track for running for president. I was trying to build up a consensus and make him into a serious candidate. This flirtation was going to delegitimize him.

Frank Morano: Everybody wanted Nicole Malliotakis at this meeting, but Mayor de Blasio was in her district for something Hurricane Sandy–related. She had to hang out with the mayor. She said to me, "Please call me as soon as it ends. Let me know how it goes. Tell him I said, 'Hello.'" All of the Trump people are asking, "Is Nicole going to come? He really likes Nicole." "Oh, Nicole said to say hi." One assembly member said, "Nicole apologized for not being here." And Mr. Trump says, "Okay, tell her I said hello too."

David DiPietro: Someone was talking about the race. Under my breath I looked at him and said, "You're going to win in a landslide." All of a sudden he stops and goes, "Let me interrupt you. Dave's got something to say." I'm like, what? He says, "Dave here thinks I'm going to win in a landslide. Dave, why do you think that? He's telling me the chance I have. I want everybody to know what you're thinking." I told the story about the cabdriver and the low-information voter. "That's the type of detail I want to hear," he said. He did not want to hear people blowing smoke at him or how great he was. He wanted to hear the details. How am I going to win this voter in West Falls, New York? What is it that they're looking for?

Frank Morano: Trump said that he was pro-life, and he wondered whether it was possible for a pro-life Republican to win in New York State. Kellyanne indicated she thought a pro-life Republican could.

Nick Langworthy: His theme was, how can you convince me that running for governor of New York was the step he needed to run for the presidency and fix the country? It might be a quick turnaround to win governor in 2014 and then run [for president] in 2016, but he could certainly make a difference in our state.

Joe Borelli: He said, "Honestly I'm not sure I need to be governor to be president. I think I can enter the [presidential] race in June of 2015. I would be essentially leading the polls in terms of just my name recognition alone." He said he would lose Iowa but win New Hampshire because of the connections he had made there, and then hopefully the campaign would take off. But he believed New York State was shedding people and the upstate economy was suffering. He understood why businesses were fleeing upstate New York because of the taxes and cost of living. It doesn't take a business genius to even explain all of these things, but it would take someone like Trump to explain them to voters.

Frank Morano: Trump said fracking was a great issue and he was afraid if people knew he would focus on fracking as a gubernatorial candidate, then Cuomo would come out in favor of fracking just to take an issue away from him. Trump suggested maybe Astorino could run for state attorney general, and then run for governor in four years. We told Trump that Astorino was not a lawyer, so he wouldn't be eligible to run for attorney general. Trump said he didn't realize that.

Michael Caputo: Cox was so upset by the meeting—and he wasn't invited—that he called another meeting down the street immediately after our meeting to disabuse them of the notion that Trump was going to be a candidate. People were getting texts and telephone calls during the meeting from his staff telling them to come to a meeting afterward. They didn't waltz over there. They were being called in. Some refused, but everybody's phone was lighting up. All the chairs were looking at each other and having these surreptitious eye-driven conversations where we all knew immediately what was going on.

Sam Nunberg: Trump says, "Fine, I'll run if you guys go talk to Ed Cox, and you tell him I don't want a primary. Then I'd run, I'd spend some money, and I'm willing to offer Astorino lieutenant governor."

Michael Caputo: At the end of the meeting Trump said, "Get your chairman to clear the field for me and I'll get in." Somebody said, "We'll be talking to him shortly." Trump said, "What do you mean?" They said, "He invited us to a meeting right now." Trump kind of laughed and said, "Tell him hello."

David DiPietro: I stood up in front of everybody and said, "Here's a chance to unify the party and unify Ed Cox. He is the party chair. He is the state chair. Let's give him that respect. When you meet with him, tell him, "Ed, if you get behind Donald Trump and make this announcement, it will be coming from you as the state chair. You will get the glory. We'll end all this little backyard bickering. You've got 90 percent of your county chairs who elect you who are for this, so get behind it, and we'll let you take the credit. Trump is running for governor, and this will be the marquee race for the entire country for the last 50 years." I can't think of a higher-profile race than Cuomo-Trump would have been in 2014.

Nick Langworthy: After things broke up and people took their pictures, I went off to the side and had some discussions with Mr. Trump. This is a guy who gets it. He understands what goes into it. He was asking how could we close out the nomination without a primary.

Dan Isaacs: I went to speak to Chairman Cox. I told Ed, "He will run but we'll need to clear the field."

Michael Lawler: Several of the chairs and Sheriff Butch Anderson from Dutchess County came and met with Ed and myself and strongly encouraged us to clear the way for Trump. Ed listened and we were both of the mindset, saying, "Rob is ready to run. Rob is committed to it. If Trump wants to run, he's got to say it and do it." Ed still had the same mindset that I did, that Trump wasn't going to run.

David DiPietro: Ed Cox wouldn't budge. He's staying with Astorino, a losing horse with no money and no name recognition. I'd say 75 percent of the chairs were totally pissed off.

Nick Langworthy: His plans were Rob Astorino would be our nominee, but I thought we could dream a little bigger.

Those who did not leave Trump Tower to see Cox got a taste of life with Trump, which went from an important political confab to a meeting with music legend Neil Young.

Frank Morano: This beautiful woman was an assistant to Donald Trump, and she was standing outside the conference room and direct-

ing us where to go. She was breathtaking. She told Joe Borelli and me
how excited she was to meet Neil Young and that he was Mr. Trump's
next meeting.

Justin McConney, *Trump Organization social media manager:* Neil Young
was doing a run of shows at Carnegie Hall, and Trump went to one.
Rhona [Graff] called me and said, "Neil Young's coming by tomorrow.
He requested a meeting. Have your camera ready."

Michael Caputo: I was sitting comfortably in Donald Trump's office,
just shooting the breeze about the Buffalo Bills, when he looked up and
exclaimed, "Neil!" I didn't think anything about it. People constantly
stopped by. I turned around and when I recognized Neil Young I
jumped up and sent my iPad flying across the office. I shook Neil's hand
and couldn't find my voice. I tried to say hello, but this weird frog sound
came out. Loudly. Trump broke out laughing. He said, "Caputo can sit
here all day talking to me no problem but you, Neil—you make him nervous." He stood up and came around from his desk, smiling really big.
It was apparent that Mr. Trump was getting a big charge out of introducing me to one of my idols. He held out his hand and said, "Give me
your phone, Caputo." I did and a photo resulted.

Justin McConney: Trump calls my name. "Justin, come in here. Neil,
this is Justin. He's my social media guy. Neil, tell him about this audio
equipment." Neil Young set this meeting to pitch Donald Trump on his
audio device called Pono—a version of an iPod that played high-quality
music. Neil Young has this MacBook and he's playing a demo video for
Trump with endorsements from about every major musician you could
think of. I'm sitting here with Neil Young and Donald Trump, and Eddie
Vedder comes up. Neil Young says to Trump, "That's the lead singer of
Pearl Jam." Trump nods his head. I'm thinking, "This is so surreal."
Trump started calling in people that were fans of Neil Young, and
started asking Neil to take pictures with these various people. Neil was
friendly about it, but you could tell he was like, "What's going on here?
Why is this a photo op? I'm here to pitch an audio product." Neil says, "I
want to do an audio demonstration." Trump tells Neil, "I have something
coming up. Why don't you go across the hall into the other conference
room with my guys and show it to them." Neil Young sits there explaining his Pono device, and then he walks around with this big set of

headphones and puts it on each of us and plays it, and asks us what we think of the quality. Trump comes in at the end and said, "Alright, we'll talk about this. Any of you guys want to go to his show?" But Neil didn't offer us any tickets, so it was very awkward. Trump was looking for an offer to come and Neil didn't, so none of us said yes. That meant we would have to ask Donald to buy a ticket. We all just sat there silent.

25.

AN ENLIGHTENING
DISTRACTION

Donald Trump made his offer—if no one else was in the primary, then he would run for governor. But Rob Astorino was staying in the race, and Ed Cox wouldn't negotiate.

Trump kept launching tweets and calling reporters, trying to blast away resistance to his bid. "You have to pick somebody and go to win," he told the New York Daily News *on January 11.[1] The next day he tweeted, "The Republican Party of New York has been conditioned to lose, and there is no excuse for this. Leadership must move fast and decisively!"*

Trump's larger goal remained a run for the White House. That campaign, Nunberg, Bossie, and others understood, would require a fight against the old guard in the national Republican Party who had knighted Mitt Romney and were likely to align behind another mainstream figure in 2016. In Cox, Trump faced a similar old-guard foe. Trump had already chewed out Sean Spicer and Reince Priebus when they came to see him in Trump Tower following Romney's loss. This battle with Cox gave Trump a new target to sharpen his attack.

Cox did not have all of Trump's tools to fight back with, but he did figure out how to land some counterpunches.

Frank Morano: I'm on the bus on the way home after the [January 10 Trump Tower] meeting and Nicole called me. "How did it go? Did he have that special connection with anybody else?" Later that night my phone starts buzzing from text messages and emails. My phone starts doing things I didn't even know it could do. People are trying to reach me, outraged that Nicole has given a public endorsement of Rob Astorino, saying he's her favorite candidate for governor.

Nicole Malliotakis: He often said he was going to run for something and then never jumped in. He had said he was going to think about it. It was already late and Astorino was ready to go. If you have a viable candidate who is a good person who wants to run, you can't hold off, waiting to see if somebody else decides to jump in at the eleventh hour.

Michael Caputo: She had a discussion with Chairman Cox, and she got back on Astorino. When I told Michael Cohen that Nicole Malliotakis had done this, he said, "Who the fuck is Nicole Malliotakis?" I told him who she was and he said, "Forget about it. We don't care. It doesn't matter to us. We have no clue who she is." She was out after that.

David DiPietro: After Nicole endorsed Astorino and crapped on Trump, she had the gall to send him a letter saying, "I'd like my donation that you promised," and Cohen went ballistic. "Do you think we're going to give her a fucking penny? Fuck her."

Frank Morano: I look like a total idiot at this point. I brought this woman into the Trump world. In the short term, the fallout for Nicole was positive because she grew in the estimation of Rob Astorino. They talked to her about being the lieutenant governor. I saw her the following week at a fundraiser, and she thanked me for coming even though she knew I was ticked off at her. She said in front of Ed Cox, "I knew he wasn't going to run, so I had no problem endorsing Rob."

Nicole Malliotakis: Sam Nunberg sent me some text message saying never to call them for anything. I'm dead to them.

Cox wasn't done using his powers. Aware that some Republican officeholders would see advantage in crossing party lines to stand with Cuomo since he was heavily favored to win the coming election, Cox released a letter on January 14 urging Republican leaders not to endorse the Democrat.[2] Trump heckled Cox the next morning, tweeting, "The Ed Cox letter to Republicans, which is being so badly ridiculed by the press, should never have been written. WEAKNESS-SAD!" Trump vowed to match the $33 million the Cuomo campaign reported in their account and spend as much as $200 million on the race if he really wanted.

"If I ran, it's a race that absolutely could be won," Trump told the Buffalo News *on January 16.[3] By the end of the week, Trump tweeted, "New York GOP leader Ed Cox's record is abysmal—no victories. Hopefully he can turn things around."*

Those who were looking to Trump saw a way to undermine Cox by bringing Trump together with Carl Paladino, a brash real estate billionaire with a thirst for state politics and contempt for political correctness—a New York Jesse Ventura with a Trumpian bankroll. Inspired by the Tea Party, Paladino spent $3 million winning the GOP primary for governor in 2010. He favored removing road tolls and cutting Medicaid, and campaigned with a baseball bat as a metaphor "for people who want to take their government back."[4]

Even though he lost to Cuomo in the general election, his Tea Party–inspired effort served as a conservative case study for a Trump candidacy. Paladino was already picking fights with Rob Astorino, demanding Astorino force out the Republican state senate leader and State Assembly minority leader or he'd mount a third-party primary challenge in 2014.[5] On January 20, 2014, Trump and Paladino had a two-hour dinner with Caputo, DiPietro, Cohen, and Langworthy at Jean-Georges, the three-star Michelin haute cuisine restaurant at the base of Trump International Hotel and Tower.

Nick Langworthy: We enlisted Carl to try to help us because we figured, here's Carl, he's a brazen developer, maybe they can have a connection.

Carl Paladino: [Nojay and DiPietro] felt they had made a good impression, and Trump was very sincere about running, and I thought it was a great idea. DiPietro called me and said, "Would you go down and see him?" I said, "Of course I will."

Jessica Proud: Carl is a lot like Trump—a very big personality and very charming when you meet him. He says crazy things in the press, and when you get behind closed doors with him, he's so loving. He hugs everybody.

Michael Caputo: We met at Trump Tower and went in a limo to Jean-Georges. Trump brought along a big shopping bag of ties and gave each of us five or six Trump ties and we took over the restaurant. A lot of striped ties. I got one on right now.

Carl Paladino: When you have a meeting with him like we did, he's got a bag of Trump stuff, Trump cologne, Trump ties, and he gives whoever he's meeting with all this stuff. It was a very elegant restaurant. Trump was very proud of it. It was Mike Cohen, Caputo, Langworthy, Trump, and me. We were up against the window.

Michael Caputo: I had steak, most people did. Trump was very generous, he kept ordering more stuff. That's when I understood Trump still didn't drink. I don't think he ever does. He didn't order a bottle of wine, and we didn't order it because we weren't the hosts.

Nick Langworthy: I had sea bass. I shared the potatoes with Mr. Trump. Dr. Oz was at a table right next to us.

Carl Paladino: We faced each other and he said, "Carl, I admired the way you handled yourself in your election and I have a few questions." I said, "Before we talk about that, why wouldn't you want to run for governor?" He said, "Because I want to run for president of the United States. Now, if I won the governorship of New York, I would only be disappointing a lot of people who would be working real hard for me, because I would have to leave within a year and start running for president." I said, "Why do you want to be president of the United States?" He told me that, like me, he had had financial success. He had a wonderful family. He had all that God could ever give him, and he was a happy guy. But he also knew he could say and do things other people could only think, and he told me he didn't have any fears. His parents gave him that base that got him going in life and he wanted to leave a true legacy for his parents, and he wanted his children to be able to see a good president of the United States doing good things.

Michael Caputo: Carl started talking to him about how he could actually do this. That he had the intestinal fortitude that was necessary, the funding, and the name ID. The two of them realized they got along very well on issues too.

Carl Paladino: I told him from my perspective it would not be a bad thing for him to leave office and run for president. What he would do for New York politics and for the people in the State of New York by running would be such an awesome change in the direction of the state. It would far offset any feelings he might have about getting people upset. I invited him to come up and speak at a gun rally [in April 2014] I was pushing in Albany. It was going to have at least 10,000 people.

David DiPietro: Mr. Trump was asking Carl a lot of questions about how he ran, what his strategy was, what he did in different areas of the counties, what groups were most receptive, where should he spend his time, and what would make a big impact.

Carl Paladino: I'm going to tell you a little side story which I'm not proud of. We came right from the airport in a cab. I started feeling irritated. By the time we sat down in the restaurant I knew what it was. It was a kidney stone coming on, and I was at a two or three in pain. Out of 10. By the time we finished the meal I was at a six or seven. I was so uncomfortable, I couldn't eat what I ordered. I was focused on talking to him and did the best I could. I told someone, "I'm having a kidney stone attack." He says, "I'll bring you to the hospital." No. It wasn't a pleasant time to be speaking. Make a long story short, I decided instead of going to the hospital after the meeting, I went home [to Buffalo]. By the time we landed I was a holy 10.[6]

Nick Langworthy: Roger always told me this was a lark. Nunberg was in the same boat. Michael Cohen was in the firm camp of wanting Trump to run for governor.

Roger Stone: It became clear he loves campaigning and he's really good at it. And that probably just reinforces his interest in running for governor. He's never had a huge respect for polling, he's more instinctual as a politician. I tend to be more data-driven. On the other hand, if he made decisions based on the polling about running for president, he wouldn't have run.

Sam Nunberg: Roger had heard through the grapevine that the Cuomo people weren't nervous about beating Trump, but they were nervous about all the money they were going to have to spend on a campaign.

David DiPietro: Trump had $8 billion, name recognition, the guy connects with the people. He wasn't a politician. Everything that Cuomo is not Trump was.

Amid the New York State drama, some of Trump's team kept him on track nationally. Sam Nunberg had arranged for Trump to appear in New Hampshire on January 21, 2014, for a "Politics and Eggs" breakfast with Manchester power brokers, and for McKay Coppins, a political reporter for Buzzfeed, to fly with Trump.

On January 24, when CNBC teased an online poll that would be part of a process of compiling a list of the country's top business leaders, Trump was among 200 nominees. Michael Cohen hired IT consultant John Gauger to rig the poll by writing a computer code that would vote for Trump repeatedly.[7] Trump's legal team would later deny his knowledge of the poll manipulation.

Michael Cohen, *excerpts of Congressional testimony February 27, 2019:* I spoke to Mr. Gauger about manipulating these online polls.

U.S. Rep. Mark DeSaulnier *(D-CA):* And did he use bots to manipulate the poll?

Cohen: He used algorithms and if that includes bots, then the answer is yes.

DeSaulnier: . . . Did the president have any involvement?

Cohen: Yes.

DeSaulnier: In directing you to do this?

Cohen: Yes.

DeSaulnier: What were the results of the poll?

Cohen: Exactly where we wanted them to be. In the CNBC poll, we came in at number nine.

Back in New York, Nick Langworthy proposed that Trump headline the Erie County Republican fundraising dinner on January 31. This time they'd invite their state GOP chairman Ed Cox so Trump could talk to him in person.

Nick Langworthy: After the Jean-Georges dinner we got into regular telephone communications with Mr. Trump. I said, "Let's try a trial. Do an event in Buffalo for me." In 10 days, we sold over 800 tickets on the speculation of him running for governor. It's exactly why I thought he'd be a great candidate, because of the attention and intrigue he brought to the public and the rank and file.

David DiPietro: We got him at the airport. We took him to Salvatore's Italian Gardens [in Depew], and there was a line of people for half a mile waiting on both sides of the street waving to him.

Michael Caputo: It had so many statues outside, dozens of statues all over the place. It was very over-the-top Italian. White marble statues of women pouring wine from a jug on their shoulders.

Sam Nunberg: There are people outside with signs, "Run, Trump, Run." They planted those people but whatever.

Nick Langworthy: His staff saw how many VIP tickets I sold. His assistant Rhona Graff said, "This is gonna be a problem. Mr. Trump doesn't like to stand and take this many pictures." I said I would personally handle that and make sure it goes rapid-fire. I busted 200 people through the line in 30 minutes.

Sam Nunberg: We get there, and Trump gives a good speech.

Michael Caputo: It was a great speech. Some big donors, Congressman Chris Collins, and Ed Cox were there. It was the biggest fundraiser in the history of the Republican Party of Erie County. He talked about how the country and New York had gone sour, how New York was over-taxed, how you couldn't even say "Merry Christmas" anymore, and how the last six years of Obama were terrible for America.

Nick Langworthy: That was certainly his first event in New York State where he was the keynote speaker at a large political gathering for a Republican Party cause.

Ed Cox: It looked like it would be a serious run at that point. I was happy because he was hitting his points well, getting a head of steam, and getting good feedback from the audience. He was sounding like a candidate, speaking about the issues well, developing his style that he would later effectively use in his run for the presidency. He sure got people excited. I was interested in seeing what would happen.

David DiPietro: Afterward there's a quick dinner in the back room for about 30 people. He's at the head of the table next to my wife, and then next to me is another person and then Ed Cox.

Sam Nunberg: Everybody's saying whatever happens after the primary, we all have to be united. That's when Cox said, "Oh, yeah, we have to be united."

David DiPietro: Mr. Trump's going around the room and saying hello. He gets to Ed and he just starts blasting at Ed.

Michael Caputo: He just started ripping into him. "You can't win, Ed. You never win. I don't understand how you can win. You don't know how to win. It's time for you to step aside and let someone else win." Ed was trying to talk and he was flabbergasted that he was being called out at the dinner. And I looked at [Congressman] Collins, and Collins made eye contact with me and just smiled. People were hanging their heads. It was very uncomfortable for a lot of the people that were there. Because it was not nice.

David DiPietro: It was crazy. He's, like, "Ed, why are you against me? I've got a chance to help you and the whole party out. Everybody in this room wants me to run. Look at all the chairmen. Why are you the only one?" Ed didn't know what to say. He started fumbling around. Trump said, "Ed, you haven't won anything in this state since you've been elected chairman. You haven't won a statewide race. You're not doing anybody any good." Trump just leveled Ed Cox, and my wife and I were right in between it. My wife felt like her hair was blown back.

Michael Caputo: I thought it was wonderful because everything he mentioned to Cox was absolutely true. Cox was trying to deny that he was standing in the way of everything. "No, that's not true." But Trump was having none of it. He said, "It is true. You can't win. You haven't won. When have you won?" And he was like hum-a-na-hum-a-na-hum-a-na.

Ed Cox: I think he was disappointed that I wouldn't come straight out and endorse him and clear the field, which is what he wanted. My job as chairman of the party at that point was to shepherd the process and develop candidates. He wasn't a declared candidate and even his most ardent supporters wanted an open state convention. I took that all in stride. My attitude is, hey, that's my job. I don't like it, but that's my job. That left me free to give him straight advice.

David DiPietro: Then others jumped in down the row, and then that was it. Trump ended it and went on.

Michael Caputo: I had never seen somebody so senior dress down a state chairman like that in front of other people. I talked to everybody afterward. They were all thrilled. Nobody likes Ed Cox in Buffalo.

Carl Paladino: I didn't want Cox to be the chairman from the time I lost that campaign. He showed up for me at different events in upstate New York, but he didn't have a nickel. He couldn't raise any money. My central problem all along was Ed Cox's failure to get in the face of our legislative leaders who had all turned RINO [Republican In Name Only].

Sam Nunberg: That's the part of it that pissed me off. The Paladino guys were using this to finish old business.

26.

STAYING SHARP

Was Trump serious about running for governor of New York in 2014? He was, but that doesn't mean he was ever going to do it.

In his business and political life, Trump has negotiated deals that he has tried to change the terms of at the last minute or backed out of. State GOP leaders were right to be afraid that Trump would drive Astorino out and then decide he wasn't interested in challenging the formidable Cuomo after all. The governor himself was aware of this. The only on-the-record comment we got directly from Cuomo about Trump's interest in the job was a quick one at a social event: "Was he ever really going to run?"[1]

To view this episode in terms of methods Trump uses, he is unpredictable, willing to go to great lengths to test ideas, and willing to drop them. Just because he was fighting for Cox and Astorino to align behind him doesn't mean he was going to run for governor if they did. There would surely have been more polls, more prodding of Cuomo's will and weak points before a campaign would begin in earnest and Trump would start writing multimillion-dollar checks. It is clear that Trump was going along a certain road to feel how the idea of a gubernatorial run felt, to gather information, and to understand what was possible before making a final, gut-level decision.

In this struggle, Trump also would display his belief that powerful people can cut through formal rules to get things done if they really want. While it's true that Ed Cox could have signaled that the state GOP was behind Trump, Cox would in the end be clear that there was a formal way to settle the matter of who would be the candidate. Trump never went for it, but the experience narrowed his path, clarifying for him and those around him where he was now more surely headed.

Carl Paladino: Trump called me up, usually in the middle of the fucking night, and he'd say, "What's happening with Ed Cox?"

David Laska: There was one conversation where Trump was sitting on his plane and called Ed and said, "Ed, I want the party to unify." Ed tried in as sober a means as he possibly could to explain to him the way that the state party nominating convention works and that he does not have the ability to unilaterally unify the party. Trump wasn't having any of it. He repeated himself, "Unify, Ed, unify the party for me, and then I'll run. Unify the party for me."

Roger Stone: There was a juncture in which it got pretty vituperative between Ed and Donald. I told him to let it roll off his back, it wasn't personal. Donald became focused on the false premise that Ed Cox could deliver the nomination to him unopposed, an ability Ed Cox never had. Therefore, Ed Cox was screwing him. I kept saying, "He's not screwing you, he can't deliver what you want. You want him to order Rob Astorino to drop out. He doesn't have that power. Astorino will laugh in his face." It's a democratic process.

David Laska: Ed went to Michael Cohen and said, "We don't think you're serious. Tell Trump to commit $15 million, then we'll get the point that this isn't a stunt." If Trump actually cut a check for $15 million, Ed would have been on board 100 percent.

Michael Lawler: Let's say you tell Rob to get out, and Rob gets out. Then Trump says, "I don't want to do it." Then you've got nobody. We couldn't take the chance that he would not run.

Carl Paladino: I tried to convince Astorino to back off two or three times. He would say, "Ed Cox is going to get me money from the billionaires because Cuomo's a shit." They were both lost in their own little worlds with no evidence why he would do any differently than I did. They believed by being nicer than me he could be a better candidate.

David DiPietro: We're on the floor of the assembly voting. I called up Rhona because I had a question for Donald. She said, "Dave, he's golfing." I go back to my seat, and 10 minutes later I pick up the phone, it's

Donald Trump. "What do you need, Dave? I'm in Scotland golfing. I'm on the eleventh tee." I said, "Mr. Trump, you don't have to call me." He goes, "Don't worry about it. We're having fun. It's a gorgeous day. I'm playing lousy, and these guys are taking all my money." He's golfing with one of these top world golfers. My jaw dropped. Here's this guy calling me, a little assemblyman in New York.

Sam Nunberg: He was flattered in the beginning, but then it got to be a pain in the ass for him because he knew Astorino was going to run. I want him to run for president. I don't want him to run for governor. I don't want him to run for this shit. It's going to be a disaster. I said to him, "I can't in good faith tell you to do this. You want me to help you. I can't. This is going to be a tough race. Cuomo's got a lot of money, and I don't know how many votes we can get downstate. I don't agree with the prognosis of Bill Nojay."

Michael Caputo: As the meetings got bigger and bigger, Roger told me to pull the plug, and I refused. "Nobody's going to run for governor, stop wasting your time," he said. "Even the speculation hurts his chances of running for president. Don't you understand? He's thought of running for office before, and another instance of his thinking about it and not doing it doesn't help us at all. So stop it." I said, "Roger, these people want more meetings." He said, "Stop it. Just stop it."

Roger Stone: I kept trying to explain to Mike the realities of Trump World, but he didn't want to grasp them. He was getting pretty good coverage out of this, and Mike Caputo is not a man who objects when his name is mentioned in the media.

With Trump set to keynote the Manhattan Republican Committee's Lincoln Day fundraiser on February 12, 2014, Caputo, DiPietro, and Nojay requested another meeting earlier that day. They hoped to nudge Trump into the race by asking him to open an exploratory committee.

Dan Isaacs: The conference room was packed. Everybody was hoping that he was going to jump in. He was reveling and basking in everyone applauding him to run. But he kept his cards close.

Michael Caputo: It was our goal there to get Donald Trump to register an exploratory committee. We had brought along all the paperwork. Ralph Lorigo, who was the chairman of the Conservative Party of Erie County, was going to notarize it for history's sake and have a Conservative Party guy on the notary. When it came time, it was me and Ralph bringing him around to that side of the table. We just waited for Trump to execute it.

Sam Nunberg: All they said to Trump was, "We want you to open an account," which Trump refused to do. People like Caputo, Nojay, and DiPietro were pushing for the campaign account as a sign to other people he's serious about this. But Trump wouldn't.

Michael Caputo: Some guy who we believe was in league with Chairman Cox said, "It's not really necessary for you to register an exploratory committee because that's just standard politics. You don't want to be standard." Trump was looking for a reason not to sign the paper, of course, because why do it if you don't have to?

Sam Nunberg: On the way down in the elevator Trump goes to Cohen, "Why the fuck did you get me into this?" Like he had already basically decided he wasn't going to do it.

Dan Isaacs: There was a lot of anticipation of what Trump was going to do that night [at the Lincoln Day dinner].

Nick Langworthy: Dan Isaacs made it awkward and put a fake campaign sign with Trump's face on it that said, "Trump for Governor." He baited Trump to announce from the stage.

Dan Isaacs: We had great entertainment there that evening. We had someone doing caricature portraits of them with Mr. Trump. We had a juggler there.

Joe Borelli: He shouted me out from the podium because I clapped at something he said. Then he saw me and he says, "Staten Island is in the house."

Sam Nunberg: He gives a terrible speech, completely disinterested. It was the fact that he knew that Astorino had planned to run in the primary.

The next day McKay Coppins's story "36 Hours on the Fake Campaign Trail with Donald Trump" ran in Buzzfeed. *Coppins observed Trump sulking at the New Hampshire Politics and Eggs breakfast because no one at the forum mentioned his gubernatorial campaign. "They didn't ask one question about running for governor. They didn't care." Coppins wrote that he told Trump the White House is "not glamorous" and wondered why he'd want the job.*

"The endgame," Trump replied, "would be that I think I could do an incredible job. I think this country has great potential. I want to make this country strong and rich again."

Isn't Trump just bored with his real estate empire and The Apprentice? *Coppins wrote that he asked Trump.*

Trump answered, "Who knows what's in the deepest part of my mind? That could be possible."[2]

On February 15, Trump tweeted, "@mckaycoppins is a failed and dishonest reporter who refuses to mention the sarcasm in my voice when referring to him or irrelevant buzzfeed." He fired Nunberg in frustration.

Four days later he tweeted, "Internal polling shows that I would swamp @RobAstorino in a NY Republican primary 77% to 23%. But won't run if party is not unified."

Sam Nunberg: I get fired for the article. It's publicized that I'm fired. I didn't really care because I knew I'd get rehired. [In his story] McKay called him a perennial tease, but McKay also said bad things about Trump's plane, the hotel room, and he attacked his property. He attacked his business and that's where I understand why I deserved to get fired.

Justin McConney: At the Trump Organization, the Donald Trump I knew rarely, if ever, fired people, and if he did so, it was never directly. Someone else did it. Even if he was upset with people or people perhaps should have been fired, he wouldn't have fired them. He had a rule that he would never take people back. That's what's odd about the whole Sam thing is not only how often he fired him but that he also brought him back. Sam was a real rare case.

Sam Nunberg: I think Michael Cohen looked at me as an impediment.

Roger Stone: Michael Cohen envisioned himself as Mr. Trump's lieutenant governor running mate. No, I'm not kidding. He was trying to show diplomacy with Astorino, and Astorino's people would call me and say, "Who is this guy Cohen, and should we really meet with him? Is anything he's telling us true?" Cohen was threatening them in his thuglike manner. "Trump is going to crush you if you don't get out of the race." That was never going to work. Finesse is not a word you ever connect to Michael Cohen. He's not a bad guy, but he has no finesse.

David DiPietro: By the end of February, Donald called me up and said, "What's going on, Dave? This is getting crazy. Why is Rob thinking he can beat me in a primary?"

Nick Langworthy: We asked Trump to come up to speak to the Onondaga County Republicans in Syracuse, March 11. We had lost some of our momentum because when you're trying to hold someone's feet to the fire and get them to announce for political office, it shouldn't linger for several months. Some leaders were getting antsy. They saw it slipping away.

Roger Stone: Trump was putting a lot of effort and time into it. I talked to him about it on the phone. I would say his interest intensified, but so did his adamance that he could not have a Republican primary. It was a way out. It was a hint toward the exit.

Sam Nunberg: Ed flew to Florida [March 5] to see Trump. Jason Weingartner, who helped plan that, told me about it. I said, "That's great because I like Ed." It's also not good to have Ed Cox upset. Despite what people say, Ed is respected. I know everybody else likes to shit on him.

Ed Cox: I wanted to make sure he understood the process. That was my purpose, it was very straightforward. And he ran right past my purpose and got to his purpose, which was "I want you to clear the field."

Michael Lawler: Ed's from Suffolk County, and his family came over on the *Mayflower*. His father-in-law was the president, and his grandfather was on the Court of Appeals in New York State. His family has been involved in New York State government for over 200 years. Ed grew up in a certain manner. He went down there to meet with him because there were a lot of chairs who were interested in seeing Trump run, and Ed wanted to show him that respect. Ed is old school and felt that a face-to-face was necessary, and if Trump were truly interested in running, Ed wanted to hear it from him directly and say, "Then let's do what we've got to do."[2]

Nick Langworthy: [A Trump candidacy] was too unconventional for Ed. There was speculation about business deals that would come out and how Ed knew people who had done business with him and it had gone poorly. The problem was our convention would not have been until June. If there were people looking to derail Mr. Trump they would have had a long time to do that.

Ed Cox: I explained that the county chairs and their committee people, including his supporters, all wanted an open convention where the declared candidates would compete for support and then see where the chips fell. That wouldn't necessarily mean there would have been a primary. But, we never got to talk it about it because we very quickly talked about the approach he wanted.

David Laska: We were asking him to do what he ultimately did do when he ran for president. Visit all of the jurisdictions that are giving you delegates and launch a campaign. We put out a release that said, "Cox to Trump: Go through the process. If you want to run, declare."

Michael Caputo: Trump told me it was a friendly meeting, and I was very disappointed. Cox is a very charming man, and he was charming Donald Trump. He didn't know that Ed was putting a knife in his back every single day. But Ed Cox is very talented. That's why they call him "Chairman."

27.

FLANNEL SHIRT

Trump listened, flattered political leaders, tested how much pressure potential new allies and enemies could withstand, and received input from his inner circle. Five months after western New York Republican activists approached him about a gubernatorial run, he was ready to announce his decision.

On March 5, 2014, the same day Cox flew down to meet with Trump at Mar-a-Lago, Astorino declared his candidacy for governor. Trump's attorney Michael Cohen brushed off the announcement: "Only Donald Trump has the ability to win the gubernatorial race."[1] When Astorino appeared at a rally in Syracuse two days later, Onondaga County GOP chairman Tom Dadey, a Trump loyalist, did not show up.

Trump toggled between state and national politics. He made a third visit to the Conservative Political Action Conference in National Harbor, Maryland, on March 6. In an 18-minute speech, Trump dinged Rubio on immigration,[2] rambled about his 2013 trip to Moscow for the Miss Universe pageant and the fact that Russian president Vladimir Putin had sent him an unnamed present, and bragged about renovating his hotel in Washington.[3]

Sam Nunberg: His speech wasn't well received at CPAC in 2014. It didn't do well in the straw poll. He had to hone his message. Ben Carson [won].[4] Plus, we didn't pay as opposed to other people who pay to win it. It's pretty meaningless. On the other hand, what it did show was even when we were doing well in the polls, Carson was doing well, and part of it was his appeal that he wasn't a politician. Americans love the notion of electing a citizen president. They love the notion of electing a CEO president.

When CNBC's list of U.S. business leaders came out on March 10 and Trump wasn't on it, he tweeted in frustration, "The #CNBC 25 poll is a joke. I was in 9th place and taken off. (Politics?) No wonder @CNBC ratings are going down the tubes" and "Other worthy people were taken off the @CNBC list as well. Stupid poll should be canceled—no credibility." Trump complained privately to TV executives, and Michael Cohen called CNBC and threatened to sue the network over the ranking, saying the station was "ignoring the will of the people." The problem was that the internet poll was only one component of compiling the list, and a panel of experts decided not to include Trump in the final list.

The next day, Trump was back at the Onondaga County GOP dinner speaking about the state's high taxes, the advantages of carrying a gun, that he's not "a big global warming person," and the greatness of Syracuse's basketball coach.[6]

Then, on March 14, he tweeted his decision: "While I won't be running for Governor of New York State, a race I would have won, I have much bigger plans in mind-stay tuned, will happen!"[7]

He said he would have run if the party wasn't so disorganized—the same reason he gave when he stopped exploring the Reform Party nomination in 2000. "I have clearly stated that if the New York State Republican Party is able to unify, I would run for Governor and win," he tweeted. "They can't unify-SAD!"

It appeared to those who didn't follow Trump's political machinations closely that once again the real estate mogul turned celebrity pitchman had faked his interest in public office. "Here's a shocker: Trump will not run," the New York Daily News tartly headlined its brief news item.[8]

Not everyone had given up. Carl Paladino made one last desperate push. Trump promised to speak at his anti–SAFE Act rally in Albany on April 1, 2014, in favor of gun rights. Paladino hoped he could convince Trump to change his mind if he saw how many conservatives wanted to hear his message.

Even though Paladino would not succeed, the trip would offer Trump a fresh, ground-level view of potential Trump voters and confirmation that he didn't need to alter his persona to mobilize them.

Nick Langworthy: We talked within 10 minutes of the tweet going out. He apologized, but he had to get the word out and make the decision official.

Michael Caputo: Trump gave it so much time, and he was so responsive and open about the process that after he said no, I could not imagine any way I could talk him out of it. He had heard everything. He took input from everyone. He squeezed every fact from every data point from every resource and then made his decision.

Carl Paladino: I called him the day before the gun rally, and I said, "Don, wear jeans and a flannel shirt." He said, "I don't have jeans and a flannel shirt." I said, "Well, can you get jeans and a flannel shirt anyway? You could start a new line of clothing." I mean, what the fuck? "There's going to be 10,000 people there, and you want to fit in with them. You don't want to come in a suit." He said, "But the suit is my uniform. That's how everybody knows me. I'll think about it." I go to pick him up at Albany Airport and he gets off the plane. He's got his suit on. He said, "How do you like my jeans and flannel shirt?" I said, "You're a prick."

Sam Nunberg: It was a mistake to continue to do this stuff. It was a mistake to associate himself with Paladino.

Carl Paladino: In the car on the way to the event I asked him, would he give me the authority to speak to Astorino and offer Astorino the lieutenant governorship? I would explain to Astorino that you're going to run for president, for at least a year you'd be running the show, but afterward, Astorino would be running the show. He'd be an incumbent running the next time out, and he'd get the name recognition that he didn't have right now.

Roger Stone: Carl fervently wanted him to run for governor and kept telling me that he would, and I kept telling Carl he would not in my opinion. But those guys do have a bond.

David DiPietro: We got on the stage. He introduced Carl. Carl got a big ovation. There were probably two, three thousand people there.

John Haggerty, *Republican political consultant:* It's the angry Tea Party–esque person who feels like their American values are being taken away.

David Laska: Cities in western New York have more in common with Cleveland and Cincinnati than they do with Manhattan. Their concern is that jobs have left and home prices are underwater. They need industry. That's not the same economic pressure you have downstate. It's a completely different economic agenda.

Carl Paladino: He's standing in front of thousands of people in jeans and flannel shirts. This was a novel thing for him.

Matt Wing: At that rally they had a doll of the governor, a figurine, and it was being lynched. We were paying attention to that rally, not because we were paying attention to Trump. Because Cuomo's strategy was to paint his opposition as extreme conservatives who have to pay homage to the base of their party.

Joe Borelli: In my three years in Albany, I've never seen that many people on the lawn of the Capitol. The grass had to be repaired. There was a lot of "Don't tread on me" signs. This was essentially the tail end of the Tea Party movement, and I don't know of any other rally that President Trump ever attended like that prior to his running for president. Perhaps that put the idea in his head that if you get a motivated, issue-based group of people, you can whip them up and get them excited about making legislative changes.

Paladino spoke first, taunting Astorino ("Rob Astorino is a good man, but we need someone who is going to get elected") before introducing Trump as the "next governor of New York State." Trump spoke briefly about the Second Amendment and held up his pistol permit, drawing cheers. "You have the constitutional right to keep and bear arms. You have that right and they want to take it away. And they are taking it away, slowly but surely, they are taking it away."[9] Trump left the stage and minutes later buzzed over the crowd of about 3,000 people in a low flyover with his helicopter emblazoned with his name.

Carl Paladino: He gave a good speech. Very pro-gun. Talked about his son Donald Jr., an avid hunter and fisherman.

Joe Borelli: He's a guy who's a billionaire and makes no secret of that fact and lives his life ostentatiously to the point where he wants his life to be seen as ostentatious, and yet he's identifying with people from lower-income counties in upstate New York, and he's bonding with them over an issue that they're both angry about.

Jessica Proud: We watched him take off in the helicopter. He wanted to make a big spectacle. People were yelling from the ground. It was lifting up. He didn't brush the crowd but he did a little circle.

Carl Paladino: The black Trump helicopter with "Trump" written on the side of it. It was 400 or 500 feet up. They did a circle around the crowd. The crowd was cheering. Astorino speaks. I chase him into the parking lot. I call him aside. "I got to talk to you for a minute. You haven't got a prayer," I said. "Will you take the lieutenant governorship?" "No, Carl," he said. "Ed Cox will raise all the money I need." I said, "You're listening to bullshit, man!" He doesn't come up with a nickel because he can't raise money from heavy donors. They don't respect him, but he said no. I told Trump he said no, and that's when Trump says, "Well, it's over, Carl."

Michael Caputo: When he decided to get out of it, Roger called me and said, "Are you done now?" I said, "I'm done." He said, "Stop getting in my way." I said, "I wasn't trying to get in your way." He said, "You almost fucked this up."

Roger Stone: The conversation went like this: "Mike, you fucking asshole. Stop pushing this stupid idea, please?"

David DiPietro: Bill and I were the only ones with Trump to start. Even at the end we were pretty much it. Me and Bill took a lot of grief in Albany.* A lot of barbs from people. One Republican senator said he already cut a deal—with the governor. "We're going to lay down," he said. "Rob's not going to get anything from anybody. He's not going to win, so we're not sticking our necks out." When Astorino got the nomination, that summer of 2014 before the election, he came out to my district. They have a Wyoming County Fair. Rob Astorino walked through this little county fair with two people. I watched him and not one person came up to him. He would stop in the middle of the causeway and they would just walk by him. Nobody recognized him or knew who he was, even with his shirt on for governor.

Roger Stone: Astorino went on to run a very good race against Cuomo considering that he had no money. He got 40 percent of the vote, and he

---

* State assemblyman Bill Nojay shot himself to death in a Rochester, New York, cemetery near a family plot on September 9, 2016. Known for advocating fiscal restraint, he was due to surrender later that day to the FBI to face fraud charges related to a trust fund he had handled. He had been implicated in a series of other schemes, including one in Cambodia related to a rice exporting company that never opened.

hit Cuomo very hard on the areas in which Cuomo is most vulnerable. He ran an amazingly good campaign, but Cuomo is very adept at turning off Republican money when he needs to.[10]

Nick Langworthy: The last time I probably spoke with Trump was shortly after Election Day 2014 to recap the elections. We weren't successful in New York. He suggested what might have been. He said he probably made the right decision.

Sam Nunberg: Trump never really said anything bad about Cuomo, and he didn't really want to attack Cuomo in case he didn't run. I'd send him suggested tweets attacking Cuomo, and he didn't want to do them. He said, "Why should I attack Cuomo now? Why have a bad relationship with him?"

Roger Stone: He's not the kind of person who suddenly says to you, "Wow, you were right all along." You have to respect his own thought process. I made my own arguments. Others made theirs. In the end, he did the right thing. He didn't run—he ran for president instead, and he won. I'm not unhappy about any of it. He's his own man. He makes his own decisions.

John Haggerty: The relationships that were established certainly helped him during the presidential primary race in New York. Carl Paladino, Caputo, Nojay, DiPietro, Langworthy: they were valuable during the presidential run because he wasn't starting from scratch in New York.

Michael Caputo: When he finally called me about it, he said, "I'm not going to do the governor thing. I'm going to do the big thing." I understood that to mean the presidency. He asked me to help him when he did the big thing, and he'd get back to me.

David DiPietro: I was the first elected official in the country to endorse him. Nicole Malliotakis used to jab me all the time. She was a Rubio person, and we would go back and forth.

Frank Morano: When Rubio dropped out, John Haggerty and Michael Caputo sent her a funeral-style bouquet with a ribbon saying, "In Memory of Your Beloved Candidate."

Nicole Malliotakis: It was terrible. [Laughs.]

Ed Cox: I attended the Pennsylvania legislators lunch [in December 2015]. Trump came right up to me and thanked me profusely. His decision to skip the governor's race and run straight for president, as Roger advised, was paying off, as he was then leading the field of Republican candidates.

Michael Caputo: I asked him one time while we were sitting around about how he would win. "You hate political consultants. You hate pollsters. You don't like ad guys," I said. "How are you going to win in the Republican primary?" He said, "I'm going to get in the race, and I'm going to say something outrageous, so newsworthy that I'm going to suck all the oxygen out of the room. And then when that story dies down, I'm going to do it again. And I'm going to do it again until every one of the other opponents dies off from lack of oxygen." Lack of news coverage. Deny everyone else media coverage until they die on the vine. I laughed, saying, "Okay. You think that's going to work?"

Carl Paladino later became New York co-chair of Trump's presidential campaign, penning an open letter to New York legislators asking them to "join 'Trump for President' and try to preserve what's left of your pathetic careers in government."

That Trump eventually decided not to run for governor does not make his foray into state politics a failure or a waste. Along the way, many of those around him would reveal their strengths and weaknesses. Michael Cohen's ambition showed itself, as did Nunberg's steadfastness. Valuable new alliances would be forged.

The exercise kept Trump and those around him sharp.

PART FIVE

TO THE ESCALATOR
2014—2015

A popularist politician emerges.

28.

OUTWIT, OUTPLAY,
OUTLAST

Trump had finally put the New York governor race behind him. The targets of his attacks would no longer be little-known New York State politicians. On April 12, 2014, David Bossie hosted a summit in New Hampshire where the mainstream media focused on Texas senator Ted Cruz and Kentucky senator Rand Paul as the most important guests.[1] It was Trump, however, viewed by some as mere celebrity bait to draw a bigger audience, whose political statements revved up the crowd and impressed a key member of the alt-right media, Steve Bannon. Trump attracted his first big applause with phraseology similar to Ross Perot's "giant sucking sound."

"Mexico," Trump told the roughly 1,000 attendees, "is beating us so bad. They're taking so many jobs out of our country. Draining jobs. It's very simple: You either have a country or you don't have a country."[2]

What really set Trump apart, though, was his unsparing, direct attack on a presumed front-runner who was not present, Jeb Bush. Bannon had been looking for someone effective to carry a populist message. Jeff Sessions wasn't the guy. Maybe Trump could be?

Bossie, whose prominence is partly owed to producing such gatherings in influential states, brands them as "Freedom" summits. The electoral advice he gave to Trump at this time resonated with the experience Trump had just gone through. Bossie suggested he approach the presidential primaries in three important states separately, tailoring unique messages, as if he were running for governor of each. Bossie introduced Trump to Corey Lewandowski, who had run New Hampshire senator Bob Smith's unsuccessful 2002 reelection campaign and nearly came aboard Trump's nascent 2012 bid.[3]

Roger Stone: We spent most of 2014 talking about and planning a campaign for president.

Sam Nunberg: I met with Trump twice in March 2014. I was going to work for [Wisconsin governor] Scott Walker. I asked Trump if I could get rehired. He said, "I can't get you rehired, are you kidding me?" He's so cheap. I called him the next day and I said, "You asked me who'd be the best campaign manager? Me. Hire me, and you'll win." The second time he took a call from Mark Burnett, I just left. I forgot that impressed him. But I didn't do it for that. I did it like, I'm gone. He doesn't want to rehire me, I'm done. Fine. The next morning he called me back. He said, "I was thinking about last night." He used to pay me $5,000 a month. I took a nice little haircut of $2,500 a month, but it was cool. I got rehired the week before we went to New Hampshire.

David Bossie: Donald Trump came and spoke in front of just under a thousand people, an enormous crowd for him at that time. Presidential politics hadn't started, so ours was basically the first big event in Manchester. We had a lot of media coverage partly because Donald Trump was *The Apprentice* guy.

Sam Nunberg: It was a big coming out for him. He gave a really good speech. It was supposed to be a coming out for Rand Paul and Ted Cruz. We just sucked up all of the energy. He absolutely killed it. He controlled the day. He talked about securing the border and trade. He's been talking about trade for years. "We're getting ripped off." He saw immigration was going to be a great wedge issue in the primary from the gang of six in 2013 and the failure of Marco Rubio.* He starts making fun of Jeb for the first time and the crowd cheers.

> **Donald Trump,** *excerpts of his 31-minute, April 12, 2014, speech:* Heard Jeb Bush the other day. People who come into this country illegally are here for love. I've never heard that one before. The one thing I never heard before is love. I understand what he's saying but it's out there. . . .

---

* Rubio was part of a bipartisan group of six senators who failed to pass immigration reform in Congress.

I would build a fence you've never seen before, nobody is climb-ing over. Nobody. . . .

I happen to love the Tea Party. They kill me for loving the Tea Party. . . .

Politicians are all talk and no action. It's all talk and it's all bullshit. They talk and talk and you go crazy. In the meantime everybody is eating our lunch. And you know whose lunch it is? Our lunch.

David Bossie: He talked about an America with borders. He talked about taxes and the economy, and our national security, and how stupid we were in our trade deals.

Steve Bannon: Trump goes to New Hampshire and blows the doors off it. Owns it.

Sam Nunberg: He faced a lot of problems because he had looked at the stupid governor's race. We had to rehabilitate him to try to make him look like a serious candidate. Immigration was great because I didn't want us to be considered birthers.

David Bossie: Part of my advice was to run three races for governor in three states: Iowa, New Hampshire, and South Carolina. Instead of running some national campaign that's spending money all over the place and building enormous machines, just run for governor in three places. That's also where I introduced him to Corey Lewandowski, who's a New Hampshire guy. I picked a local partner in each of the three states. Corey was the first one. Steve Bannon came to the event and did his live radio show from there. And we had Mr. Trump do a live segment with him.[4]

Steve Bannon: I'm sitting there with the SiriusXM show, and [*New York Times* reporter] Jeremy Peters is one of our first guests, and I said, "As soon as Trump comes offstage he's going to do an interview. If you hang out here, I'll tell Trump, and maybe you can interview him." He says, "If my editor heard that I approached Donald Trump for an interview, I would be fired from the *New York Times*." And I said, "What are you talking about?" He says, "Trump's a joke. Nobody takes Trump seri-ously. He's doing this to get a better deal for his TV show. You guys are being played." I said, "What are you talking about? He's blowing guys away." He says, "He'll be mentioned. But trust me, Trump's not a thing."

Peters's article for the New York Times *did mention Trump in four paragraphs, noting that Newt Gingrich, Mike Huckabee, and Trump had "been speaking at events like the Freedom Summit for years and have loyal followers but are not likely to bring with them any constituencies that will expand the party's reach. . . ." Trump "tossed out a few one-liners that lighted up an otherwise sedate crowd."[5]*

Steve Bannon: The guy in the room was 10 times more impressive than the guy I'd seen on TV. He's a much more serious guy. When he came on SiriusXM radio as a guest, he was unbelievable. Every mark, if you go back it will look like we scripted it. I'd throw the questions out. Boom! Cruz, it's talking points. Trump speaks in a very different vernacular. It was very powerful. I saw it right then. I said, "He grasped trade and he grasped immigration."

Sam Nunberg: We had taken a helicopter there in the morning. We went back and we stopped and played golf at one of his clubs in Westchester afterward. And we looked at all of the press coverage. We had a good meal. We got good coverage from everyone. Even Molly Ball [in *The Atlantic*]. She was very tough on us in 2011. The next day, Chuck Todd said on *Meet the Press*, "They're booing Jeb Bush while Donald Trump speaks." He was shocked. We weren't.

Ball concluded her article by quoting an audience member whose favorite candidate was Trump. "He gets to the point. He gets what's wrong with our country." That Sunday, Meet the Press *was hosted by David Gregory, who did not mention Trump but made note of Bush's comments about illegal immigrants and love and wondered if Bush was serious about winning a Republican primary. Chuck Todd did not appear, but the first month he took over as the regular host, January 2015, he said, "Nobody is going to mistake Donald Trump for a presidential candidate."*

Steve Bannon: You've got to remember where people in the media come from. Trump is a true barbarian. He's not from the system. Even a conservative like Cruz doesn't trigger them like this. Since he was four years old, Chuck Todd has watched Sunday *Meet the Press*. You haven't, and I haven't, and Donald Trump hasn't. We don't give a shit. We're playing golf or going to church or doing things that normal humans do. Or sleeping until noon to sober up. But what you're not doing at four years old is watching *Meet the Press*, which is what all these guys do. That's why they can still relate to Jeb Bush and Ted Cruz. And that's why Trump triggers them. He's Archie Bunker from Queens.

Sam Nunberg: Roger was having eye surgery and wearing a patch. Trump called Roger during a car ride, and Roger said, "Isn't this more fun than governor?" He started laughing. He goes, "Yeah, it is. The governor is small potatoes."

David Bossie: He was cultivating his message. He learned from people, from giving those speeches. He would test out language. That was really the beginning.

Steve Bannon: All that shit about "Lyin' Ted," "Crooked Hillary," "Low Energy Jeb." These are archetypes. He's not like [George W. Bush] throwing names out like "Turd Blossom."[6] Because that's a rich prep school kid putting you down. Trump is collective unconscious. Best story on "Low Energy Jeb." Because I'm a filmmaker and I make spots, my spot guy came to me early on and said, "Hey, I've got a thing on Bush's campaign." I said, "Go. It would be great experience for you." He's down there, and he said Jeb showed up to a staff meeting in a hoodie, gets the guys around him, and the first thing he says, "We've got to get the energy up in these ads. These ads suck." And they're sitting there saying, "I wish he hadn't used that phrase."

Sam Nunberg: He thought W was a terrible president. I don't think he liked Jeb because of business dealings in Florida. Gambling, things that Jeb wouldn't legalize. The line I suggested originally was, "We need another Bush about as much as we need another Clinton." He didn't want to do that because I always felt that he was going to endorse Hillary had he lost the primary. He said to me in 2013, "How can I run against her? She's my friend." I said, "So what?" He had donated to the [Clinton] Foundation. They went to his wedding. He had thought she was very popular. "No she's hated," I said. He donated and voted for her [Senate campaign]. Bill played golf with him. They had a lot of banter. You could imagine about what. [Laughs.] So Bill liked him. He liked Bill.

Steve Bannon: He's got something else that you can't coach. It's not star power. It's a way he carries himself like a leader. Sarah Palin had it and lost it. It's very tribal. It's very emotional. Something about what the Greeks told us he's got, this physical presence. One time he said, "I've had that since I was a kid. I've always had it. I noticed it when I went to military school. But I've always had it." I've never met Obama personally, and I've never met Clinton personally, but I hear that it's what they got.

Sam Nunberg: Trump said he had a 30 percent chance to win the primary because of a big field. I was worried about Scott Walker. Trump was right. He flamed out. I was wrong. Trump thought Marco wasn't going to be great, and too sweaty. But we were worried about Jeb because of the money, and when was the last time a Bush lost a primary? I said to Trump, "We may not win the primary, but Jeb ain't winning it either. No matter what, we are going to take out Jeb. And that could be something you did. If this doesn't work out, you go back to *Apprentice* and everything else, that's one kill shot for us. You took out Jeb."

Glenn Beck, *conservative radio and TV host:* A couple of years ago, I was on this special diet that had to have certain foods, eight ingredients. It was a pain in the ass, given by my doctor. I was traveling to New York and had to bring this chef and all the special ingredients. So I'm trying to find a hotel that would allow my chef to cook, and the only one that would was Trump's hotel, the one on the park. I was supposed to stay a week. I got there on a Friday, and I ended up leaving Sunday or Monday because I got a call that my father was dying so I had to fly out to Seattle and be with him. A couple of weeks later, I get a phone call, Donald Trump, and he said, "I noticed that you didn't stay the whole time, was there a problem with the hotel?" I said, "Oh no, Don, my father has passed away, and I had to go." And he said, "Oh, I'm sorry to hear that." And I said, "While you're on, I wanted to tell you your chef and his crew, they treated me and the guy who was cooking for me just so well and I really want"—and I was gonna say I really wanted to point them out so you could thank them. He interrupted me and he said, "Well, of course, I only hire the best, and you know you have a guy like me running a company and a hotel . . ." And he proceeded to go on for like three minutes about how great he was and I wanted to say, "Well, Don, you weren't there, like maybe it's your hotel, but it was your people that did that and you should probably say something to the people," but I realized about two and a half minutes into it that he wouldn't have recognized that. I hung up the phone, and I was walking out of my office and I'm thinking, why did Donald Trump call me about my hotel stay? That's when I stopped. I realized in the hallway, oh my gosh, this guy's gonna run for president.

29.

TEAM OF APPRENTI[1]

Trump still ran his company, but politics began to take up more time. There were conferences, dinners, and fairs to attend, each with opportunities to differentiate himself from his potential opponents and convince conservatives in Iowa, New Hampshire, and South Carolina to give him a closer look. Trump recognized that he needed a staff beyond Sam Nunberg, including a campaign manager and a press secretary.

Trump engaged in a hiring process that was chaotic, capricious, and, at times, vicious. Many he brought on had never worked on a political campaign, let alone a presidential one. It may seem a stretch to view this battle royale as reasoned, an attempt to graft rhyme to madness. But for Trump it was like assembling a team of apprentices, an uneven, youngish cast who fought for his attention and favor. He, in the seat of power, could pick and choose the ideas he liked and fire people he didn't. This model offers a prism for viewing his White House, where almost none of this cast of candidates stayed employed.

Lewandowski was as controversial as Omarosa had been on the first season of The Apprentice. *He was a blunt force despised by others in Trump's circle soon after he was brought aboard to manage the campaign in January 2015 (and like Omarosa in her debut season, he would not make it to the final boardroom). Hope Hicks was a winning hire, earning Trump's trust before becoming the campaign's press secretary at age 26. Veteran operatives Roger Stone and David Bossie—the George Ross and Carolyn Kepcher of the campaign—contributed guidance, as did Breitbart's tumultuous Steve Bannon (the Gary Busey?), while Trump's fixer/attorney Michael Cohen was an offscreen producer handling de-*

tails and solving problems. Trump's children were drawn into this project as they'd been drawn into so many others, including his TV show.

Some very promising "apprenti" bowed out before the boardroom, like Washington-based lobbyist and marketer Doug Davenport. In 1992, Davenport had gotten his start with Black, Manafort, Stone & Kelly, and was known in DC for the fully tricked-out rock-and-roll club he built in his home's basement. He had worked as an aide on the McCain presidential campaign but quit in May 2008 when a Newsweek *report revealed that his lobbying firm, DCI Group, was paid in 2002 to represent Burma's repressive regime.[2] On July 10, 2014, Trump met Davenport in New York and spent three hours talking about primary politics.*

Doug Davenport, *lobbyist, Black Diamond Strategies:* Roger had put me up in front of him in 2012 when he was considering running, but it never went anywhere. Roger had been pimping me like he had pimped Nunberg, although Sam and I are very, very different kinds of people. If it weren't for Roger or Paul [Manafort],[3] regardless of what you may think of them or anything else, I wouldn't have the life I have, i.e., a career in Washington, so I just don't want something taken out of context when I'm ball-busting about them.

Sam Nunberg: Trump first had interviewed Doug Davenport.

Doug Davenport: In 2014, I had been begging Roger for six months, "I've got this really cool fucking thing, man. It allows people to bet and trade options on hotel rooms for a city getting a marquee event like the Super Bowl. The CEO is a crazy fucker who drinks bourbon and smokes. Get me in front of Trump." One night, I'm laying there in bed just about to go to bed with my wife at 10:30 on a Tuesday night, and Roger calls. "Dougie. Trump, tomorrow, New York City, you have 30 minutes with him." I said, "Roger, I've got clients." Roger said, "Listen, asshole, this is what you asked for, I got you time with the man. If you go in looking for something without bringing something, you're going to be like every other fuckface. You've been traveling this country, you've done a lot of campaigns, convention and delegate work. You ought to put together a bunch of reasons why he ought to listen to you politically."

So I stayed up for a couple hours, took the train with my client the next morning, walked into his office. We sit down in those red chairs in front of his desk. All Roger told him is I'm coming to interview for the campaign. My client's sitting there with cowboy boots on, reeking of booze and cigarettes, and we spend 45 minutes going through the 99 counties in the Iowa Caucus. He's asking me who to hire, he's taking notes, he's asking me for cell phone numbers, and I'm thinking, holy shit, this dude's going to go. We get to about the 40-minute mark in a 30-minute meeting and he looks at my client and says, "So what do you do?" My client hadn't said a word. He says, "Well I'm actually here to sell . . ." and I said, "Hold on a second. Mr. Trump, would your hotel people take a look at this plan?" He says, "Yeah, you got it." This guy comes in the room who I recognize from *The Apprentice*. And Trump says, "Hey, Tom, take this guy up to your office and see what you guys can do." I get up with him to leave and Trump says, "No, no, sit back down." We sit there for another two fucking hours discussing politics. I've worked in 48 out of 50 state capitals, so he knew I understood the business. Finally, my client comes back and says, "Hey, we got a deal."

I walk out not knowing what just happened, and so Sam Nunberg rides down in the elevator with me and says, "That was pretty fucking great! So are you going to come and be the campaign manager?" I said, "Well, no, Sam, we were just shooting the shit there," and he said, "No, you just had a three-hour job interview," and I said, "I don't really look at it that way."

The next day I get a call from Trump: "Hey, it was really great to meet you yesterday, I was talking with Sam. You said you had some ideas how to approach launching a campaign. Would you mind putting that together in a memo?" In about 96 hours, I put a three-page memo together, and I sent it in. Fucking crickets for four months. I'm thinking, "Well, you know what, I got a story to tell my grandchildren, this is hilarious."

Among Davenport's advice in the memo, dated August 6, 2014, was the following:

> There has never been a more appropriate time in your or our country's history for a Trump candidacy and ultimately, a Trump presidency. If your message is unique, serious and disciplined, and your campaign is well organized and singularly focused, you stand the best chance of prevailing over the likely GOP Presidential field and ultimately the Democrat's nominee for President.

This is not to say that you need to change your overall persona to run for President. People still expect you to show up in YOUR plane, with YOUR name on the side. The presidency is a "larger than life" position—Leader of the Free World—and I personally see no down side to YOUR larger than life personality—if managed thru a disciplined governing message and strict adherence to a common sense plan.

The time is now—if you are serious about this—it is your last window to do it. BUT, you must have the right messages, the right team around you and align yourself with the right players overall. AND, you must show people you are deadly serious and focused on this race and it is by no means some grand media stunt.

At the same time Trump was soliciting campaign advice, he kept himself relevant in pop culture. A philanthropic promotion called the Ice Bucket Challenge, where participants dumped ice water over their heads and invited others to do so to raise money for ALS, swept across the internet starting in June, catching on with celebrities who challenged each other to take part. By August, several had goaded Trump to join in.

Justin McConney: Vince McMahon was the first one who challenged him, but Trump was in Scotland at that time. Then Mike Tyson challenged him, but Trump didn't want to do it. I asked, "Is it the hair?" He said, "No, I actually don't care about that. Shouldn't this be something I do on TV?" I said, "No, the whole point is to do it online." The third challenge came from *The Simpsons* [on August 26].[4] They had animated Homer Simpson doing it, and he challenges Donald Trump. I go into his office and I play it for him, and he says, "Alright, let's do it."[5] I suggest doing it right in front of Trump Tower in the atrium. He says, "I have something better. What about the rooftop?" Then he says, "Who's going to do it?" I say, "What about Miss USA and Miss Universe?" He says, "That's great. See if they're around."

I call up my contact at the Miss Universe organization. "Are Miss USA and Miss Universe here? I've got a huge favor to ask of you. And this has got to be done quickly before he changes his mind. I just convinced him to do the Ice Bucket Challenge, and I need Miss USA and Miss Universe to be in it and I need a video crew. Can I borrow your videographers?" They got there right away. Getting up to that rooftop of

Trump Tower was a catastrophe because you had to go through the residential section and through another set of stairs. It was a whole process getting up to that rooftop. We set up a second camera because I was so afraid if something got screwed up with the first one. "You better get this right," he said to me. No pressure at all.

But he sat down and he did it, and he loved it. I added in a joke afterwards where they're using Trump Ice to dump into the bucket. We're literally packing up the equipment and my phone rings. "Mr. Trump wants to see the video. He's in his apartment." I go into his apartment. It was the only time I've seen him in a t-shirt. He was in jeans. It could have been khakis. There were two ways I was used to seeing Trump. There was the business suit or golf clothes. He had a towel around his neck. The hair was still dripping. We were at the center of his apartment. "Play it for me," he says. "This is amazing. Release it." He had me email it to George Stephanopoulos, *Morning Joe*, just about any journalist you could think of.

A week later, on September 3, Trump and Melania attended an Aerosmith concert at the Prudential Center in New Jersey. McConney attended part of the show with them. The set list gave Trump an idea.

Justin McConney: The next morning, Trump calls me into his office because I watched part of the show from the front row with him. He started to bring up "Dream On." "I really like that song," he said. "I want to use that song when I run for president." He's always been a huge rock-and-roll fan. He loves the Beatles. Neil Young was his favorite. He would go see Neil Young every time he was in town. Aerosmith he liked. He had an Elton John DVD that was the only DVD ever played on his airplane. He also liked pop music. He was a big Taylor Swift fan. *Phantom of the Opera* he's seen multiple times.

Stone, Nunberg, and Bossie were fighting to persuade Trump whom to hire to manage his campaign. Stone recommended Davenport, but Nunberg pushed for Gregg Keller, a St. Louis–based Republican consultant. Bossie was for Corey Lewandowski.

Sam Nunberg: In November 2014, Trump finally brings me in full time. I'm working on the twenty-fourth floor.

Doug Davenport: One night in the middle of November, Sam forwards me an email from Roger saying, "Oh no I just found this plan Davenport put together for the boss at the bottom of a stack of stuff that got re-disorganized." Trump's handwriting said, "Sam I really like Doug, this memo is great, please set up another meeting." I went from, "Great story, whatever," to sitting in the red fucking chair again 48 hours later and we're right back at it. This time it was maybe two hours. He says, "The next step would be for you to go on a couple of these early trips with us to Iowa and to New Hampshire into 2015."

David Bossie: I talked to Mr. Trump. But I didn't work there. I was an outside adviser. I talked to Corey multiple times a day.

Doug Davenport: I have every email where Sam says, "Mr. Trump would like you to meet with Corey Lewandowski." I said, "Who the fuck is Corey Lewandowski?" He said, "He's been working for Koch[6] and knows people and has done voter registration." We ended up having three or four calls. What became obvious to me was, unlike Corey, I already had a 20-year, pretty good career in DC. The irony of Trump being interested in me is, number one, I hate a lot of people in the swamp for all the same reasons, but I'm part of the swamp. I did not think that was a good thing. Number two, I had twin five-year-olds and a second wife. I don't want to go to every fucking town hall meeting in Iowa. I finally said to Corey, "Why aren't you manager? I'll help informally, but the timing's wrong, plus I don't think you want somebody like me, even though I'm a Stone guy."

Sam Nunberg: We decided not to go with Doug. He then interviewed Gregg Keller, who I was pushing for. But Bossie fucked Gregg because he wanted Corey to get the job.

On January 5, 2015, Corey Lewandowski got up at 3:30 a.m. and drove from his home in Windham, New Hampshire, to midtown Manhattan to meet Trump. Nunberg told him to meet at the Starbucks at the Trump Tower atrium at noon. Nunberg was running 15 minutes late, according to Let Trump Be Trump, *the campaign book by Lewandowski and Bossie. "A good-looking guy," Trump said as Nunberg introduced them. Lewandowski estimated Trump's odds of winning at 5 percent. Trump shot back that he thought it was 10 percent but told Lewandowski, "You're hired, you start tomorrow."*

Doug Davenport: Three weeks later I'm watching TV, and they're saying Trump's going to name Corey Lewandowski, and I'm like, great. This was right at the time when Stone, Lewandowski, and Nunberg were all having their fucking fits and tantrums because that's typically how those things have happened in normal campaigns, let alone one like this. If it wasn't for Donald Trump, Corey Lewandowski wouldn't exist. Corey will not be Roger Stone. Corey is not going have a 30-year career. Corey was not a master strategist. He was an advance/logistics/events man. When Trump is gone, Corey is going to go be Bob Newhart and run a bed-and-breakfast in New Hampshire.[7]

John McLaughlin: Corey Lewandowski called me up in January and said, "Do you want to do some polls for Mr. Trump?" I said, "I would, but is he going to run?" He says, "Yep. He's definitely running. I have a contract. He's paying me money. I'm going to be the campaign manager." I was in the middle of a campaign for Benjamin Netanyahu, in Israel doing his polling, and I had to go back to Israel the next day. I said, "Let me focus on Netanyahu now and then I'll do it."

A few days later, Trump also hired Hope Hicks, who'd promoted his daughter's fashion brand.

Sam Nunberg: Hope was brought in through a PR firm that was doing Ivanka's PR. She wasn't political. Trump picked her and said she would be doing it. He liked her father, who worked at the NFL. She's a very quick learner. She's not a friend of mine. She fucked me over, but I have nothing bad to say about her abilities The other thing we had problems with was people didn't want to work for us. Republicans. Operatives. I contacted some people. They didn't get back to us. We thought Lewandowski killed two birds with one stone. We thought he could manage the campaign, number one. And number two, he could handle New Hampshire for us. Trump let it be known that Corey was top guy. Within two weeks, I was told that Corey had said to him, "Am I Sam's boss?" Trump said, "Yeah, you're Sam's boss." Why was he my boss? Fuck you. I'm not in the business of being friendly with Corey. He wanted to push Roger and me out. This is where I blame David Bossie because I was going to get my own guy in and Bossie sandbagged him because Corey needed a job. And I trusted Bossie.

David Bossie: At some stages of the campaign early on when Sam was around maybe it was a little bit more true [that people didn't get along]. Trump prefers lots of direct reports, as opposed to a filter. Executives want to speak directly to their top management, learn what they know, hear what they have to say, get as much information, and then make a good decision. That's what he prefers.

Sam Nunberg: Corey gets me fired within six weeks. I fucking hate him. I came back six weeks later. I had asked to go back. He rehired me. Lewandowski said, "You're going to have to work offsite, you can't talk to anybody besides me, you can't even talk to Trump, and you're going to go from $10,000 to $5,000 a month," for which I threatened to sue him. Corey wanted to take control of the whole thing, and Trump gave him the opportunity. Here's the difference between Roger and me. Roger blames it all on Lewandowski. To me, no. Trump let him do that. Because he never appreciated me or valued me.

David Bossie: I don't have [a relationship with Roger]. Never dealt with him. Never talked to him about this stuff. Never.

Roger Stone: [His number is] 1-202-ASS-HOLE. If his IQ was one point lower, you'd have to water him.

David Bossie: Getting into personality stuff. Not going to do it.

Sam Nunberg: I like Michael [Cohen] a lot. Michael and I ended up being competitors in the beginning. Probably a lot of it was because of Roger. We could have been friends. As opposed to Rhona [Graff], who I really helped situate in the political stuff. Rhona abandoned me. Michael and I were allies. Michael would have been an asset in the White House. Michael cleaned up messes for him.

David Bossie: Don McGahn called me in December of '14 and said, "Hey, how serious is Mr. Trump about running?" I said, "Very." And he said, "Well, I'd like a chance to meet him because if he does run, I'd like to have him consider me for the legal side." So I told him, "We're doing the event in Des Moines. Come on out. I'll put you in the room with him and you can visit."

The environment favored a candidate promising change. Americans disapproved of President Obama's job performance 55–43 percent in a May CNN poll.[8] Of those polled, 63 percent of Americans thought their children would grow up worse off than them, and 59 percent believed the American dream had become "impossible" for people to achieve.[9] By September, 83 percent of voters were fed up with Congress.[10] The national mood, rife with a sense of insatiability, was in the condition Trump had said, in 1999, would be favorable for him to run.

While Trump's campaign staffers bickered, his political rivals loomed. Florida governor Jeb Bush, who had announced on December 16, 2014, that he would "actively explore" a bid,[11] took pole position with 23 percent of the vote in a December 2014 CNN/ORC poll[12] and set an ambitious goal of raising $100 million in the first quarter of the year.[13] New Jersey governor Chris Christie, second in the CNN poll with 13 percent, surgeon Ben Carson, and Wisconsin governor Scott Walker sought the attention of the political press. And Mitt Romney was contemplating a third presidential run.

At the South Carolina Tea Party Convention on January 19, 2015, Trump met Katrina Pierson, a longtime Tea Party activist who would become his national campaign spokeswoman.

Katrina Pierson, *Trump national campaign spokeswoman:* I was on the board of the South Carolina Tea Party Convention. I heard he was going to be there, so I made sure to hang around. In the holding room I went up to him and said, "I heard the rumor again that you were thinking about running." He didn't want to say. He didn't know me from Eve at that point, but he knew I was in the media. I said, "Look, this is all off the record. I'm a Cruz girl, as a Texan." He just shook his head. "But he can't win," I said. "You can win." He was a little taken back by that. He said, "You think so?" I said, "I know so. If you run, you're going to win and you're going to win big. You have to run." He said, "We're thinking about it." I went over to Cruz's holding room and told him what I told Trump. I said, "I'm telling you guys out of a courtesy I told Trump if he runs, I'll support him 100 percent."

Steve Bannon: Bossie got Trump to hire Corey. Bossie swore about Corey as being a practical guy. Sam was there. I didn't know Hope at the time. But they had the beginning of a little nucleus of something.

30

HOW THE WALL
GOT BUILT

The idea for a barrier on the southern border had been touted in the 1990s by Pat Buchanan and in 2006 by Iowa congressman Steve King, an anti-immigrant Republican who hosted one of Bossie's Freedom Summits in Des Moines in January 2015, where Trump spoke forcefully about border security—but didn't yet utter the term "wall."[1] In the 2012 campaign, Republican hopefuls had talked about various forms of a barrier, the most extreme being Herman Cain's idea for an electrified fence that would kill would-be crossers but have, in fairness, posted signs on the Mexico side saying, "It will kill you. Warning."[2] Candidate Rick Perry was pilloried as soft for suggesting that there were better ways of dealing with immigration than a physical barrier.

Pat Buchanan: We called it the "Buchanan Fence." When I was in the hospital [during the 1992 campaign], my sister got it written into the 1992 platform. It calls for structures on the border. If you're going to secure the border, how are you going to secure it? You're either going to put a fence on the border or you're going to put a wall on the border. It doesn't take a genius. His wall and the fact that the Mexicans are going to pay for it, that's probably his innovation. But the Buchanan Fence was mine.

Roger Stone: Parts of it [are Buchanan's idea] but not all of it. Trump absorbed the America First concept.

David Bossie: He found his own way of having his own thing. A blunt New York fashion, but he came up with "Make America Great Again" and "Build the Wall." All of these different sayings that he would intertwine in his speeches and these events became like a rock show. There's tremendous energy out there. He won over the conservative movement, which was skeptical of his team.

Over about a year's time, Trump's anti-immigrant message was built from the raw material of his broad ideas along the mental workbenches of his disparate team, who tinkered with and tested it before it was sent back into Trump's mind for polishing. It finally came out of his mouth in memorable, rabble-rousing, hard-line form.

He was mentioning a border fence in a roundabout way at least as early as a March 6, 2014, CPAC speech in Maryland. There, though, he focused on the idea that granting amnesty to those in the country illegally was not going to help Republicans.

"No matter how soft you are, no matter how many times you say rip down the fence and let everybody in, you're not going to get the votes," he said. This was not Trump taking a principled position. He was talking mostly about strategy, what position was going to get votes, which made a certain sense since the room was filled largely by activists. The audience was listless, applauding with a smattering of strength only at the top of his immigration remarks when he said, "If you don't have a border, what are we? Just a nothing."[3]

Sam Nunberg: The wall was my idea. The wall was about immigration, but it involved Trump and his political, marketing, and business brand. It was our idea. Roger and I had spoken about it. I called up Bannon about it and ran it off him.

Steve Bannon: It was Sam who actually came up with the concept.

Roger Stone: Trump saw that he would have to move right to win the party's nomination, but this idea that Roger Stone or Sam Nunberg or Steve Bannon provided him his agenda is just not true. Sam deserves a lot of credit for helping Trump frame some of the things he wanted to say in memorable ways, but it's all pure Trump. Trump is the one who sees immigration as an issue, who has been talking about trade imbalances and our NATO allies not paying their fair share all the way back to 1988. He formulates his own platform, and he road tests it. He knows where the applause lines are.

Sam Nunberg: I was on the phone with Roger. It was sometime in July of 2014. Roger knew Trump was going to be very strong on border security, but we wanted to make sure that, frankly, he gave speeches where he didn't just talk about himself. So this policy platform, in terms of saying he will build a wall and get Mexico to pay for it, was something we thought he would like and use frequently. So I sent it to Roger and then Roger called Trump and Trump loved it.

On August 5, 2014, Trump tweeted: "SECURE THE BORDER! BUILD A WALL!" He would not regularly add the term "wall" to speeches until the next spring.

Despite numerous accounts of Trump first beginning to speak of a "wall" in a January 2015 Iowa Freedom Summit speech, a C-SPAN video records Trump advocating only for a "fence" and adding, "Who can build better than Trump?"[4] He also doesn't yet say terrorists "are" coming across the southern border. He says they "can." He refers to "criminals" and "crooks" crossing, not, as he would later, rapists. Trump's rhetoric was not yet honed to an edge that would dependably cut to the core of his target audience. Just as he'd pushed gossip writers decades earlier to refer to him as a billionaire at every mention, truth was not the end goal. What would motivate a crowd and sell like sensuously edged Breccia Pernice marble was.

Sam Nunberg: Look, I don't want to take credit for all of it or Trump will say, "Oh, you're taking credit." When he tweeted about immigration, that was the equivalent of our focus group, and we'd get a lot of retweets. Trump was a little ambivalent about it at first, but it was a perfect vehicle for him. Donald had consistently said, "I don't want to be told what to say. I don't want to be handled." Roger says to Trump, "I'm helping you sell yourself as a product in a different market. You're gold. You know the classic is gold. You're gold. Let's figure out a way to make this gold valuable and political." Trump thought maybe the wall proposal could hurt his business, which is something he never talked about. I don't know if he used the word "fence" in that speech, but he was already tweeting about it. I mean, we had already suggested to him it should be a wall. I don't know why he said "fence."

A lot of business got done in Iowa in January 2015. In his speech, Trump turned on Republican politicians who "disappointed" him. "It can't be Mitt. Because

Mitt ran and failed. He failed. He choked. He had that election won." And *"the last thing we need is another Bush."*

Steve Bannon: Bossie started putting on these forums. I'm going because we have a SiriusXM show and Breitbart's on fire. Breitbart's the voice of this. Trump's there with these other guys. Rand Paul's on the cover of *Time* magazine. You've got Ted Cruz. And you've got Newt Gingrich and Rick Santorum and Rick Perry. Chris Christie. Marco Rubio. The cattle calls are very important because there's 500 people in the room who are activists who are going to organize people and ring doorbells. They're not in big arenas. I noticed right away Rubio and particularly Jeb Bush had no command presence. These activists are there for the emotional part, but they're also pros. Trump kind of phones it in. He's good but he's not great. Scott Walker comes in and fucking takes the microphone and walks around the stage and owns it. And the whole media jumps on him, and Scott Walker's now the hot guy.

David Bossie: We were in a VIP room where some of the candidates were. Everybody had 20 minutes onstage, so we had multiple candidates in the greenroom at any one time. There were donors, VIP types in there, maybe a member of Congress or two from Iowa. Mr. Trump rolled in, and I introduced Don [McGahn, a campaign lawyer]. I told Trump he was the best in the business, and that's who he should have. We stood there and chatted for a few minutes. And Corey ended up hiring him.

Jeff Jorgensen, *Pottawattamie County, Iowa, Republican Party chairman:* Me and Margaret Stoldorf, our district executive committee chairwoman, went to Des Moines to see if we couldn't get somebody to deliver the keynote address to the Pottawattamie County Lincoln–Reagan Day dinner in May. I was really interested in meeting with Carly Fiorina. There were 17 potential candidates. It was still early in the election cycle. We told Carly what we were out here for, Pottawattamie County. She would tell her staff, she would think about it, and she would get back to us. But as Margaret and I were walking out of Carly's suite to the lobby, there's a television crew interviewing Donald Trump. So I thought, "Here's a fella." There's another fella standing there that I knew wasn't from Iowa, the way he dressed. Sharkskin suit. He's got to be with Donald Trump. I gave him my card. "We're having a Lincoln–Reagan Day Dinner in May and looking for a keynote speaker."

He looked at my card and said, "This is you?" I said, "Yeah, chairman, Pottawattamie County Republican Party." He brought Mr. Trump over and introduced us. We had our picture taken. The fact that he knew who I was tells me that they were doing some advanced research in Iowa. I'm guessing that they knew that I had endorsed a former businessman in the last presidential election cycle—Herman Cain. We left and I'm thinking, I will never hear from Donald Trump.

Carly Fiorina—her staff didn't get back to us right away. I called and pressed. "We'd like to find out." "Well, we don't know yet. We're not sure yet. We'll look at her schedule." About two weeks later I get a phone call from Rhona Graff, his personal secretary. "Mr. Trump has accepted your invitation." I said I'm going to have to bring it up with my central committee at our next meeting and as soon as I get their approval, I will notify you. She said, "That's fine." She's a very nice gal. We had an interesting discussion about the weather in Iowa. She was kind of impressed with the state of Iowa. I don't know if she had ever been here or not. I really started pressing the issue with Fiorina. "If you guys don't want to be here for our event, Donald Trump will. So you guys have to make a decision right now." Again they declined to get back to me. And then I brought it up to my central committee and they said, "Sure, why not?" I called Rhona back and said that we'd certainly like to have Mr. Trump out here.

Katrina Pierson: At Steve King's event [in Iowa], I was in the back and Trump was coming through, and he saw me. I gave him the nod, and he said, "You should come see me."

Steve Bannon: Trump goes to South Carolina next. Trump doesn't own it down there. He's good, but it's not like before. He's not owning these things. I think he's great and he's talking this language. But Scott Walker and these other guys got some heat.

Trump had attended the Conservative Political Action Conference nearly every year since 2011. He had grown frustrated with his poor showings in the event's straw polls. He'd never won and often finished below fifth place. On February 27, 2015, Trump brought the recently rehired Sam Nunberg with him to CPAC in Maryland and finished in eighth place. It got ugly.

David Bossie: I had Trump come to CPAC several times because I wanted to make sure we highlighted him. The conservative movement was incredibly skeptical of any newcomer who is trying to run for president who didn't have a pedigree. And then they were even more skeptical because Mr. Trump is a New York tabloid-ish TV personality with no grounding in the conservative movement or in conservative policy.

Sam Nunberg: The secret is, when you start appealing to the base, you get the moderates too. They start coming around. You start getting the whole smorgasbord of support.

Marji Ross: At CPAC, he surprised some people by sounding more conservative and being more articulate and passionate than what was expected. He exceeded expectations, and that added to the reaction he got because especially early on there were plenty of conservatives who approached candidate Trump warily.

In his CPAC speech, Trump said: "A lot of people think I am doing this for fun. I am not doing this for fun. Washington is totally broken and it's not going to get fixed unless we put the right person in that top position."

After the speech, Fox News' Sean Hannity asked Trump how likely it was that he would run, on a scale of 1 to 100. Trump answered between 75 and 80, adding, "I am really inclined. I really want to do it so badly."[5] Trump also revealed to CNN that NBC executives wanted to bring back The Apprentice *for a fifteenth season, saying, "They want to renew it and I told them I have to put it on hold because I'm doing something that's far more important."[6]*

Steve Bannon: Trump goes to CPAC and he only finishes sixth, fourth, or fifth in the poll.* Rand Paul wins it with all the Paulbots. But Trump's not second. I'm talking to my guys, and Sam walks up and says, "The phone is blowing up. Will you talk to him?" Sam stinks of whiskey. I take it, and a voice says, "The fucking guy's drunk, isn't he?" I said, "What?" He said, "Steve, this is Trump. The fucking guy's drunk, right?" I said, "I don't know, Mr. Trump. I don't know." I always call him Mr. Trump. I never call him Donald. He says, "How the fuck did I write

---

* Trump finished eighth. When we asked Nunberg about this incident, he addressed Trump's expectations about the straw poll but ignored the issue of sobriety.

a $25,000 check to sponsor this fucking thing and I lose? Nunberg's a loser."

David Bossie: I do recall that being an issue.

Sam Nunberg: Bannon spoke with Trump via phone. I put him on. I also put Trump on the phone with Kellyanne. We all wanted to explain that the results showed that there was an opening for an outsider non-conventional candidate. Ben Carson was overperforming. It is not accurate that Trump wanted to win the straw poll. But he was concerned that he underperformed.

David Bossie: Mr. Trump was unhappy because he did spend some time and resources to be involved at a high level, and it didn't pay off. I try to tell him it's a marathon, not a sprint, so you've got to be prepared for the long run, to not have too high a high and too low a low. It's good to win, but it's part of the process. Rand Paul, who won that, ended up not being the nominee. "People who win these things spend their whole year organizing a win and then they don't end up doing anything after that," I told him. "So don't worry about it."

Steve Bannon: I said, "The poll thing's not bad. The Paulbots come down with all the college kids. Your speech was great. Don't worry about it." Trump says, "He told me I was a lock in to win it." Nunberg's sitting there going, "Tell him good stuff. Tell him good stuff." And Trump is crawling through the phone. "That fucking loser," he said. "This is fucked up. Fuck this." One F-bomb after another. "Listen, let me deal with Sam and I'll call you back." When I got off I said, "What the fuck did you tell this guy?" "He had to be a sponsor," Sam said, "and he never would have written the check if I didn't tell him he was going to win the poll." "He can't win the poll," I said. "They bring 2,000 Libertarian kids to this thing. That's how CPAC rolls." "I know," he said. "It was a mistake. I shouldn't have done it." Sam Nunberg is a genius. Now, he's got some drawbacks.*

---

* After Nunberg made a series of infamously loquacious cable TV appearances in March 2018, rambling about the Mueller investigation, he told WABC radio, "I'll listen to people, and see if there's proper programs. That's fine. I'm not a 24-hour-a-day alcoholic." (*Election Central with Rita Cosby*, aired March 8, 2018, on WABC-AM.)

Sam Nunberg: The fact of the matter is I was essential to Trump. And at the end of it, he treated me like shit the minute Corey came. Inexcusable to me. He never respected me. The reason he somewhat appreciated me was I was underpaid, which was always something I did with Trump so I could get rehired.

David Bossie: Sam was fundamentally a good guy to work with. I'm sorry he had his own troubles. I like Sam. He just spiraled a little bit. Bringing in Sam helped bring a little bit of organization to the campaign.

Sam Nunberg: During the exploratory period in 2015, I was surprised he did a lot of events. He went to South Carolina and New Hampshire a lot. He went to Iowa more than I thought he would. Roger and I were worried we were overworking him. He was willing to do that because he figured he had to. He said to me in early 2015, "If I'm going to do this, I'm really going to do this."

Jeff Jorgensen: There were people who had concerns that this is going to be a no-show. Donald Trump never had an Iowa campaign staff at that time. I was dealing with people that were directly working under him in New York. Sam Nunberg said, "Do us a favor, put together a list of things you'd like to see happen in Council Bluffs, and then we'll submit it and get everybody on board." So we got together, brainstorming. We ought to have a business roundtable discussion at the Omaha Press Club. We ought to have a VIP reception and get pictures taken. Then we have a dinner. From three o'clock until nine we had events scheduled with Donald Trump in Omaha and Council Bluffs. I said, "He's going to need a little downtime." We told them we've got an hour that he can relax. And Sam Nunberg gets back to me. "We want his time filled up. He doesn't want any downtime." I've never worked with campaign people that were more accommodating, ever. I've worked with quite a few of them. The only thing I got was positive feedback. "Mr. Trump is going to be there. Mr. Trump is going to enter the race." Sam Nunberg would call and say, "Is there anything we can do for you? How's ticket sales to the event going?" And I'd say, "Oh, it might be a little slow. We're still about two months out." The next day they would have Donald Trump being interviewed on KFAB. "If you want tickets to see Donald Trump, Pottawattamie County Republican Party's event." They called me.

"What else can we do for you?" I said it would be nice if Mr. Trump would provide some gift bag items for our sponsors. Three days later I had United Parcel deliver a box filled with books, ties, tie clasps, and cuff links.

A news database search shows that the first time Trump is recorded speaking publicly about a wall and not a fence was in an interview with Fox News' Bret Baier on April 10, 2015, in advance of Hillary Clinton's anticipated April 12 announcement of her candidacy. Trump told Baier he would have his own announcement by June on whether he was going to run.

> **Donald Trump:** People don't realize Mexico is not our friend. We have to build the wall. We have to stop people from coming in, and you have to stop it now. Nobody can build a wall like Trump can build a wall—believe me. That's one thing everybody agrees on.

> **Sam Nunberg:** A lot of it, which Trump totally knew and Roger and I loved, was gonzo politics. Grabbing people's attention. Everybody takes everything so personally. We said this is like one of his licensing deals. You build something, somebody else pays for it, and you have your name on it. That's like the birth certificate because it's like a mass deportation thing. Everybody else is going to say they're tough on immigration. And we said, "Oh, yeah? You're not as tough as us."

> **Roger Stone:** He's not not open to suggestions. He's very much his own man, but he'll always listen. He road tested it and he liked it, and it got a good response. It became a signature phrase, kind of like "Make America Great Again." It's that simple.

Two weeks later, on April 27, 2015, at a forum in Salem, New Hampshire, Trump was asked how he'd tackle border security. "I will build the best wall, the biggest, the strongest, not penetrable, they won't be crawling over it, like giving it a little jump and they're over the wall, it costs us trillions," he said. "And I'll have Mexico pay for the wall."[7]

> **Steve Bannon:** When he threw out the wall, people fucking jumped on it. And when he said Mexico would pay for it, they jumped on it more. These other politicians are stiffs. Trump reads a room better than anybody and understands the zeitgeist.

Sam Nunberg: He had said "fence" as early as 2013. So maybe he just mixed them up, and then he finally would just use "the wall" because it had been written down so many times for him. We didn't view it as interchangeable. It was also one of those things where he doesn't want to be handled, so he didn't want to immediately do what we were suggesting, but then he eventually does it. Because a wall is bigger than a fence. It's grander, it's bigger, and Trump's a builder. So what's bigger? What's more of a barrier? A wall. Right? Because we wanted—his candidacy was going to be the hardest on immigration to the right. So, others would say, "We'll build a fence." Trump would say, "I'll build a wall and I'll get Mexico to pay for it."

Anthony Scaramucci, *White House communications director July 21–31, 2017:* There's a blend of things that Mr. Trump firmly believes. The trade stuff, that tax cuts would help incentivize growth in the economy, deregulating the economy from unnecessary regulation. How far along the spectrum he believes the immigration stuff and the racial undertones, that I can't say.

By the time Trump was an official candidate later in the year, he would be saying "rapists" are crossing the border.[8] Then, as president in January 2019, he said, "We have terrorists coming through the southern border."[9] So he ended up with the image of an indomitable wall and the shock value of invading rapists and terrorists—a potent combination that could play to a certain audience's fear of the Other and of change, like the birther attacks on Obama. "The wall" was a carefully crafted catchphrase that crystallized the emotion of something Trump had been talking about for years.

31.

THE ANNOUNCEMENT

On March 17, 2015, one year after abandoning the New York governor's race, Trump announced he would form a presidential exploratory committee.[1] Trump was putting in the legwork, but it was the rare political figure or pundit, even on the right, who took him seriously. Three out of four voters said they definitely or probably would not vote for Trump, according to a March 2015 Quinnipiac poll. On March 1, 2015, Fox News' Media Buzz host Howard Kurtz led a segment titled "Should Journalists Believe Donald Trump Will Run for President?" National Journal editor Ron Fournier quipped, "He is a carnival barker." And conservative commentator Mary Katharine Ham followed with, "He has a long and flawless record of thinking that he's awesome."

In teasing a possible announcement of his candidacy, Trump was doing what he'd done as far back as 1999. In that Reform Party contemplation, he'd tried out the idea on the public, watched polls, and rolled out a book. A new book, Crippled America: How to Make America Great Again, was to be published by Simon & Schuster in October, and Marji Ross's Regnery Books prepared to print a paperback version of his 2011 book Time to Get Tough in August 2015. Most political reporters, who were holding on to the incorrect idea that Trump was never serious about 2000 or 2012, smugly propagated this canard as evidence that he would not run in 2016. The fact is that Trump did exactly as he'd done before: he explored the idea. In the past, he'd found the timing, the national mood, or his personal situation not right. Trump knew what the pundits thought, and at the Iowa GOP Lincoln Dinner in Des Moines on May 16, 2015, he mentioned a June announcement that's "going to surprise a lot of people."[2] The Des Moines Register noted that he was there but ignored *him, highlighting another business executive, former Hewlett-Packard CEO Carly Fiorina.[3] She had skipped Jeff Jorgensen's Lincoln–Reagan Day Dinner in Council Bluffs a night earlier, but Trump made both.[4] Politico declared Scott Walker the front-runner in Iowa.[5] The* New York Post's *Kyle Smith wrote a column headlined "Trump Is Not Running."[6]*

David Bossie: Right up until the escalator ride, you didn't know if he was actually going to do it. He didn't want to build an expectation that he was 100 percent going to do it because it didn't fit his modus operandi. He was a deal maker. You let the guy you're negotiating with figure out for himself or make assumptions, and it puts you in a firmer position. He was always somebody who said, "Yeah, I might do it, I might not." But the way he talked and carried himself was very serious. If he didn't do the escalator ride, he wanted to say, "I thought about it and I didn't do it." It was part of his mystique.

Sam Nunberg: One thing Michael [Cohen] and I disagreed on was timing. Michael wanted Trump to get in really, really early. I said, "No, later." I even discussed it with Roger. Trump wanted to announce during the summer because he was going to go back to *The Apprentice* if it didn't work out. That was the option. In October 2015 he could have started filming.

Katrina Pierson, *Trump 2016 campaign spokesperson:* No one believed he was going to get in the race. I told Ted Cruz and two of his staffers, "He could win. He could beat Jeb. You guys would be smart if you went with him." One of them said, "He's not gonna run." Somebody else said, "I bet he doesn't even file his paperwork." I said, "I understand why you would believe that, but he's going to run hard."

Anthony Scaramucci: He invited me to breakfast the day after *The Apprentice* finale [in February 2015]. We were discussing that his career as a television entertainer was over, that he was moving into politics and he was going to announce a run for the presidency. I didn't believe him. I said, "That's ridiculous. You're not going to do it." He then insisted he was going to do it. I had explained to Mr. Trump at that time that I was already involved with Governor Scott Walker's campaign as his cofundraising chair. I had an obligation to Jeb Bush if Scott Walker came out of the race. But I also told Mr. Trump in the event he was going to take it seriously and beat those two guys, then I would go work for him.

He respected that, and he was very highly confident that he was going to beat those two guys.

Tucker Carlson: Trump called me in March 2015 as I was in a car from the airport. "I'm going to make an announcement, and I think it's going to surprise you." I said, I'll never forget it, "You're going to have another fake run for president?" Because I remember so vividly his 2000 one, which was timed so coincidentally with the release of his book. [Laughs.] He was just grooming the media for his book tour, so I brought that up, and he sounded a little wounded, and said, "I'm going to surprise you, this time I really mean it. I'm not kidding around." I did not believe it. I really didn't. Shows you what I know.

Jeff Jorgensen: Donald Trump flew into town for five hours. He got to speak with [Omaha talk radio host] Chris Baker. Chris gave Mr. Trump a heads up on local issues. One, a year later, was Sarah Root.* She made a very big impact on that particular issue of illegal immigration in Iowa. Donald Trump was the one that was aggressively [taps table on "aggressively" for emphasis] addressing that issue. We had quite a few state party dignitaries there. Our national committeeman and national committeewoman from Iowa chatted with Mr. Trump. The other person to speak at our event was Sam Clovis. Sam ran for U.S. Senate in the primary in Iowa. He is a radio personality up in Sioux City. Donald Trump called him up later on. Covered the state of Iowa for the Trump campaign. Trump invited him into his administration.[7] Every one of these people gave credibility, which is what Trump had to have in Iowa. He said at our event, "I'm going to have an announcement here very quickly." He said, "You're going to like what I've got to say."

Steve Bannon: I spoke with Trump in May. He hadn't told me it's coming in June. The only thing I told him before is, "Hey, as soon as they know you're in, you're going to own this. But, right now, a lot of people just think you're doing it for TV ratings."

Sam Nunberg: We did one poll. One thing we saw was nobody took us seriously. We're hiring these people. We're doing this exploratory phase.

---

* Sarah Root was killed in a January 2016 car crash by a street-racing drunk driver who was an illegal immigrant and had skipped bail.

I only cared about our fave and unfave, and it consistently started going up the more visits he did to Iowa and New Hampshire. So the state polls went up, and I said to him, "These are the states. It takes longer for the national. When you announce, it will be the same thing."

David Bossie: Anybody who says they knew [that he was going to announce that day], they're lying to you.

Sam Nunberg: Melania really believed. She wasn't blowing smoke up his ass. She thought he was going to win the whole thing. I like her a lot, by the way. She gets a raw deal in all of this. She gets very high ratings. She said, "People don't think you're serious. When they know you're serious, you'll get a lot of support."

Roger Stone: He would always joke, "You know who my absolute best pollster is? Melania."

Sam Nunberg: I asked him, "What's our biggest problem going to be?" And he said, "You know what our biggest problem's going to be, and I'm going to get in trouble upstairs." Meaning Melania. He didn't specify anything. To me the whole Stormy Daniels thing, I feel bad for Melania; otherwise, it's fucking funny to me.[8]

Trump's campaign team had debated how they would prepare the stage for his presidential announcement. Lewandowski wanted a "dignified" announcement. Stone, Nunberg, and Cohen wanted a "smashmouth" display of opulence inside Trump Tower. Guess who won?

Roger Stone: His greatest advantage was that everyone knew who he is from the get-go. The average voter does not know who Marco Rubio is. Also true of Ted Cruz. They become well known through the process, but first they have to achieve critical mass before they can impart a message or idea. Trump doesn't have that issue. He's universally known from the beginning, so he can go right to his agenda. Then there's the entertainment factor. People think his candidacy is so improbable, but they want to tune in to see what he has to say.

Sam Nunberg: There were two lines of thought. Lewandowski and this guy he brought in, George [Gigicos], wanted it to be dignified.[9] He should just take the elevator down, give a 10-minute speech, and come out and then leave. We were like, "No." Michael, me, and Roger, and of course Trump himself, wanted this to be the most smashmouth, disgusting—I mean in a good way—fuck you to everything. It was glorious. Terrible. We're different. We're here. Get over it. It's not only about the TV image. We wanted to say this is new. This is fun. This is something exciting.

Roger Stone: It was a relatively chaotic period. I had a detached retina from my own stupidity of boxing at my advanced age. And I couldn't fly, so I was not actually at that announcement.

Sam Nunberg: Roger and I spoke to Trump, saying, "Dude, you gotta do the escalator." Be yourself. Of course he was going to do the escalator. That's what he always does. The first scene of *The Apprentice* he's coming down the escalator. That's him. That's his schtick. Trump was going to be himself. It didn't take much. Like all the music, he picked it himself.

Justin McConney: He calls me in, and he says, "Alright, we've got to talk about music, what songs I'm going to run out to." I wasn't someone that was into politics, but I did know every time there was a campaign, especially for Republican candidates, there was an issue where someone would play a song and the band would get really upset. He started naming off all these rock bands that he liked. "I don't think a lot of these guys are going to want you playing their song," I said. "Yeah, but I'm friends with these guys," he said. "I want Aerosmith in there. Neil Young. *Phantom of the Opera. Cats.* Adele." "Mr. Trump," I said, "that doesn't make any sense. Those don't really go together." "Look," he said, "these are just songs I like, okay? It's about what I like." Then he starts playing musical *Jeopardy!* where he just starts naming the bands and then asks me, "Name a few songs by them. Rolling Stones." I said, "If you're going to go with them, 'Start Me Up' would make sense." "I was never a fan of that one," he said. "I want to do 'You Can't Always Get What You Want.'" "That really doesn't make any sense," I said. "I don't care," he said. "I love the chorus to that song."

We start going back and forth and putting together this list and how he's going to walk onto the stage. He says, "I can't just walk out there. I can't just walk onstage. I either come out through the elevator, but that's not much of an entrance. Or there's the escalator." I said to him, "The escalator, that's kind of your shot. In *The Apprentice*, over and over again, they show you coming down an escalator and you've done it on news shoots." He said, "You know, you're right. That is my shot. I'm going to come down the escalator."

Then he says, "I want to use 'Dream On,' but I'm not sure it's the last song. What about a Neil Young song?" I said, "I really don't think Neil Young's going to like it." He said, "This guy's a friend of mine. He was up here. Just start naming them." I start naming Neil Young songs. He says, "No, no, no. What's the big one?" I said, "Rockin' in the Free World." "That's it," he said. "That's the song. I'm going to come down to 'Rockin' in the Free World.'"

Sam Nunberg: Trump had very good instincts. If it were up to me, we would have had strippers, clowns, and elephants. Michael had this great quote. I love Michael saying this: "I know how to do this stuff. You should see my kid's bar mitzvah." I thought, "Awesome, I love this." I loved it, and I don't mean that as a criticism. It was a sentiment we needed. The bar mitzvah.

Donny Deutsch, *CNBC host:* I really got to know Michael Cohen through Donald. We traveled in the same social circles, and we got to be friendly outside of Trump. He was at my kid's bar mitzvah. No, he did not give advice how to plan it. Why would you ask that? [*Deutsch is told about Cohen's bar mitzvah take on Trump.*] That's great. That's so genius. That pretty much says it all, doesn't it? Let's do it like it's a bar mitzvah boy coming in for his grand entrance.

Trump's advisers began making preparations for his presidential announcement. Michael Cohen sent letters to his boss's alma maters, demanding they not release Trump's grades or transcripts, lest they face "substantial fines, penalties and even the potential loss of government aid and other funding."[10]

Sam Nunberg tipped reporters to come to Trump Tower. Some reporters didn't want to show up, doubting he would do it. Trump himself got cold feet. A week before the announcement, he called Lewandowski from an overseas trip asking to postpone it indefinitely.

Sam Nunberg: People didn't believe he was going to announce. I tried to get Maggie [Haberman, of the *New York Times*] to report it. She didn't want to. She didn't want to get used. I had to tell Kasie Hunt [of

MSNBC] the week before because Jeb announced the week before us. I said, "Kasie, we're running. I'll be off the record with you. I'm reading the announcement speech right now. I swear on my life we're running." People still didn't believe it.

Justin McConney: He's going to announce. He's definitely going to run for president. In my head I'm thinking, "Well, the guy's always saying this and not running." But once they started to put together the stage and he was sitting there talking to me about the songs, I'm thinking, "I've got to get out of here. I don't want to be involved with this."

Sam Nunberg: Trump travels to Europe the week before he announces. It was a business thing. Trump was bothering Corey. He said he didn't want to go do the campaign stops. He only wanted to do TV interviews in Trump Tower.

Roger Stone: He called Corey from Scotland[11] and said, "Put the announcement on hold." Corey was relatively panicked, and I said, "I'll talk to him, but don't worry about it if he's just in a bad mood today." Which he was. By the time he returned to the United States, that moment had passed and he was full speed ahead.

Sam Nunberg: That's like Madonna saying she doesn't want to perform at a sold-out Madison Square Garden. I knew he was going to go.

Steve Bannon: We sent a team. We had no New York operation at that time. I sent [Breitbart reporter] Matt Boyle and a five-man team to cover that thing. That's how important we thought it was. Coverage from every angle.

Justin McConney: Periscope [the live-streaming app] had just come out. I wanted him to get on Periscope, and the best way to use Periscope would be to stream his announcement speech on it. The first Periscope we did was the day before, where he announced, "Tune in to my Periscope tomorrow for my big announcement."

Steve Bannon: The only thing I did on the speech was say, "Stick to yourself. Particularly if your signature thing's going to be trade and immigration, throw down. You've got to break through the white noise. The reason you're in seventh place is nobody thinks you're committed to do this." I told him, "The moment people think you're in, you're going to capture the Tea Party. Because nobody's got that Tea Party vote right now."

At 11:00 a.m. on June 16, 2015, press and invited guests assembled in the atrium of Trump Tower. On a raised stage adorned with eight American flags and a blue "Trump: Make America Great Again" campaign sign, family and aides looked on as Neil Young's "Rockin' in the Free World" began to play.

Trump and Melania walked out of a private elevator one floor above the crowd. Trump gave two thumbs up and gestured for Melania to follow him to the escalator in front of campaign volunteers and paid actors wearing "Make America Great Again" t-shirts and hats. They descended.

It was the culmination of years of work. Almost nothing was random. The setting was the marble-lined atrium that had been extolled for its luxury and tasteful use of expensive materials by the most important architecture critic in New York when it opened 35 years earlier. The candidate's entrance had been honed both by the most successful reality producers in television and by his close political, media, and tech advisers.

What he said was market tested, harkening back to his very first interview that touched on politics, with Rona Barrett, drawing from the policy books he'd co-authored over the past decade and a half, steering straight into applause lines he'd buffed at CPAC, freedom summits, and Lincoln dinners, aimed not at everyone but at an audience he knew was out there because he'd met them at the upstate gun rally during his almost-run for governor, with Jesse Ventura in Minnesota, in arena tour stops with Tony Robbins, tantalized them by tweeting, listened to them call in to conservative radio, been told about them by Bannon and the memos from Caputo and Davenport, scanned printouts of web pages they read from alt-right news sources. He'd investigated the particular power of his own brand, from asking questions and listening during the phone calls with Tucker Carlson, Don King, Roger Stone, Roy Cohn, and Howard Stern; in the huddles with Dick Morris, David Bossie, his ghostwriters, Justin McConney, people high and low sent into his office by Rhona Graff, by Norma Foerderer, by Nunberg. He used a brashness that was part his father's, part New York City birthright, part having gotten away with so much for so long, solidified in tussles with Pat Buchanan, Gloria Allred, and Rosie O'Donnell and a thousand sparring phone calls to reporters, rivals, friends, and frenemies like Al Sharpton, Ralph Nader, Donny Deutsch, and the editors of the New York Post—*his onrushing undergirded by what Carl Jung suggested, trusting in a finely tuned intuition. Now was right. Now. When he walked out to "Rockin' in the Free World," he was striding to a famous song about trampled American pride by someone who'd come to this very building and been shown up that elevator to ask him for money, a final ego-fortifying thought if he needed any more of a boost—"There's colors on the street / red, white and blue . . ." He did not know he would win, but he'd always said he wouldn't run if he didn't think he could win. Now he thought he could, now, and now he was as ready as he knew how to be.*

In his 45-minute speech, the culmination of this part of a staggering American journey, the kickoff of a new phase that would engender its own near-impossible twists, Trump touched on foreign policy, trade, terrorism, the economy, health-care, and immigration. "Our country needs and deserves a comeback," he said. "But, we are not going to get that comeback with politicians. Politicians," he said, sounding like the hero of the old Reform Party, Jesse Ventura, and, know-ing he'd spent what for him was loose change to turn politicians, elected beggars he'd made cool their heels in his waiting room, into rubber stamps for his real estate developments, "are not the solution to our problems. They are the problem."[12]

His reference to some Mexican migrants as "rapists" provided his most in-flammatory line:

> The U.S. has become a dumping ground for everybody else's prob-lems. And these aren't the best or the finest. When Mexico sends its people, they're not sending their best. They're not sending you. They're sending people that have lots of problems, and they're bringing those problems to us. They're bringing drugs, they're bringing crime, they're rapists . . . [13]

The immigration issue was near the top of the speech, minutes before he finally said that which he had never said before:

> So ladies and gentlemen, I am officially running for president of the United States, and we are going to make our country great again. . . . You know, all of these politicians that I'm running against now—it's so nice to say I'm running as opposed to if I run, if I run. I'm running. . . . But they all said, a lot of the pundits on television, "Well, Donald will never run, and one of the main reasons is he's private and he's probably not as successful as everybody thinks." So I said to myself, you know, nobody's ever going to know unless I run.

Justin McConney: I was on the press riser in the atrium. My iPhone was on a tripod, and I had an extension cord. I was Periscoping. I had the whole social media plan laid out. I had a picture up beforehand. I got the family photo of them onstage. My own camera guy next to me filming, so we could put the whole video on YouTube and Facebook. Then there was the music, which I worked on with Trump. I don't think anyone knew the speech was going to go that long. Someone explained, "It's just going to be 10 minutes." It ended up being 46 minutes or so. When he started going and going, I thought, what's going on here? That was a big surprise. I don't think people knew really what to expect with this because he had been teasing it for years. I got text messages on my phone, "Is this real? Is this really happening?"

Steve Bannon: At the top of the escalator, he's in seventh place. After the speech he's number one. Because the left bit on the border, rapist stuff, thought they were going to destroy him. The Huffington Post and the rest of these guys were triggered. And he didn't back down. That was so extraordinary.

Anthony Scaramucci: He invited me to that. Unfortunately, I couldn't make it that day. I sent my political director. She heard the speech, brought back some of the "Make America Great Again" placards and "The Silent Majority Stands with Candidate Trump," and buttons and a few "Make America Great Again" hats. But we were with Governor Walker at that time. So we said, "Okay, let's see how this goes." He shot right to the top of the polls and he stayed there.

Sean Spicer, *White House communications director January–July 2017:* I was in my office in DC. I was thinking, "I wonder how they're going to raise money." I knew a few of the guys up there and was thinking, "This is going to be interesting how they handle this."

Glenn Beck, *conservative radio and TV host:* When he was coming down the escalator, I was on air, and we were laughing about it. There's a good chance the whole thing was a publicity stunt that threw him into a presidency. I wasn't on the Trump train.

Neera Tanden: I never had any thoughts of him as a serious candidate for anything before he went down that escalator. When he first ran, I thought he was going to drag down the Republicans.

Steve Bannon: The Republican donor class has spent 25 years to create the Class of 2016. In every vertical you had the best. If you're a Christian, you've got Cruz. If you're a libertarian, you've got Rand Paul. If your big thing is governors, you've got Christie. If you're this, you've got a Bush. You've got Rubio. You had 16 people who spent a billion dollars to be the flower of the Republican Party, and I said, "He's going to cut through that like a scythe through grass. It's not even going to make a sound."

Marji Ross: When it became obvious that Trump was very serious about a presidential run in 2015, we said, "Let's release the paperback of *Time to Get Tough*. We better go back and read that book again." There was nothing in the book of a policy nature or an opinion of his that needed to be changed. It was all very consistent, and that impressed me. For all the talk, "He's just an opportunist," or "He's not a real conservative." No, he's saying the same thing and has the same positions as he did four years ago. The original subtitle was *Making America #1 Again*. We just switched it, a very easy change, to "Make America Great Again.".

Reverend Al Sharpton, *civil rights activist:* When he announced it, I said, "Ah, he's not really going to do it." Because I never saw him as a kind of guy who can build an organization and build an infrastructure.

Justin McConney: My boss was running for president and now I was doing his social media unwillingly. It wasn't something I wanted to do or work on. I was trying to leave before it happened.*

Trump concluded his announcement:

> Sadly, the American dream is dead. But if I get elected president I will bring it back bigger and better and stronger than ever before, and we will make America great again.

---

* McConney stayed with the Trump Organization until 2017.

THE CENTRE CANNOT HOLD

We're about to leave these players to their fates. Taking a parting glance at the waves caused by Trump's full-throated entry into the presidential race demonstrates that something new was rising from the east, if not in substance then in form.

The shock that Trump had actually announced his candidacy was soon replaced by the shock of what he'd said while doing it. Mexico sending rapists! Reporters who might have been impelled to ignore a candidacy that many still saw as a publicity stunt were nevertheless drawn to report on the outrageous words. If he was a clown to them, he was one of those scary, threatening ones, the grinning kind you don't dare turn your eyes—or your cameras—from.

Democratic front-runner Hillary Clinton chided him with a classic politician's distance and decorum, not even mentioning Trump by name as she explained to a Nevada journalist her opposition to placing children in large detention centers. "A recent entry into the Republican presidential campaign said some very inflammatory things about Mexicans," Clinton said, building on her earlier comment that "unfortunately, the public discourse is sometimes hotter and more negative than it should be, which can, in my opinion, trigger people who are less than stable." She was referring to a shooting that claimed nine lives in a Charleston, South Carolina, church.[1]

Trump hammered back, casting himself as the victim by saying in an Instagram video, "Wow, it's pretty pathetic that Hillary Clinton just blamed me for the horrendous attack that took place in South Carolina. This is why politicians are just no good. Our country's in trouble." The caption was, "Hillary Clinton *reaches new low #TrumpVlog." He no longer had to phone the* New York Post *and trade gossip that he'd collected in exchange for a next-day mention of him blasting his opponent. He knew the game of pillorying better than Clinton and had no compunction about insulting a woman by name. Hillary Clinton would be his new Rosie O'Donnell, social media his Page Six. Trump, who'd turned 69 years old two days before his announcement, had honed his methods for the world of 2015, and he was applying them ruthlessly.*

It turned out McConney was right about rock stars. Three days after the announcement, Neil Young put out a statement that Trump did not have permission to use his song. Trump fired back on June 24, tweeting a photo of Young's business proposal and saying the musician was a "total hypocrite" and that he "didn't love [the song] anyway."

That wasn't the only relationship that soured after the announcement. On June 29, 2015, NBC severed ties with Trump "due to recent derogatory statements" he made about immigrants.

Sam Nunberg: He announces. The next week he's dropped by everyone. It helped us politically, but it was killing his business. He lost a lot of money. Part of it too was he didn't know where this was going to go. He got pushed into wanting to go the full distance after they fucked him after his announcement speech, especially when he got *The Apprentice* taken away. I don't want to betray his trust here, but I'll put it to you one way. It didn't happen immediately, but eventually it hit him. And boy, boy, boy, did you not want to be around him then. I don't think he was upset at [Mark] Burnett. He was upset at NBC. The irony was, whenever they hurt his business it was going to help him. He would prefer they didn't hurt his business, but it would help him politically to become a martyr.

Justin McConney: Once *The Apprentice* was done, he took his chair from the show and moved it up into his office and put a sign on it that says, "The chair from *The Apprentice*. 2004 to 2015. Number One show." Then he had a couch, which was full of sports memorabilia: boxing gloves, Shaq's sneakers. If you were a reporter that would go in during that time period, he would walk you over to his couch of memorabilia.

Jonathan Wald, *cable news producer:* He was a spectacle that we couldn't get enough of. No guilt. None whatsoever. At the time it was the best story going.

Sam Nunberg: There was a time he liked Hillary. When I saw him really not like her was two days after our announcement. There was a terrible terrorist shooting in South Carolina. The racist went into the black church. It was disgusting, and she blamed him, his speech, for it. And Trump said, "She's a nasty, nasty . . ." I won't use the word he used.*

Jonathan Wald: There were a couple of interviews we did with Don Lemon, who he now calls the dumbest man on television, at Trump Tower in which they got along famously. My favorite moment was when we were told that Mr. Trump wanted to speak with us before an interview. There's a table with a map on it with pins in it for the states he's focusing on and what he's targeting and what his strategy is going to be to win the presidency. He sidles up and walks us into his office and says, "You guys wanna see Tom Brady's helmet?" [Laughs.] I said, "Yeah, I would love to see Tom Brady's helmet!"

Roger Stone: People wanted to see a man working without a net. You never knew what he might say, including me, or anyone around him, and he was endlessly entertaining. He understood that you need to engage a voter before you could educate them. I did not think that you could combat hundreds of millions of dollars of paid negative media with a free media blitz of your own, where it meant being seen and heard everywhere that you possibly could, even if it meant six interviews a day. He did think you could out-communicate paid media. He was right and I was wrong.

Katie Couric: I was at Yahoo!, and I was kissing the ring to see if he'd do an interview. I went to see him in his office, and he had magazines piled up high that he was on the cover of. He said, "Can you believe this?" I said, "Wow, no, I can't."

Steve Bannon: The guy who missed it, and missed it hard, my good buddy Mr. Roger Ailes and Rupert Fucking Murdoch. Fuck them. They

---

* Nunberg would be fired from the Trump campaign for the final time 47 days after the escalator announcement, on August 2, 2015, amid allegations he'd left racist Facebook posts dating back to 2007, including one calling Barack Obama a "Socialist Marxist Islamo Fascist Nazi Appeaser" and another that used the N-word in reference to Reverend Al Sharpton's daughter. Nunberg denied he wrote the posts, but he was out. Lewandowski explained the firing to CNN: "They do not reflect Mr. Trump's position."

were dead wrong on this thing from the beginning. They thought Trump was a fucking goombah. And they're supposed to be media geniuses? Fox was the never-Trump network until they weren't. He's got an ability to viscerally connect into people's guts and hearts. I always tell people, "I'm always arguing with him, and I'm always wrong eventually." You can go anywhere in the world today, and it's all him. He's saturated everything.

Tucker Carlson: Bannon's not smart enough to understand the implications. He has no fine motor skills, that's his problem. But Bannon also had the quality that Trump has, the ability to look at everybody else in your peer group and say to their face, "You're wrong."

Reverend Al Sharpton: I go do *Morning Joe* in early December a month after Trump won, and Joe [Scarborough] was asking me, "You and Trump know each other for years. Tell me about Donald Trump. I don't understand how he translated to these working-class poor people."

I said, "Trump is an outer-borough guy who was never accepted by the real estate moguls and downtown barons of that industry. So he always had a chip on his shoulder. He felt that they looked down on him and his father. And you'd have to be a New Yorker to understand an outer-borough status. I had it double because I was from Brooklyn and black. But he felt like that. You didn't see him at the power breakfasts. He didn't hang out at the Regency. He wasn't a member of those clubs. That's why he wanted to splash his name. And he translated that chip on his shoulder, that resentment, to those blue-collar workers in Appalachia and Kentucky because that was really how he felt. The fact that he was a billionaire, if he is, it was us against them, and he felt that."

I get off the show. Get in the car. We were having a board meeting of the National Action Network, and in the middle of the meeting, my phone rings. I look at the number. It ended with 2000. I didn't know the number. And the voice comes on, "Would you hold on for the president-elect?" And Trump comes on. "Al, I saw you this morning. I was telling my wife, 'He got me. This guy knows me.' You've got to be a New Yorker to know that. You're absolutely right. They look down on us, Al. Look at what you did to the black establishment. And can you believe I'm the president of the United States?"

I said, "No, I'm having a hard time getting my head around it." And he laughed. "I want you to come to Mar-a-Lago." I said, "The only way we meet is if I can bring the other civil rights leaders." He said, "No, I don't know them. I know you. We fight, but I know you. Anybody who knows race knows Al Sharpton." "I'm not doing that," I said. "You're not going to get me in a photo op. We know each other too well. It's going to be a serious meeting. The head of Urban League, NAACP, same group that would meet with Obama." "I ain't doing that," he said. "Well, we'll talk," I said. "As things come up, I'm sure we'll talk," he said. I asked, "Who's the contact to you?" "Call me," he said. "Nobody talks for me. You know that, Al. You call me when I'm in the White House, you just tell them it's you." That was the last conversation we had.

Sam Nunberg: Anyway, I'm done with these fucking interviews. I'm done in general. This is the last time I'm ever talking about the elections. This is it. When I write a book, it's going to say, "I worked for Donald Trump." Now you understand my personal feelings. To me, honestly, it's water under the bridge now because I already vented on national TV [on March 5, 2018, when he made numerous rambling cable-TV appearances]. I loved that day. You know me. I loved that day. Everybody knows who I am. They know I'm not a low-level, part-time consultant. I'm getting booked now.

ACKNOWLEDGMENTS

We are grateful for the talents, kindnesses, suggestions, and time of those who supported us during the year and a half we spent on this fascinating project. Yfat Reiss Gendell, Adam Bellow, Sara Ventiera, David Dunbar, Becky Wisdom, Adam Park, Tyler Allen, Amanda Morris, Jennifer Litton, Kristine Rakowsky, Betsy Goldman, Lisa Ferri, Alexandra Pelosi, Victoria C. Rowan, Jon Rosen, Sheryl Hastalis, Jolie Parcher, Angel Dean Lopez, Claudia Borzutsky, Gersh Kuntzman, Kevin Reilly, Brad Hamilton, Marjorie Short, Edwina and Allen Berliner, Adam Lubow and Sarah Siegel, Matt O'Dowd, Matt Cowherd, Lacey Tauber, Leslie Josephs, Harry Siegel, Matt Taylor, Ben Adler, Matt Clark, Godfrey and Cassy, Dante and Sandy Amenta, Francis Pickering, David Seifman, Carl Campanile, Alan Bradshaw, Katherine Haigler, Steve Cohen, Ryan Masteller, Gabrielle Gantz, Guy Oldfield, Craig Young, Nina Sander, Nora Isaacs, Mathew Klickstein, Dakota Smith, Mandy Stadtmiller, Laura Harris, Rebecca McBane, Dan Patterson, CarolLee Kidd, Matthew Lynch, Marshall Poe, Geoffrey Gray, Mia Stageberg, Susan Shapiro, the newsletters of Brian Stelter, Mike Allen, and Michael Calderone, Caleb Stark, Abby Ellin, Alison Brower, Joelle Goldstein, Ron Dodd, Laurel Touby, Jon Fine, Julyne Derrick, Jessica Felleman, Kiri Tannenbaum, Mark Rozzo, Norah Lawlor, Jeffrey Bradford, Faye Penn, David Wallis, Erik Huey, Curtis Stone, Mitchell Davis, Amy Brightfield, Jonathan Bloom, Laura Begley, Cezary Podkul, Cathering Ngai, Shady, Stubbs, Martha, Daniel Boy, Emma,

Zoya, Mocha, Juliet Linderman, Rebecca Federman and the New York Public Library, Joyce Litt, Nadia Sussman, Toby Salkin Jacobson, and Doug, Jenny, Alex, Lilly, and Max Salkin. Aaron and Allen are also grateful to each other. We put a lot into it. Thank you for reading.

NOTES

INTRODUCTION: YES, THERE IS A METHOD

1. The Central Park Five were convicted in 1990 and exonerated in 2002.

2. Ginger Gibson and Grant Smith, "Figures Show Trump Spent $66 Million of His Own Cash on Election Campaign," Reuters, December 8, 2016.

3. David Barstow, Susanne Craig, and Russ Buettner, "Trump Engaged in Suspect Tax Schemes as He Reaped Riches from His Father," *New York Times*, October 2, 2018.

4. Rona Barrett, interview with Allen Salkin, September 6, 2018.

5. Figuring out how long Trump was actually in the Soviet Union on this 1987 trip proved difficult, but it appears that six days is about right. A *New York Times* article with a dateline of Thursday, July 2 (Donald Janson, "Trump Wins Approval for a 3d Casino in Jersey"), said he would leave for Russia the next day, a Friday, and would spend six days in Moscow. On July 15, a Wednesday, the *Los Angeles Times* printed an interview ("Trump May Develop a Hotel in Moscow") conducted at the Plaza Athne hotel in Paris "this weekend," likely meaning July 11 or 12, where Trump was staying "for a few days of vacation on his way back from the Soviet Union."

6. Joyce Barnathan, "Trump Lands in Red Square," *Newsweek*, July 20, 1987.

7. Michael Oreskes, "Trump Gives a Vague Hint of Candidacy," *New York Times*, Sepember 2, 1987.

8. Fox Butterfield, "New Hampshire Speech Earns Praise for Trump," *New York Times*, October 23, 1987.

9. *Hardball with Chris Matthews*, August 27, 1998. This segment was re-aired on the show on July 3, 2017 (http://www.msnbc.com/transcripts/hardball/2017-07-03).

10. Allen Salkin wrote the first major profile of Kushner when he purchased the

New York Observer at the age of 26. Salkin, "The Education of a Publisher," *New York Times*, March 11, 2007.

1. TIPSTER

1. Paul Goldberger, "Architecture: Atrium of Trump Tower Is a Pleasant Surprise," *New York Times*, April 4, 1983.
2. Katherine Love, "34 Years of Donald Trump in the Pages of Forbes," *Forbes*, July, 16, 2016, online.
3. Allen Salkin, "Trump: The Smarts of the Deal," *New York Post*, April 18, 1999.
4. Jason Horowitz, "For Donald Trump, Lessons from a Brother's Suffering," *New York Times*, January 2, 2016.
5. Barrett's assistant at the time, Timothy L. O'Brien, got into the Atlantic City birthday event and was not arrested. In 2005, O'Brien published the book *Trump Nation: The Art of Being the Donald.* He was sued by Trump for questioning Trump's wealth. After three years, O'Brien won.
6. Barrett's book was a sales failure, but the work in it was widely used by other reporters in the years to come. In the summer of 2016, it was republished under the updated title *Trump: The Greatest Show on Earth; The Deals, the Downfall, the Reinvention.*

2. THE TOUGH AND TIRELESS ROGER STONE

1. Jonathan Mahler and Matt Flegenheimer, "What Donald Trump Learned from Joseph McCarthy's Right-Hand Man," *New York Times*, June 20, 2016.
2. Stephanie Mansfield, "The Rise and Gall of Roger Stone," *Washington Post*, June 16, 1986.
3. John M. Crewdson, "Sabotaging the G.O.P.'s Rivals: Story of a $100,000 Operation," *New York Times*, July 9, 1973; Matt Labash, "Roger Stone, Political Animal," *Weekly Standard*, November 5, 2007.
4. Michael Oreskes, "Trump Gives a Vague Hint of Candidacy," *New York Times*, September 2, 1987.
5. Fox Butterfield, "New Hampshire Speech Earns Praise for Trump," *New York Times*, October 23, 1987.
6. Ed Rendell, "A Letter to the President," *Philadelphia Daily News*, June 8, 2018.

3. ROSS FOR BOSS

1. Brian Elzweig, Katherine Roberto, and Andrew F. Johnson, "Political Ideology as a Proxy for Disparate Impact Discrimination," *Southern Law Journal* 27, no. 2 (2017): 277–92.
2. Pam Belluck, "A 'Bad Boy' Wrestler's Unscripted Upset," *New York Times*, November 5, 1998, p. 2.

4. THE AMERICA WE DESERVE

1. Michael Lind, "The Radical Center or the Moderate Middle?" *New York Times*, December 3, 1995, p. 2.
2. Michael Janofsky and B. Drummond Ayres Jr., "Rift on Buchanan Leads to a Split in Reform Party," *New York Times*, August 11, 2000.

5. THE TRUMP RV

1. Matt Bai, "Jesse Finds His Big Guy," *Newsweek*, July 19, 1999, p. 32.
2. Seth Gitell, "Fulani, Perot Pact Spurs Talk about 'Red-Brown Coalition,'" *The Forward*, August 30, 1996, p. 1.
3. Mike Allen, "Weicker Cool to Reform Bid," *New York Times*, Late Edition (East Coast), October 5, 1999, p. 22.

6. STANDING PAT

1. Kenneth R. Bazinet, "Trump Rips Buchanan Hitler Talk," New York *Daily News*, September 20, 1999.
2. Adam Nagourney, "President? Why Not? Says a Man at the Top," *New York Times*, September 25, 1999, p. 1.
3. Tom Squitieri, "A Look Back at Trump's First Run," The Hill, October 7, 2015.
4. Joel Siegel, "See Donald Run: Looking to Presidency, with Oprah as His Veep," New York *Daily News*, October 8, 1999, p. 4.
5. Deborah Orin and Mark Stamey, "Trump Pumped to Hit Stump: Wants to Run with Oprah on His Ticket," *New York Post*, October 8, 1999, p. 4.
6. Gallup Poll, October 8–10 1999, https://news.gallup.com/poll/184115/1999-not-trump-serious-candidate.aspx.
7. Glen Johnson, Associated Press, "Donald Trump Eyes the White House," New York *Daily News*, October 8, 1999, p. N1.
8. Frank Newport, "Trump Enters Presidential Fray with Unfavorable Image and Low Poll Positioning," Gallup News Service, October 8, 1999.
9. Francis X. Clines, "Trump to Quit GOP, Join Reform Party," *Chicago Tribune*, October 25, 1999, p. 4.
10. Glen Johnson, "Reform Party May Gain Trump, Buchanan Today," *Chicago Sun-Times*, October 25, 1999, p. 24.
11. Theresa Conroy, "Trump at Penn to Talk Oval Office Ambition," *Philadelphia Daily News*, November 18, 1999, p. 13.
12. Frederick Cusick, "Trump Plays It Coy on *Hardball* Show," *Philadelphia Inquirer*, November 19, 1999, p. 43.
13. Joel Siegel, "Trump 100G Speech Fee," New York *Daily News*, December 2, 1999, p. 74.
14. Carla Marinucci, "Trump to Stump in Southern Cal: The Donald's Campaign

Stop Includes Sellout Talk, Jay Leno Show," *San Francisco Chronicle*, December 2, 1999, p. A3.

15. Scott Lindlaw, "Reform Party Activists Ask Trump Some Tough Questions," *The Columbian*, December 8, 1999, p. A8.

16. Carla Marinucci, "Trump Counting on His Fame, Wealth," *San Francisco Chronicle*, December 7, 1999, p. A3.

17. *The Tonight Show with Jay Leno*, NBC, December 7, 1999, available at: https://www.youtube.com/watch?reload=9&v=MGLNb0JE8uc&feature=youtu.be.

7. I PLEDGE I WILL NOT RENAME THE WHITE HOUSE

1. C-SPAN, January 5, 2000, https://www.c-span.org/video/?154645-1/the-america-deserve.

2. Gersh Kuntzman, "Trump's Not Quakin' over Shakin' Anymore," *New York Post*, January 6, 2000.

3. Allen Salkin, "For Him, the Web Was No Safety Net," *New York Times*, August 28, 2009, p. ST1.

4. Walter Kirn, "In Trump We Trust," *New York* magazine, January 17, 2000.

5. Jerry Useem, "What Does Donald Trump Really Want?" *Fortune*, April 3, 2000, p. 188.

6. Rochelle Olson, "Trump Closing in on Presidential Bid: Ventura Says He'll Consider an Endorsement," *Chicago Sun-Times*, January 8, 2000, p. 9.

7. C-SPAN, January 7, 2000, https://www.c-span.org/video/?154581-1/trump-news-conference.

8. Richard Johnson and Bill Hoffman, "Trump Knixes Knauss: Donald-Dumped Supermodel Is 'Heartbroken,'" *New York Post*, January 11, 2000, p. 7.

9. Jared Paul Stern, "Model Dumped the Donald," *New York Post*, January 13, 2000, pp. 4–5.

10. Vincent Morris, "The Suddenly Single Trump's Still a Political Party Animal," *New York Post*, January 14, 2000.

11. Brian E. Crowley, "Trump Woos Reform Leaders with Soiree at Mar-a-Lago," *Palm Beach Post*, January 15, 2000, p. 3A.

12. Richard Johnson and Bill Hoffman, "Trump and Melania Rekindle Flame," *New York Post*, January 27, 2000, p. 3.

8. THE UNREFORMED

1. Peter Carlson, "Outriders' Roughrider: With the Foam-Flecked Fury That Made Jack Gargan Great, Reform Follows Dysfunction," *Washington Post*, January 18, 2000, p. C1.

2. Michael Janofsky, "Factions Fracture Reform Party: Infighting Between Texas, Minnesota Groups Weakens Party as Elections Approach," *Austin American-Statesman*, January 23, 2000, p. H1.

3. Tom Squitieri, "Reform Wanted to Break Out, Not Break Down," *USA Today,* January 17, 2000, p. 10A.

4. "Reform Party Infighting Gives Trump Pause," *Los Angeles Times*, January 21, 2000, p. 23.

5. Jo Mannies,"Trump Will Speak at Seminar Here, Meet with Reform Party," *St. Louis Post-Dispatch*, February 8, 2000.

6. Associated Press, "Trump Backs Health-Care Vouchers," *The Columbian*, February 8, 2000, p. A4.

7. "Daily Briefing," *Seattle Times*, February 7, 2000, p. A4.

8. Rochelle Olson, "Ventura Delivers Slam to Reform Party," *Milwaukee Journal Sentinel*, February 12, 2000, p. 1A.

9. Adam Nagourney, "Reform Bid Said to Be a No-Go for Trump," *New York Times*, February 14, 2000, p. A18.

10. Ellis Henican, "Who Was Donald Trying to Kid?" *Newsday*, February 16, 2000, p. A08.

11. "Liberal Activist Fulani Resigns from Buchanan Campaign," *Los Angeles Times,* June 20, 2000, p. 16.

9. C.E.O.

1. Mark Burnett, *Jump In! Even If You Don't Know How to Swim* (New York: Ballantine Books, 2005), pp. 186–94.

2. Mark Bethea, pitch document for *C.E.O.*, in authors' possession.

3. Jim Gilmore, "The Frontline Interview: Jim Dowd," *Frontline,* September 27, 2016, https://www.pbs.org/wgbh/frontline/article/the-frontline-interview-jim-dowd/.

4. Mark Burnett, Keynote Presentation, Entrepreneurial Leaders Conference, Vancouver, BC, November 14, 2013, available at: https://www.youtube.com/watch?v=DlfVJL4mSfI.

10. BOUND FOR GLORY

1. Charles V. Bagli, "Due Diligence on the Donald," *New York Times*, Late Edition (East Coast), January 25, 2004.

2. "The Apprentice: Omarosa Manigault: Herself, Herself - Contestant, Herself - Reality Star," IMDB, https://www.imdb.com/title/tt0364782/characters/nm1524098.

11. THE N-WORD

1. https://www.vanityfair.com/news/2018/11/michael-cohen-trump-racist-language. In the original article the quote is "black f_g." Allen Salkin confirmed in an email with a *Vanity Fair* editor that the word was "fag."

12. TRUMP ASCENDANT

1. "NBC Names Head of Entertainment Unit," *New York Times*, May 4, 2004, p. C4.
2. Keith Naughton and Marc Peyser, "The World According to Trump," *Newsweek*, March 1, 2004, pp. 48, 54, 57.
3. Charles Passy, "I Do, I Do, I Do: Will a Third Trip Down the Aisle Be the Charm for the Donald?" *The Spectator*, January 22, 2005, p. G3.
4. Cathy Horyn, "Reports of Couture's Death Were Exaggerated," *New York Times*, July 11, 2004.
5. Jennifer Fermino, Braden Keil, Rich Alder, and Bridget Harrison, "Trump Rings Up Number 3: Weds Melania in Celeb-Filled Seaside $how," *New York Post*, January 23, 2005, p. 2.
6. Georgia Dullea, "Vows: It's a Wedding Blitz for Trump and Maples," *New York Times*, December 21, 1993, p. B1.
7. Megan Specia, "Why a Journalist's Killing Has Resonated around the World," *New York Times*, October 25, 2018, p. A6; "Jamal Khashoggi's Killing: Here's What We Know," *New York Times*, October 19, 2018, web.
8. Joyce Wadler, "Boldface Names," *New York Times*, January 25, 2005, p. 2.

13. WOLFGANG DOES NOT HAVE ANY RECOLLECTION

1. An astute reporter, Jacob Clifton, who was writing weekly recaps of the season for *Television Without Pity*, picked up that something seemed odd about Jenn suddenly advocating for go-karts, wondering how "frankendoodled" the episode was in the editing (March 3, 2007).

14. BELOW THE BELT

1. From an unpublished portion of an interview conducted by reporter Andrew Corsello, January 26, 2017.
2. Donny Deutsch, "Trump in His Own Words," *The Big Idea with Donny Deutsch*, aired January 12, 2007, on CNBC.
3. Larry King, "Interview with Donald Trump," *Larry King Live*, aired October 15, 2007, on CNN.
4. "Donald Trump: Gloria Would Be Impressed with My Genitals," TMZ, April 3, 2012, www.tmz.com/2012/04/03/donald-trump-no-apology-transgender-miss -universe/.
5. Gideon Resnick, "Donald Trump Said in 2012 Gloria Allred Would Be 'Very, Very Impressed' with His Penis," Daily Beast, October 8, 2016.

15. STAYING TUNED

1. Roger Friedman, "Donald Trump Offered Rosie O'Donnell $2 Million to Go on *The Apprentice*," Fox News, July 30, 2007.

2. Andor B. Michael, "A Timeline of Trump's Tenure on Twitter," *Boston Globe*, May 18, 2017.

16. CREATING A BRAIN TRUST

1. Alex Frangos, "Trump Fights Chicago Headwinds: Credit Crunch, Shift in Housing Market Pressure Big Project," *Wall Street Journal*, October 30, 2008, p. 25.
2. Don Kaplan, "Recession Hits *Apprentice*: Rocky Economy Is Star of Latest Celeb Biz Series," *New York Post*, January 15, 2009, p. 90.
3. Lauren Price, "Upping the Ante," *New York Post*, February 27, 2007.
4. Rebecca Ballhaus, Michael Rothfeld, Joe Palazzolo, and Alexandra Berzon, "Cohen–Trump Relations Were Rocky for Years," *Wall Street Journal*, June 16, 2018, p. A1.
5. "Generation Zero: A Hannity Special," *Hannity*, aired February 23, 2010, on Fox News Channel.
6. Joseph Berger. "Still No Place in New York for Qaddafi to Pitch a Tent," *New York Times*, September 24, 2009, p. A34.
7. Mike Allen, "Dems See Key Races Tightening," *Time*, October 4, 2010.
8. "You're Fired, Mr. President! Donald Trump's New Hampshire Poll May Just Be a Front for Billionaire Businessman Michael Bloomberg," *Wall Street Journal*, October 6, 2010.
9. "Donald Trump Interview, MSNBC," *CEO Wire*, October 5, 2010.

17. A PARTY TRUMP LIKES THE SOUND OF

1. Phil Rosenthal, "In Battle of Ideals, 'Rick's Revolt' Dials Volume to 11," *Chicago Tribune*, February 22, 2009, p. 4.1.
2. Jeff Zeleny, "Republicans Take Control of House, Setting Back Democratic Agenda," *New York Times*, November 3, 2010.
3. Giles Whittell, "Obama Takes Blame: 'I Took a Shellacking,'" *The Times*, November 4, 2010, p. 1.
4. Pat Boone, "It's Time for Another Tea Party" WND, March 7, 2009, https://www.wnd.com/2009/03/90948/.
5. Anti-Obamacare protestors were carrying swastikas. Pierson and others felt that it was unfair to imply that this made the protestors Nazis, that the protestors' point was that Obamacare was something a totalitarian state would impose. Pelosi did not call the protestors Nazis. She referred to them as "Astroturf," meaning that they were fake grassroots protestors working at the bidding of larger forces. James Taranto, "Desperately Seeking Swastikas," *Wall Street Journal*, August 7, 2009, https://www.wsj.com/articles/SB10001424052970204908604574336462379328406.
6. Danny Hakim, "Politics Seen in Nasty Call to Spitzer's Father," *New York Times*, August 22, 2007, p. A1.
7. Danny Hakim and Nicholas Confessore, "Political Consultant Resigns after

Allegations of Threatening Spitzer's Father," *New York Times*, August 23, 2007, p. B1.

8. Jeffrey Toobin, "The Dirty Trickster," *New Yorker*, June 2, 2008, p. 54.

9. Danny Hakim, "Opposing Campaigns, with One Unlikely Link," *New York Times*, August 12, 2010, p. A25.

10. "Donald Trump's Accounting: Debt Debate," *International Wire*, April 21, 2011.

11. Stephanie Mencimer, "The Time a Trump Aide Sued a Trump Adviser over an Anti-Hillary Group Called C.U.N.T.," *Mother Jones*, September 29, 2016.

12. Margot Adler, "Islamic Center Near Ground Zero Sparks Anger," *All Things Considered*, July 15, 2010.

13. Molly Ball, "The 2012 Trump Card," Politico, February 2, 2011.

14. Philip Elliott and Liz Sidoti, "A Crowded Field: Trump Dangles Potential '12 Bid before Conservatives; Republican Presidential Hopefuls Abound at D.C. Conference," *Houston Chronicle*, February 11, 2011, p. 6.

15. Chris Cillizza, "By the Way, Ron Paul Cannot Get Elected, I'm Sorry to Tell You. . . . I Like Ron Paul, I Think He's a Good Guy, but Honestly He just Has Zero Chance of Getting Elected," *Washington Post*, February 14, 2011.

16. Maggie Haberman, "Stone: Donald's Cash a Trump Card," Politico, February 25, 2011.

17. Maggie Haberman, "The Donald Reins in Roger Stone," Politico, February 25, 2011.

18. Maggie Haberman, "Trump: Ready for Iowa Hand-Shaking," Politico, March 3, 2011.

19. Juana Summers, "Trump Aide in Iowa: Run Would Be 'Big Personal Sacrifice,'" Politico, March 7, 2011.

20. Jeff Zeleny, "G.O.P. Voters Are Ready for the 2012 Race. Now Somebody Tell the Candidates," *New York Times*, March 7, 2011.

18. BORN IN THE USA

1. "Public Trust in Government: 1958–2017," Pew Research Center, December 14, 2017.

2. Lymari Morales, "U.S. Distrust in Media Hits New High," Gallup News Service, September 21, 2012.

3. Maggie Haberman, "Breitbart Takes Over Weiner Presser," Politico, June 6, 2011.

4. Sarah Posner, "How Donald Trump's New Campaign Chief Created an Online Haven for White Nationalists," *Mother Jones*, August 22, 2016.

5. Ashley Parker and Steve Eder, "How Trump's 'Birther' Claims Helped to Stir Presidential Bid," *New York Times*, July 3, 2016, p. A1.

6. David Weigel, "Birther Speaker Takes Heat at Tea Party Convention," *Washington Independent*, February 6, 2010: https://web.archive.org/web/20140301055830

/http://washingtonindependent.com/75949/birther-speaker-takes-heat-at-tea
-party-convention.

7. Ashleigh Banfield, Rich McHugh, and Suzan Clarke, "Exclusive: Donald Trump Would Spend $600 Million of His Own Money on Presidential Bid," video, ABC News, March 17, 2011.

8. Ibid.

9. Maggie Haberman, "Giuliani: Time to Bury the Birthers," Politico, March 18, 2011.

10. Maureen Callahan, "Trump, Card—Behind the Donald's Latest Fake Run for President—and His Weird Embrace of the Birthers," *New York Post,* April 3, 2011, p. 23.

11. Alexander Mooney, "Trump Sends Investigators to Hawaii to Look at Obama," CNN Political Ticker April 7, 2011, Web.

12. Kendra Marr, "Trump Sides with Birthers," Politico, March 23, 2011.

13. Jane Mayer, "The Making of the Fox News White House," *New Yorker,* March 11, 2019.

14. Alana Abramson, "How Donald Trump Perpetuated the Birther Movement for Years," ABC News, September 16, 2016.

15. Laura Ingraham radio show, March 30, 2011, https://youtu.be/WqaS9OCoTZs.

16. Juana Summers, "Trump: I Stand with Tea Party," Politico, April 7, 2011.

17. "WSJ BLOG/Washington Wire: WSJ/NBC Poll: A Donald Trump Surprise," *Dow Jones Institutional News,* April 6, 2011.

18. Maggie Haberman, "Trump Aide Defends, Downplays Birther Focus," Politico, March 29, 2011.

19. Olivia Messer, "Mika Brzezinski: Trump Told Me He Knew Birtherism Was 'Bad. But It Works,'" Daily Beast, November 5, 2018.

19. ROASTED

1. Ben Smith and Maggie Haberman, "What's Donald Trump Really After?" Politico, April 18, 2011.

2. Ashley Parker and Steve Eder, "How Trump's 'Birther' Claims Helped to Stir Presidential Bid," *New York Times,* July 3, 2016, p. A1.

3. Michael D. Shear, "Citing 'Silliness,' Obama Shows Birth Certificate," *New York Times,* April 28, 2011, p. A1.

4. Maggie Haberman, "Trump's New Hampshire Victory Lap," Politico, April 27, 2011.

5. E. Alex Jung, "This Joke Was Off-Limits at Donald Trump's Comedy Central Roast," Vulture, August 3, 2016.

6. Roxanne Roberts, "I Sat Next to Donald Trump at the Infamous 2011 White House Correspondents' Dinner," *Washington Post,* April 29, 2016, p. C3.

7. For Busey's 2018 book *Buseyisms,* Trump contributed a cover blurb, but at the last

minute Busey's partner Steffanie Sampson decided it might hurt sales and had it removed.

8. Nick Gass, "31 Times Trump Got Roasted," Politico, April 29, 2016.

9. Roberts, "I Sat Next to Donald Trump at the Infamous 2011 White House Correspondents' Dinner."

10. Ibid.

11. Maggie Haberman, "Trump's Poll Numbers Collapse," Politico, May 10, 2011.

12. Nia-Malika Henderson, "Trump Drops 'Birther' Talk in N.H. Speech," Washington Post, May 12, 2011.

13. Karen Tumulty and Nia-Malika Henderson, "Trump Won't Run—But Says He'd Win if He Did," Washington Post, May 17, 2011.

14. Ewen MacAskill, "Trump Rules Himself Out of Election Race," Guardian, May 17, 2011, p. 22.

15. Tumulty and Henderson, "Trump Won't Run—But Says He'd Win if He Did."

20. THE TWITTERER

1. Shushannah Walshe, "Sarah Palin and Donald Trump's Pizza Summit," Newsweek Web Exclusives, June 1, 2011.

2. The authors believe in picking up a pizza slice but not in the fold, as this hides the flavorful cheese and creates a fast-moving grease channel down the crease that can stain clothes.

21. REMAINING A PLAYER

1. Jonathan Lemire, "Donald's Debate Dud Could Die Early," New York Daily News, December 10, 2011, p. 6.

2. Sarah Huisenga, "Trump Pulls Out as Debate Moderator," National Journal, December 13, 2011.

3. Ryan Creed, "Christine O'Donnell: 'I Dabbled in Witchcraft,'" September 18, 2010, https://abcnews.go.com/News/christine-odonnell-dabbled-witchcraft-story?id=11671277.

4. Sean Hannity, Fox News Channel, August 15, 2011.

5. Fox News, On the Record with Greta Van Susteren, "Interview with Donald Trump," December 6, 2011.

6. Brian Montopoli, "Donald Trump Switches Party Affiliation to Independent," CBS News, December 23, 2011.

7. Aman Batheja, "Report: Paperwork Filed in Texas for Donald Trump Third-Party Run for President," Fort Worth Star-Telegram, January 2, 2012.

8. https://www.snopes.com/fact-check/trump-patent-maga-2012/.

9. Corey R. Lewandowski and David N. Bossie, Let Trump Be Trump (New York: Hachette, 2017).

10. "Unpopular Nationally, Romney Holds Solid Lead," Pew Research Center, January 18, 2012.

11. Chris Cillizza, "What Does Romney See in Trump?" *Washington Post*, May 30, 2012.

12. Mark Leibovich, "Over-the-Top Setting, Run-of-the Mill Endorsement," *New York Times*, February 3, 2012, p. A14.

13. Allan Smith, "Donald Trump's 4-Year-Old Endorsement of Mitt Romney Seems Surreal Today," Business Insider, March 3, 2016.

14. Maggie Haberman, Sharon Lafraniere, and Danny Hakim, "Punching Bag for President Now Has Clout," *New York Times*, April 21, 2018, p. A1.

15. Cillizza, "What Does Romney See in Trump?"

16. Manu Raju, "Trump Gets 'Surprise' Convention Role," Politico, August 19, 2012.

17. "RNC Cancels First Convention Day, as Isaac Approaches Florida," *Florida Today*, August 25, 2012.

18. Emily Schultheis, "Trump Plays Up Birth Certificate Issue in Fla.," Politico, August 26, 2012.

19. Beth Fouhy, "Trump to Obama: $5 Million Donation for Passport, College Records Release," Associated Press, October 24, 2012.

20. Carson Griffith and Kristen A. Lee, "WHAT AN ASS! Trump's Absurd $5M Offer on Bam Files," New York *Daily News*, October 25, 2012, p. 11.

21. Jonathan Capehart, "Donald Trump Knows 'Mean-Spirited,'" *Washington Post*, November 27, 2012.

22. Sean Trende, "The Case of the Missing White Voters, Revisited," RealClearPolitics, June 21, 25, 28, and July 2, 2013.

22. SITTING ON THE HOOD OF A CAR

1. "Cuomo Approval Tops 70 Percent, Highest In 11 Years, Quinnipiac University Poll Finds," Quinnipiac University, May 30, 2012.

2. Thomas Kaplan, "Sweeping Limits on Guns Become Law in New York," *New York Times*, January 15, 2013.

3. Danny Hakim, "New York Governor Puts Off Decision on Drilling," *New York Times*, February 12, 2013.

4. "New York's Cuomo Opens Election Year with a Roar, Quinnipiac University Poll Finds; 2-1 Approval and Huge Lead over Unknown Contender," Quinnipiac University, November 26, 2013.

5. Nick Reisman, "Most Cuomo Contributions Are Big Dollar Checks," State of Politics, July 15, 2013.

6. Vivian Yee, "Bill Nojay, Upstate Assemblyman, Dies after Shooting Himself at a Cemetery," *New York Times*, September 9, 2016.

7. Fredric U. Dicker, "GOPers Eye Donald Trump for Governor Run," *New York Post*, October 14, 2013.

8. Ibid.

9. Winnie Hu, "Mayoral Ambitions and Sharp Elbows; Councilwoman Spars Way into Position of Influence," *New York Times,* April 29, 2004.

10. Susanne Craig and David W. Chen, "Trump Flirted with State Bid Before '16 Race," *New York Times,* March 6, 2016, p. A1.

11. Poll details and Conway's memo can be seen at greater length in Joshua Green's book, *Devils Bargain,* Penguin Press, 2017.

23. SELLING TRUMP TO TRUMP

1. Nicole Malliotakis only tweeted the photo with fellow assembly member Joe Borelli and Donald Trump, not the one Trump asked her to post of only Trump and her together.

2. Rob Astorino was a founder of ESPN Radio in New York and worked as executive producer of *The Michael Kay Show* before serving as a county legislator in Westchester.

3. "December 5, 2013 (Page 6A A)," *Journal News,* Westchester/Putnam Zone ed., December 5, 2013, p. 1.

4. Joseph Spector, Gannett Albany Bureau, "Trump Gets In-Person GOP Pitch to Run for N.Y. Governor," *USA Today,* December 4, 2013.

24. LIKE A HURRICANE

1. Susanne Craig and David Chen, "Trump Flirted with State Bid Before '16 Race," *New York Times,* March 6, 2016, p. A1.

2. Andrea Peyser, "'Fire'd Up for Gov Race," *New York Post,* December 23, 2013, p. 14.

3. Jon Campbell, "Trump, Again, Flirting with Public Office," *Poughkeepsie Journal,* December 24, 2013.

4. Peyser, "'Fire'd Up for Gov Race."

5. Joseph Berger, "Westchester County Leader Weighs a Run for Governor," *New York Times,* December 24, 2013, p. A3.

6. Rob Astorino did not reply to repeated requests for comment, both in person and through a spokesperson.

7. Jon Campbell, "Trump, Again, Flirting with Public Office," *Poughkeepsie Journal,* December 24, 2013.

25. AN ENLIGHTENING DISTRACTION

1. Kenneth Lovett, "Trump in Gov Pump," New York *Daily News,* January 11, 2014, p. 2.

2. Carl Campanile, "NY GOP Chair Asks Party Leaders to Not Support Cuomo," *New York Post,* January 14, 2014.

3. Robert J. McCarthy, "Trump: 'I Can Put Up $200 Million if I Want' for a Gubernatorial Campaign," *McClatchy-Tribune Business News,* January 16, 2014.

4. Maureen Miller, "Paladino Concedes with a Baseball Bat," *CNN Politics*, November 3, 2010.

5. Jill Terreri, "Astorino Run for Governor Cited by Cox," *Buffalo News*, January 7, 2014.

6. As he recuperated, Paladino reflected on the dinner conversation with Trump. Paladino bet a Binghamton journalist an Italian dinner in Buffalo that Trump would not enter the governor's race.

7. Michael Rothfeld, Rob Barry, and Joe Palazzolo, "Cohen Tried to Rig Polls to Favor Trump: Lawyer Had Tech Firm Promote His Boss Pre-Campaign, Then Allegedly Stiffed It," *Wall Street Journal*, January 18, 2019, A4.

26. STAYING SHARP

1. To Allen Salkin, at Park City party for *RX Early Detection: A Cancer Journey with Sandra Lee*, January 22, 2018, Sundance Film Festival.

2. McKay Coppins, "36 Hours on the Fake Campaign Trail with Donald Trump," BuzzFeed, February 13, 2014.

27. FLANNEL SHIRT

1. Jesse McKinley, "Westchester Leader Opens Bid to Deny Cuomo a Second Term," *New York Times*, March 5, 2014.

2. Elizabeth Titus, "Trump Warns Rubio on Immigration," Politico, March 6, 2014.

3. Nikki Schwab, "Donald Trump Peppers CPAC Speeches with Humblebrags," *U.S. News & World Report*, March 6, 2014.

4. Kentucky senator Rand Paul won that year, followed by Texas senator Ted Cruz. Ben Carson came in third. Chris Gentilviso, "CPAC Straw Poll Results 2014: Rand Paul Wins Conservative Vote," Huffington Post, March 8, 2014.

5. Joe Palazzolo, Michael Siconolfi, and Michael Rothfeld, "Cohen Threatened CNBC," *Wall Street Journal*, January 22, 2019, A7.

6. Teri Weaver, "Donald Trump: I'll Be Making a Decision Shortly,'" *Syracuse Post-Standard*, March 12, 2014, p. A8.

7. Philip Bump, "Breaking: Donald Trump Is Not Running for New York Governor or Anything Else, Ever," *The Atlantic*, March 14, 2014.

8. Glenn Blain, "Here's a Shocker: Trump Will Not Run," New York *Daily News*, March 15, 2014, p. 2.

9. Rick Karlin, "Albany Anti–NY SAFE Act Rally Draws Trump, Astorino, Paladino," *Albany Times Union*, April 2, 2014.

10. In addition to losing the governor's race by 14 percentage points in 2014, Astorino lost his bid for a third term as Westchester County executive in November 2017 by 14 percentage points, despite outspending his Democratic rival three to one.

28. OUTWIT, OUTPLAY, OUTLAST

1. Jaime Fuller, "Freedom Summit Draws GOP Hopefuls," *Washington Post*, April 13, 2014.

2. C-SPAN, "Donald Trump at New Hampshire Freedom Summit," April 12, 2014, https://www.c-span.org/video/?c4495435/donald-trump-nh-freedom-summit &start=336.

3. Jonathan Pincus, "Exclusive: Trump Campaign Mgrs Explain Where 'Make America Great Again' Slogan Really Started," *Western Journal*, December 17, 2017.

4. The show was *Breitbart News Saturday*, and this event was on April 12, 2014.

5. Jeremy W. Peters, "New Hampshire Republicans Get a Preview of 2016," *New York Times*, April 12, 2014.

6. "Turd Blossom" was President George W. Bush's nickname for his political adviser, Karl Rove. "Pootie-Poot" was Vladimir Putin. He did not appear to have a nickname for Donald Trump. Veronika Bondarenko, "'Turd Blossom,' 'Pootie Poot'—Here Are the Nicknames George W. Bush Gave to World Leaders, Politicians, and Journalists," Business Insider, August 1, 2017.

29. TEAM OF APPRENTI

1. Apprenti is not the grammatically proper plural of apprentice, but Trump has used it. https://www.businesswritingblog.com/business_writing/2011/12/is-donald -trump-wrong-about-apprenti.html.

2. Jonathan Martin, "Second McCain Aide Quits over DCI Ties," Politico, May 11, 2008.

3. Convicted of financial crimes in 2018 as part of the Mueller investigation, Manafort was taken into federal custody.

4. Here's *The Simpsons* challenging him: https://www.youtube.com/watch?v=kYNPt Dbykp0.

5. Trump's Ice Bucket Challenge. He challenged his two eldest sons. https://www .youtube.com/watch?v=xaHR9a7sJTY.

6. The conservative brothers David and Charles Koch funded Americans for Prosperity, an advocacy group that helped finance Bossie's Freedom Summits and employed Lewandowski as head of the group's New Hampshire office.

7. Corey Lewandowski did not reply to numerous requests for comment.

8. Paul Steinhauser, "CNN Poll: GOP Advantage in Midterms," Political Ticker, CNN Politics, May 5, 2014.

9. "Interviews with 1,003 Adult Americans Conducted by Telephone by ORC International on May 29–June 1, 2014," CNN/ORC Poll, June 4, 2014.

10. Mark Preston, "CNN/ORC Poll: Most Think Congress Is Worst in Their Lifetime," CNN Politics, September 10, 2014.

11. Alexandra Jaffe, "Jeb Bush to 'Actively Explore' 2016 Presidential Bid," CNN Politics, December 31, 2014.

12. Alexandra Jaffe, "CNN/ORC Poll: Bush Surges to 2016 GOP Frontrunner," CNN Politics, December 29, 2014.

13. Michael C. Bender and Jonathan Allen, "Bush Team Sets Bold Fundraising Goal: $100 Million in Three Months," Bloomberg, January 9, 2015.

30. HOW THE WALL GOT BUILT

1. Trip Gabriel, "Before Trump, Steve King Set the Agenda for the Wall and Anti-Immigrant Politics," *New York Times*, January 10, 2019.

2. Beth Reinhard and Jim O'Sullivan, "Hispanic Panic," *National Journal*, December 15, 2011.

3. American Conservative Union, "CPAC 2014 – Donald Trump, the Trump Organization," March 6, 2014, https://www.youtube.com/watch?v=3nzaemPHSU0.

4. "Iowa Freedom Summit, Donald Trump," C-SPAN, January 24, 2014.

5. Seth McLaughlin, "Donald Trump: I Want to Run for President 'So Badly,'" *Washington Times*, February 27, 2015.

6. Jeremy Diamond, "Donald Trump Launches Presidential Exploratory Committee," CNN Wire Service, March 18, 2015.

7. Paul Steinhauser and NH1 News, "Why Donald Trump's Campaign Push Is Different this Time Around," *Washington Post* - Blogs, April 27, 2015.

8. http://time.com/3923128/donald-trump-announcement-speech/.

9. Calvin Woodward, "AP Fact Check: Trump's Myth of Terrorist Tide from Mexico," Associated Press, January 7, 2019.

31. THE ANNOUNCEMENT

1. Jeremy Diamond, "Donald Trump Launches Presidential Exploratory Committee," CNN Wire Service, March 18, 2015.

2. "Donald Trump Iowa Lincoln Dinner," C-SPAN, May 16, 2015.

3. Jennifer Jacobs, "8 Takeaways from Iowa's Lincoln Dinner, Its Aftermath," *Des Moines Register,* May 18, 2015, p. 9.

4. Robynn Tysver, "In Visit to Omaha Area, Donald Trump Assails Politicians and Touts His Credentials," *Omaha World-Herald,* May 15, 2015.

5. Eli Stokols, "Iowa GOP Lincoln Dinner: 5 Takeaways," Politico, May 18, 2015.

6. Kyle Smith, "Trump Is Not Running!" *New York Post*, May 31, 2015, p. 32.

7. Sam Clovis, a climate-science denier and steadfast Obama birther, was withdrawn for consideration for a science post with the U.S. Department of Agriculture in 2017 after it became known that as Trump campaign national co-chair he had authorized aide George Papadopoulos to meet with Russian officials in Moscow for an "off-the-record" talk.

8. Payoffs to silence Daniels and Karen McDougal about affairs with Trump were arranged with Cohen's help in 2016.

9. George Gigicos was a campaign consultant who specialized in planning events. He stayed with the campaign and joined the Trump administration as White House Director of Scheduling and Advance before leaving in August 2017.

10. Grace Ashford, "Michael Cohen Says Trump Told Him to Threaten Schools Not to Release Grades," *New York Times,* February 27, 2019.

11. Trump was in Scotland to handle matters concerning his golf course, Trump Turnberry.

12. "Donald Trump Presidential Campaign Announcement", C-SPAN, June 16, 2015, https://www.c-span.org/video/?326473-1/donald-trump-presidential-campaign-announcement.

13. Ibid.

32. EPILOGUE

1. Ralston Reports, June 18, 2015, https://www.ralstonreports.com/blog/hillary-clinton-ralston-live-video-and-transcript.

INDEX